TOXIC MASCULINITY

EDITED BY ESTHER DE DAUW

AND DANIEL J. CONNELL

UNIVERSITY PRESS OF MISSISSIPPI • JACKSON

TOXIC MASCULINITY

MAPPING THE MONSTROUS IN OUR HEROES

The University Press of Mississippi is the scholarly publishing agency of
the Mississippi Institutions of Higher Learning: Alcorn State University,
Delta State University, Jackson State University, Mississippi State University,
Mississippi University for Women, Mississippi Valley State University,
University of Mississippi, and University of Southern Mississippi.

www.upress.state.ms.us

Designed by Peter D. Halverson

The University Press of Mississippi is a member of the Association of University Presses.

Copyright © 2020 by University Press of Mississippi
All rights reserved

First printing 2020

∞

Library of Congress Cataloging-in-Publication Data
Names: De Dauw, Esther, editor. | Connell, Daniel James, editor.
Title: Toxic masculinity : mapping the monstrous in our heroes / edited by Esther De Dauw and Daniel J. Connell.
Description: Jackson : University Press of Mississippi, 2020. | Includes bibliographical references and index.
Identifiers: LCCN 2020014582 (print) | LCCN 2020014583 (ebook) | ISBN 9781496828934 (hardback) | ISBN 9781496828941 (trade paperback) | ISBN 9781496828958 | ISBN 9781496828965 | ISBN 9781496828972 | ISBN 9781496828989
Subjects: LCSH: Masculinity in motion pictures. | Superhero films.
Classification: LCC PN1995.9.M34 T69 2020 (print) | LCC PN1995.9.M34 (ebook) | DDC 791.43/65211dc23
LC record available at https://lccn.loc.gov/2020014582
LC ebook record available at https://lccn.loc.gov/2020014583

British Library Cataloging-in-Publication Data available

CONTENTS

vii   Acknowledgments

3   Introduction: The Subaltern and the Hegemonic

PART I: UNDERSTANDING SUPER MEN

19   The Simulacrum of Hypermasculinity in Comic Book Cinema
     DANIEL J. CONNELL

34   Renewing Hegemonic Masculinity Every Wednesday: *Arrow* and Television Form
     JAMES C. TAYLOR

52   "I'll Show You What It Means to Be a Man": Hegemonic Masculinity of *Batman v Superman: Dawn of Justice*
     JANNE SALMINEN

PART II: THE MONSTROUS OTHER

71   The Monstrous in *Batwoman*: Military Masculinity and Domestic Spaces
     ESTHER DE DAUW

89   *Days of Future Past*: Queer Identities and the X-Men
     DREW MURPHY

103   *Torchwood*'s Supermen: Bisexuality as a Hypermasculine Superpower
     CRAIG HASLOP

PART III: STRATEGIES OF RESISTANCE

121   Emma Frost, the White Queen: Superpowers as the Performance of Gender
     RICHARD REYNOLDS

142   Albus Dumbledore and the Curse of Toxic Masculinity
     KAREN SUGRUE

157   Conclusion: Reflecting on Toxic Masculinity

163   Bibliography

178   Contributors

180   Index

ACKNOWLEDGMENTS

We would like to take this opportunity to thank all our collaborators for their hard work in getting this book out. Throughout the two years that we worked on this book, our contributors moved house, got married, campaigned for social reform, completed PhDs, and took on new teaching commitments. Nonetheless, they continued to work on the book with us, updating and editing their chapters. We cannot thank them enough for their commitment, time and efforts.

We are also grateful to all the authors, creators, editors, and scholars who helped shape this book by providing guidance, general advice, or feedback. In particular, we would like to thank Lindsay Catt, Jason Dittmer, Zalfa Feghali, Sean Guynes, Joanna Wilson, and Emily Bandy.

TOXIC MASCULINITY

INTRODUCTION

THE SUBALTERN AND THE HEGEMONIC

"Like our '70s sisters who proclaimed that the personal is political, we know that so, too, is the popular."
—**DEBBIE STOLLER**, *The Best Guide to the New Girl Order*

It would be easy to dismiss popular culture—that miasma of television, film, comic books, internet culture, and consumerist branding—as only entertainment. "It's just a commercial, just a movie, just a meme"—as if storytelling were not the way we have made sense of the world and ourselves for centuries and as if storytelling were not inherently political. Hegemonic forces (government, media, mega corporations, universities, etc.) still largely determine who gets to tell their story, what kind of stories can be told, and the size of the platform on which these stories are delivered. These stories both entertain and disseminate cultural values. As Dawn Heinecken writes, "[the] media are seen as major instruments of cultural expression."[1] In this book, we will investigate how the (super)hero in popular culture conveys messages about heroism and masculinity, considering the social implications of this narrative within a cultural (re)production of dominant, hegemonic values and the possibility of subaltern ideas, norms, and values to be imagined within that (re)production.

(Super)Heroes produce gendered scripts that influence the way popular media interacts with gender and sex in general. Cultural ideas about sex and gender, in turn, are influenced by popular media, their creators, corporate concerns, and executive decisions (all of which influence and are influenced by popular culture as well). Through these processes of mutual influence, media demonstrates how people must adhere to sex and gender norms. Judith Butler writes that gender is "the repeated stylization of the body, a set of repeated acts in a highly regulatory frame that congeal over time to produce the appearance of substance, of a natural sort of being."[2] In effect, gender is a cultural construct that works to present the idea of a biologically defined gender that determines cultural roles and values. These gender roles are often influenced by other outside factors—race, (dis)ability, sexuality—but are ultimately modeled on the "ideal," "true," and more "natural" or "correct" way to do gender that exists within the cultural hegemony. Raewyn Connell discussed this concept through the idea of hegemonic masculinity, which is the "culturally exalted" version of masculinity.[3] While there continuously exist multiple forms of masculinity competing with each other, there are specific forms that are framed as illustrious and presented as a singular ideal within popular culture. This singular masculine ideal often folds in elements of competing subaltern masculinities that have become marketable and fashionable, ultimately producing an ideal that comprises many contradictory elements and presents a unified illusion. This deradicalizes the potential of resistance inherent to subaltern masculinities by increasingly marketing these elements as part of the cultural norm within capitalist production of popular culture. Therefore, hegemonic masculinity "can be defined as the configuration of gender practice which embodies the currently accepted answer to the problem of the legitimacy of patriarchy, which guarantees (or is taken to guarantee) the dominant position of men and the subordination of women."[4] This hegemonic masculinity is straight, able-bodied, white, and "hard," i.e., not feminine. Depending on the context and relevance of other elements, some elements can be dismissed in order for subaltern identities to gain acceptance temporarily or exist peacefully within the hegemonic hierarchy. However, this ideal remains the starting point of the hierarchy which determines the rights and power of people within specific demographics. For example, a white gay man, who is not "camp" and can deflect accusations of being a "sissy" (nonmasculine) through the over-performance of his whiteness and able-bodied strength *in comparison* to a black man, can temporarily gain acceptance in extreme right-wing circles and evade persecution as this group targets black minorities. This is, in fact, a common tactic used in extreme right-wing online communities to bolster support and is sometimes referred to as the pink-washing of white nationalism.[5]

It is important to distinguish between hegemonic masculinity, hypermasculinity, and toxic masculinity, even as these different categories have mutually reinforcing relationships. Hypermasculinity has been identified as "a gender-based ideology of exaggerated beliefs about what it is to be a man," which contains "four inter-related beliefs, namely toughness as emotional self-control, violence as manly, danger as exciting and calloused attitudes towards women and sex."[6] Hypermasculinity focuses predominantly on violence as a way to success and defines success as the appropriation of property—which includes women—to achieve high status and accumulate social capital. These same attributes are also considered part of toxic masculinity, which differs slightly in that it considers masculinity as "threatened by anything associated with femininity (whether that is pink yoghurt or emotions)."[7] Toxic masculinity focuses on the way that the extreme rejection of femininity through the performance of hypermasculinity creates unhealthy behavioral patterns and ideological beliefs that become toxic to men and, on a structural level, to their environments. The reciprocal relationship between these three different concepts of masculinity is best understood through the concept of hybrid masculinities. Tristan Bridges and C. J. Pascoe describe how society includes increasingly different forms of masculinity, which cannot be accounted for by local differences. However, instead of opening up hegemonic masculinity and offering new, nontoxic forms of masculinity, these "hybrid masculinities work in ways that not only reproduce contemporary systems of gendered, raced, and sexual inequalities but also obscure this process as it is happening."[8] These hybrid masculinities incorporate elements or forms of masculinity that have historically existed outside of hegemonic masculinity and are culturally identified as Other. While this might seem like positive resistance strategies, the way these elements are divorced from a structural position of power weaken hybrid masculinities' ability to truly resist hegemonic masculinity. Instead, men are encouraged to wield a performative "woke-ness," which allows them to act personally in ways that are seemingly divorced from hegemonic or toxic masculinity while simultaneously reinforcing structural inequalities. Hegemonic masculinity has an unfixed nature, encompassing hybrid masculinities, hypermasculinity, and toxic masculinity.

Considering hegemonic masculinity's unfixed nature, this volume seeks to understand to what extent it is possible to provide any alternatives to the hegemonic order, whose appropriative nature purges the radical from any resistance by enfolding its palatable and marketable elements into its contradictory mass. Similarly, "media forms, such as film, TV, and advertising are notorious for the ways in which they adopt and absorb oppositional points of view or modes of expression, reframing them in ways that are beneficial to big business and the ruling corporate class."[9] When writing on comics or any aspect of popular culture in terms of the reproduction of dominant cultural values, it is important to understand how everything produced within capitalism works to strengthen it, as described by Gilles Deleuze and Felix Guattari's concept of folding in.[10] Like an Ouroboros devouring its own tail, resistance becomes consumed, integrated, and sold back to the masses. Like capitalism and the consistently reiterated story of the hero, hegemonic masculinity continuously renews itself, only to perpetuate its old archetypes and gender roles.

In the light of this understanding of gender and hegemony, this volume seeks to analyze superheroes, the masculinity they represent, the behavioral patterns they model for their readers, and the impact these behaviors have on the representation of nonmale characters. It wouldn't be an exaggeration to say that most (super)hero narratives maintain a male-centric point of view. The current popularity of the superhero blockbuster film, with the advent of the MCU in 2008, has produced nineteen male-centric films and two female-centric films (with nine ensemble films with a majority of male characters) by both DC and Marvel.[11] These male-centric films often include an origin story and produce a hero who functions within a "lone wolf" narrative, removing the hero from a wider social network. They might have sidekicks, civilian friends, and family members or even fellow superheroes they team up with at moments of extreme crisis, but they often exist as the sole arbiter of power and protection without other heroes (true equals) to share the load. As Jennifer K. Stuller notes, such "lone wolf" social constructs are "rooted in traditional uber-masculinity and isolationism."[12] The "lone wolf" hero is the template for the superhero, who is the only one who can protect the world from the various dangers that threaten it. The template promotes an ethics of self-reliance that casts the nonhero civilians (usually white women, people of color, disabled people, LGBTQIA+ identities, etc.) as victims who can only be protected by the overwhelming might and masculinity of the hero. Heinecken concurs when she writes that "[the] individualism and images of bodily hardness found in most male-centerd texts convey a sense that the hero is unique and separate from others."[13] The male superhero's abilities set him apart as a model and pinnacle of masculinity that is defined by the ability to protect through the application of violence, physical supremacy and self-reliance. As Heinecken writes "[male] heroes' ability to master and dominate their bodies functions as a display of ephemeral qualities such as their spirit, drive, and willpower. Male-centerd texts reveal these qualities, not the body, to be 'the self,' and their heroic subjectivity is thus one that exists outside the body."[14] The hero's mastery over the body and his construction of the powerful body form a display of mind over matter and, not only extreme self-reliance, but also extreme willpower. Comparatively, as Heinecken notes, women have not been provided with opportunities to express their heroic subjectivity in the same way. The male superhero and his heroism rooted

NBC News Covers Kamala Khan Bus Activism © 2015 NBC News

in extreme physicality, violence and isolation remain the dominant form of heroism promulgated throughout popular culture. This dominant heroic ideal becomes the form of heroism we use to define all others.

Consider the ubiquitous nature of the superhero, who we can find everywhere in contemporary life in the Anglo American world. Superheroes are in blockbusters (2018 alone had *Black Panther*, *Ant-Man and The Wasp*, *Aquaman*, *Avengers: Infinity War*, and others), television series (*Daredevil*, *Luke Cage*, *Jessica Jones*, *Arrow*, *Gotham*, *Supergirl*, and more), internet memes, podcasts, and, of course, comic books. Heroes who exist outside of classical superhero narratives but who perform superheroism also feature heavily in our lives, such as characters from *Doctor Who*, *Harry Potter*, *Star Trek*, and *Star Wars*, with more franchises gaining purchase every day. Beyond the digital/online spheres and paper comics, (super)hero merchandise is everywhere: in clothing stores, home improvement stores, and grocery stores. An increasing number of stores is dedicated only to selling superhero merchandise. While these developments are not completely new, the intensity with which superheroes are saturating the market at the expense of other narratives is new, especially with advances in digital and social media. Superheroes are even in our street art and social activism. For instance, in 2015, activists covered anti-Islam advertisements on buses with an image of Ms. Marvel—the sixteen-year-old Pakistani American and Muslim superhero, Kamala Khan—with messages to combat bigotry and resist hate speech.[15]

Considering the importance of heroes and their omnipresence—the almost sinister way they penetrate all aspects of our public and personal lives—we must consider what they say about and to us. Of course, the concept of superheroes and the medium in which they appear do not remain static: it would be an oversimplification to claim that they are all exactly the same or say the exact same thing about and to everyone. However, it cannot be denied that these heroes are preserved "in their most archetypical, recognizable, and marketable states," as Marc Singer writes.[16] Once brought into existence, superhero characters are preserved in their archetypical state to increase their commercial market potential. In conversation with Danny Graydon at The Superhero conference in 2016, Graydon pointed out that the recent changes to Superman's costume—its muted colors and the removal of the characteristic red briefs—would either be temporary or remain less "real" or "legitimate," compared to his original costume. Merchandise depicting Superman in this new version or any other alternative suit identifies it as merchandise for a specific iteration, such as the DCCU's Superman as depicted in *Man of Steel* (2013), *Batman v Superman: Dawn of Justice* (2016) and *Justice League* (2017), but not the original or "real one."[17] The primary version still remains the Superman dressed in bright colors with briefs over his tights.[18] As Federic Pagello writes, "the history of superhero comics therefore shows the structure of the genre, based on its economic logic and the established expectations of its audience, to consist of endless variations on the same fundamental elements made possible by replacing a linear, temporal narrative with a proliferation of co-existing parallel universes."[19] Comic books wield an economic logic of taking well-established and popular characters, putting them into new and different scenarios and then rebooting or dismissing the new storylines in order to return the popular character to his initial starting point and thus, undoing the potential changes that make the character less popular and less financially viable. Furthermore, it also allows for the sale of never-ending "what if" scenarios. This logic is no longer limited to superhero comics or the superhero genre. The hero can increasingly be found in a universe that spans transmedial texts, reiterating and repeating the same stories. Consider how shows like *Doctor Who* (1963–1989, 1996, 2005–present) and *Torchwood* (2006–11) have a primary canon aired on television. As universes, however, the shows are supplemented through novels, comic books, and radio serials. The *Star Trek* franchise, first aired in 1966, includes several series, films, comics, novels, and videogames, and is currently enjoying a reboot facilitated through Hollywood blockbusters and Netflix series where the same stories are told but "reimagined" in a new version of the *Star Trek* universe. In this transmedial, reboot world, who is the (super)hero who demands the repackaging and reworking of their serialization?

> *Superhero.* A heroic character with a selfless, pro-social mission; with superpowers—extraordinary abilities, advanced technology, or highly developed physical, mental, or mystical skills; who has a superhero identity embodied in a codename and iconic costume, which typically express his biography, character powers, or origin (transformation from ordinary person to superhero); and who is generically distinct, i.e. can be distinguished from characters of related genres (fantasy, science fiction, detective, etc.) by a preponderance of generic conventions. Often superheroes have dual identities, the ordinary one of which is usually a closely guarded secret.[20]

In his discussion of Judge Hand's above definition of the superhero, Peter Coogan highlights how the costume and, by extension, the dual identities are what sets the superhero apart from other heroes in the fantasy or science fiction genres. Ostensibly, this makes the concept of the superhero easier to wield, even as superheroes themselves increasingly complicate this definition. For instance, Tony Stark has abandoned the secrecy of his "civilian" or ordinary identity and is known to be Iron Man. Alternatively, the Netflix series *Jessica Jones* (2015–present) has a protagonist clearly marketed as a superhero, but she does not have a superhero identity or costume. By poking fun at superhero conventions, *Jessica Jones* asks us whether these elements are still appropriate in a genre that is seemingly gravitating towards "realistic" (meaning "serious" and "gritty") depictions of superheroes in television and movie formats. If these superhero elements are slowly fading from the most visible of superhero media, what happens if we consider heroes who exist outside of the "superhero" genre, such as Captain Jack Harkness in *Torchwood*? Harkness's immortality is his super power, and it can be argued that his staple coat and recognizable World-War-II-era sense of style, which set him apart in the show's 2006–11 setting, function as a superhero costume. However, he does not have dual identities and it is the ordinary, civilian identity that is missing. It is clear that this early definition of the superhero becomes untenable when considering the current state of (super)hero narratives. Any attempts to clearly define the superhero might superficially draw a hard, clear line, but nebulous and shifting categories and narratives inevitably complicate it. This volume does not seek to find a clear definition of the superhero or define who is and is not a superhero. Instead, it will use characters and narratives that, in several ways, fit the definition of popular understandings of the superhero in order to grapple with the gendered scripts that they produce.

Just as not all heroes are exactly the same, the gendered scripts or the meaning of heroism that they project is not exactly the same for all audience members. Depending on the sociocultural context in which a text is produced and delivered to an audience and that audience's own sociocultural context, different readings of a text are produced. However, this does not negate that a dominant reading of a text exists. In fact, as Bonnie Dow writes, "resistance or opposition assumes that the viewer 'gets' the preferred meaning of the text ... prior to resisting."[21] Both the creation and reading of a text are created by people shaped by their own natures and cultures at a specific sociocultural point in time. They can shift, depending on the social cultural context. Resistant readings often require the reader to be well versed in codes of resistance and dominance *prior* to reading the text.[22] The readings produced in this volume examine texts produced within a Western, Anglo American context and seek to understand or unravel dominant readings of those transmedial heroic texts in order to get at the specific Anglo American, gendered scripts within the narratives.

(Super)Hero narratives and their treatment of gender increasingly enjoy considerable attention in the field of comics, media, and popular culture studies, and they are frequently critiqued on social media and the internet news industry. With a history of analyzing female or LGBTQIA+ superheroes' gender performance, scholarly and academic writing is now increasingly turning its attention towards masculinity and male characters. Building on this groundbreaking work, this volume investigates the ways in which toxic and hegemonic masculinity appears in (super)hero narratives. While discussion of masculinity in superhero comics often focuses on subaltern masculinities existing in the spaces of hegemonic masculinities or nonmasculine identities responding to hegemonic masculinity, few texts focus on superheroes demonstrating toxic masculinity. Focusing on heroes within popular culture and utilizing hero-focused cinema and television, this volume provides an interdisciplinary perspective to argue for a reconsideration of the hero in popular media through an analysis of representations of masculinity and the demonization of femininity and LGBTQIA+ identities, while providing examples of progress and new ways to conceptualize superheroism. In an age when the sitting president of the United States was elected despite "grab them by the pussy" remarks, when #MeToo went viral, and when transgender people are increasingly targeted by the extreme right in an attempt to fold transphobic gender and sex equality activists into their ranks, the gender debate has never been more alive.[23] At this time, identifying the texts that promote toxic masculinity is crucial in order to help young boys and men think critically about the identities or roles they are encouraged to adopt, helping them formulate healthier and happier behavioral patterns.

By deconstructing the toxicity of hypermasculinity and monstrous femininity by mapping its roots in various forms (from writers to artists and actors), this volume will help develop a broader understanding of how the sociological phenomenon of hypermasculinity and its participation in hegemonic masculinity present themselves in Western, Anglo American culture. It will provide a platform on which calls for a more diverse presentation of creators, characters, and actors can be ideologically supported and will offer strategies for resistance to dominant narratives that enshrine traditional gender roles (within the capitalist promotion of subaltern gender identities). This volume contributes to wider discourses concerning popular media's advances and shortcomings in accommodating diversity. Consisting of three separate sections, this volume seeks to understand how the superhero interacts with these toxic forces of masculinity and what alternative strategies (if any) are possible.

The first part of this manuscript, "Understanding Super Men," focuses on the construction of toxic masculinity. These first three chapters demonstrate how, in television or movie format, the actor is increasingly pressured to embody the hypermasculine. This super body, with its bulging muscles and hyper-toned abs, is increasingly on display and embodies the hegemonic qualities of both the eroticized object and commanding subject. While men are increasingly eroticized for a female gaze, they often remain a commanding subject, a role unavailable to female characters. While it is tempting to say that both male and female bodies are equally exploited, men's combined powers and authority positions retain privilege. Yet, the cost of that privilege is the demand that men only inhabit this powerful position, which leaves no room for emotional vulnerability or even the weakness of basic humanity (needing rest, getting hurt, being afraid, etc.).

"Understanding Super Men" opens with Daniel J. Connell's chapter, "The Simulacrum of Hypermasculinity in Comic Book Cinema," which discusses the intensification of hypermasculinity's physical aspect through the character of Wolverine as portrayed by Hugh Jackman. Delving into Jean Baudrillard's concept of the simulacrum and the hyperreal, Connell's chapter discusses the impact of live action actors depicting our superheroes, blurring the line between what is physically achievable and what is not. This chapter posits that this proliferation of muscularity—a near requisite of male actors portraying hero roles—has paradoxically moved the aesthetics of the film further along Baudrillard's phases of the image even while bringing the reality of the film closer to its source material.

The second chapter, "Renewing Hegemonic Masculinity Every Wednesday: *Arrow* and Television Form," written by James C. Taylor, elaborates on the link between hypermasculinity and physicality—the powerful body—through textual and extratextual strategies. Drawing from Umberto Eco and Federic Pagello, this chapter discusses superhero texts' serialized narration in light of the repetition of storylines and how that repetition is (or is not) produced in both comics and television format. This chapter explores the way the main actor—Stephen Amell—narrates his masculinity and interlocks it with Oliver/Arrow's, including Amell's continuous communication with fans over social media and his forays into WWE wrestling. The use of textual and extratextual strategies highlights how serialization ritualizes the display of gendered bodies while also potentially opening a space for destabilizing gender norms. Meanwhile, television, with its use of live actors who can extend their performances across multiple texts and social media, further erodes the lines between reality and fiction.

In the final chapter of Part I, Janne Salminen's "'I'll Show You What It Means to Be a Man': Hegemonic Masculinity in *Batman v Superman: Dawn of Justice*," considers how Zack Snyder's film perpetuates the idea that only men constitute humanity. Any deviation from the concept of biological cisgendered males occupying key positions in society are treated as anomalous. Wonder Woman can be as strong as Superman, but physically, she does not disrupt the heterosexual matrix in any way. She is also explicitly mentioned as not being part of the same society or "world" as Batman and Superman, implying that women who are equal to men are an exceptional rarity. Other female characters are reduced to damsels in distress or window dressing. Comparatively, male characters can inhabit the hero role through the demonstration of superior physical strength and a performative suffering that legitimizes their law-breaking vigilantism.

The next section, "Part II: The Monstrous Other," focuses on the characters who are impacted by toxic masculinity but do not fit the hegemonic mold. The three chapters in this section highlight how those outside hegemonic masculinity are pressured to incorporate exalted masculine traits while maintaining their clearly nonhegemonic identity. If they can be accused of trying to take a man's place (in authority or power), the performance of masculinity becomes monstrous instead of mandatory. Whether modeling "Straight Acting," "Butch," or other behavioral strategies, the performance of hegemonic masculinity by nonhegemonic identities must be aspirational or mimetic to avoid being threatening. Simultaneously, these chapters question the viability of hegemonic performance as an equalizing strategy by nonhegemonic identities if it perpetuates the toxicity of hegemonic masculinity.

The first chapter, "The Monstrous in *Batwoman*: Military Masculinity and Domestic Spaces," by Esther De Dauw discusses the demonization of powerful women in superhero narratives. In these narratives, military masculinity is infused with toxic masculinity, impacting Batwoman's childhood, subsequent military career, and lesbian identity. Batwoman is consistently doubled and cast as the Other. Surrounded by Gothic monsters and haunted by her own Otherness, this chapter investigates if the lesbian superhero can sustain superheroism or if she is doomed to failure. It discusses to what degree superhero narratives tend to align military masculinity with superhero masculinity, which draws a line between the heroic combatant and the feminine civilian.

This chapter is followed by Drew Murphy's "*Days of Future Past*: Queer Identities and the X-Men." Since the 1960s, the X-Men have functioned as an allegory for various minority communities and have long served as symbolic interpretations of social ills and discourses of change while their journeys are perhaps most relatable to those of the LGBTQIA+ community. The X-Men must go through a coming out when their powers develop, are often targeted by hate groups, and are subject to discriminatory violence. The vast majority of the X-Men protect themselves by hiding their mutant identities, similar to the way that superherose traditionally hide their superhero identity under their "normal" civilian identities. This concealment mirrors very closely the lives of many LGBTQIA+ people, who often juggle dual identities as both heterosexual and homosexual. This chapter explores the recurring themes in the *Days of Future Past* comic series, published in 1981, and the 2015 movie, drawing comparisons to current and real journeys that LGBTQIA+ people are undertaking both on a personal and a community level.

The final chapter of Part II is "*Torchwood*'s Superman: Bisexuality as a Hypermasculine Superpower" by Craig Haslop, which focuses on the spin-off series *Torchwood*, lauded by academics and popular media for its liberating and frank representations of fluid sexuality. This chapter discusses audience research using focus groups exploring *Torchwood*'s representations of queer masculinity, analyzing respondents' responses to the masculinity of the leading character, Captain Jack Harkness, and the recurring character, Captain John Hart. While not ostensibly superheroes or supervillains in the comic-book sense, research participants positioned them as superhuman or godlike. Using the notion of homonormativity—the pressure on queer people to conform to heteronormativity—this chapter highlights how, despite foregrounding the leading man as fluidly sexual, *Torchwood* suggests a homonormative hypermasculinity dominating much of Western gay male culture, which deradicalizes queer identity and renders it safe for heteronormativity and, by association, hypermasculinity.

This brings us to the final section of this volume: "Part III: Strategies of Resistance." This section offers an insight into representations of gender identities that model alternative superheroic identities. It analyzes narratives that highlight the benefits of resistance and encourages the reader to find more hopeful ways forward even while it questions the possibility of escaping the hegemony and its folding in of the subaltern identity. The two strategies under consideration range from a hyper-performance of traditional gender roles as a way to achieve hidden goals and, essentially, using elements of the patriarchy in order to transgress the patriarchy's boundaries. Alternatively, this section also considers behavior that lies outside the scope of permissible gender identity and behavioral patterns. Are either of these strategies a viable approach to breaking with toxic masculinity?

Attempting to answer the above question, the third section opens with Richard Reynolds's "Emma Frost, the White Queen: Super-Powers as the Performance of Gender." Emma Frost has been a key character and enigma within the Marvel Universe since her first appearance in 1979. Initially a ruthless and hypersexualized operative for the Hellfire Club, Frost has transformed into a core member and leader of the X-Men. Frost engages with the world on her own terms, bypassing many of the stereotypes attached to superheroines. Her challenging personality functions as a dark mirror for other characters in the saga, inscribing emotions and attitudes that implicitly question the values of the X-Men and of the genre to which they belong. Focusing chiefly on her membership in the X-Men and her part in key developments of the Marvel Universe in the twenty-first century, this chapter examines Emma Frost as exemplifying Butler's concept of gender performativity as an explicit aspect of her superpowers. It explores whether the limitations of hegemonic masculinity can offer a way out and asks whether it is possible to consciously exploit hegemonic narratives in order to affect change.

This section closes with "Albus Dumbledore and the Curse of Toxic Masculinity" by Karen Sugrue. In both the worlds of sociology and psychotherapy, a crisis of masculinity can be seen in a number of very concerning trends in violence, mental health, education, media, and in wider social domains. Having explored the traditional representations of "superhero" masculinity through the discussion of superheroes and villains in the previous sections, this chapter analyzes how Albus Dumbledore represents the old superhero masculine archetype by contrasting it with Harry Potter's, who provides a newer and more hopeful model of masculine behavior based on friendship, connection, teamwork, and love. This chapter delves into how characters can model alternative masculinities as an effective strategy to combat the pervasiveness of toxic masculinity and its effects on children and adults alike.

This volume identifies the ways in which (super)hero narratives have promulgated and glorified toxic masculinity. It offers alternative strategies to consider how characters (and their effect on the audience) can resist the hegemonic model and productively demonstrate new masculinities. Despite the difficulties of offering alternative strategies and resistance narratives, this volume highlights that one of the key ways in which we can bring about change is through representation. As Stuller writes, "Sex and Gender do not and should not define us or what we do, but a combination of nature and nurture colors our lives regardless. Who we are influences the stories we tell and the stories we want to hear."[24] When we consider how popular culture and its stories give us a lens through which we can learn how to empathize with and love those different from us, it becomes clear that representation is a promising start, even if it cannot be the whole of our strategy to increase equality. Through new narratives, we can actively imagine the possibility of moving beyond a traditional binary of gender roles defined by mutually exclusive behavioral characteristics that lessens the humanity of us all.

NOTES

1. Dawn Heinecken, *The Warrior Women of Television: A Feminist Cultural Analysis of the New Female Body in Popular Media* (New York: Peter Lang Publishing, 2003), 3.

2. Judith Butler, *Gender Trouble: Feminism and the Subversion of Identity* (London and New York: Routledge, 2007), 45.

3. Raewyn Connell, *Masculinities: Second Edition* (Cambridge: Polity, 2005), 77.

4. Connell.

5. Arwa Mahdawi, "The Troubling Ascent of the LGBT Right Wing," *The Guardian*, October 26, 2017, https://www.theguardian.com/commentisfree/2017/oct/26/ascent-lgbt-right-wing-afd.

6. Megan Vokey et al., "An Analysis of Hyper-Masculinity in Magazine Advertisements," *Sex Roles* 68, no. 9 (2013): 562.

7. Sarah Banet-Weiser and Kate M. Miltner, "#MasculinitySoFragile: culture, structure, and networked misogyny," *Feminist Media Studies* 16, no. 1 (2016): 171.

8. Tristan Bridges and C. J. Pascoe, "Hybrid Masculinities: New Direction in the Sociology of Men and Masculinities," *Sociology Compass* 8, no. 3 (2014): 247.

9. Heinecken, *The Warrior Women of Television*, 5.

10. Brian Massumi, *A User's Guide to Capitalism and Schizophrenia: Deviations from Deleuze and Guattari* (Cambridge: MIT Press, 1992), 51.

11. This count does not include the *X-Men* franchise or various *Fantastic Four* films produced by 20th Century Fox.

12. Jennifer K. Stuller, *Ink-Stained Amazons and Cinematic Warriors: Superwomen in Modern Mythology* (London: I. B. Tauris, 2010), 7.

13. Heinecken, *The Warrior Women of Television*, 91.

14. Heinecken, *The Warrior Women of Television*, 129–30.

15. "Comic Heroine Ms. Marvel Saves San Francisco from Anti-Islam Ads," Asian America, *NBC News*, January 27, 2015, https://www.nbcnews.com/news/asian-america/comic-heroine-ms-marvel-saves-san-francisco-anti-islam-ads-n294751.

16. Marc Singer, "The Myth of Eco: Cultural Populism and Comics Studies," *Studies in Comics* 4, no. 2 (2013): 359.

17. DCCU is used here to refer to the DC Cinematic Universe.

18. Danny Graydon, conversation at The Superhero Project: 2nd Global Meeting, September 9, 2016.

19. Federico Pagello, "'The Origin Story' is the Only Story: Seriality and Temporality in Superhero Fiction from Comics to Post-Television," *Quarterly Review of Film and Video* 34, no. 8 (2017): 728.

20. Billings Learned Hand, quoted in Peter Coogan, "The Definition of the Superhero," in *A Comic Studies Reader*, ed. Jeet Heer and Kent Worcester (Jackson: University Press of Mississippi, 2009), 77.

21. Bonnie Dow, *Prime-Time Feminism: Television, Media Culture, and the Women's Movement since 1970* (Philadelphia: University of Pennsylvania Press, 1996), 12.

22. Heinecken, *The Warrior Women of Television*, 17.

23. Cole Parke, "The Christian Right's Love Affair with Anti-Trans Feminists," *Political Research Associates*, August 11, 2016, https://www.politicalresearch.org/2016/08/11/the-christian-rights-love-affair-with-anti-trans-feminists/.

24. Stuller, *Ink-Stained Amazons*, 155.

PART I

UNDERSTANDING SUPER MEN

THE SIMULACRUM OF HYPERMASCULINITY IN COMIC BOOK CINEMA

DANIEL J. CONNELL

When Jean Baudrillard released his prescient philosophical treatise *Simulacres et Simulation* in 1981, only two examples existed of blockbuster Hollywood superhero films: *Superman* (1978) and *Superman II* (1980). The notional simulacrum Baudrillard spoke of—a simulacrum being a world shorn of external references, disconnected from reality—was not related to Reeve's Superman, given that Baudrillard's main theory was that media culture was primarily concerned with interpreting and reflecting some hyperreal image not truly connected with reality. Reeve, an excellent athlete after whom the Sportsmanship Award at Princeton Day School's invitational hockey tournament was named, stood 6 ft. 4 in (1.93m) tall and was by all accounts an outstanding physical specimen. Although he did weightlifting with David Prowse (of Darth Vader fame) and added some 30 lbs (14kg) to his frame in preparation for the role, the base was already there: someone at the pinnacle representing someone at the pinnacle.[1]

Reeve's Superman fit in perfectly with Orrin E. Klapp's analysis regarding popular models of masculinity: "The purpose of hero-worship behaviour seems to be to convert a selected individual to an ideal, a durable symbol of supernormal performance—to capture and make a norm of the exceptional."[2] Where Klapp's research on popular heroes in the 1950s reflected and preceded archetypes like Reeve's Superman, Baudrillard's theories attached themselves via the work of Lacan to a world he saw as unraveling at an increasing pace just after Reeve's debut.[3] What is fascinating about the intertwining events—the first true superhero blockbusters and Baudrillard's theories of hyperreality—is how they set a groundwork that would not truly reveal its connectedness until far later: the year 2000.

Perhaps the delay occurred because of the need for technology—explicitly CGI—to develop further so that audiences could be convinced of a fantastical world's reality. Or, maybe the explosion and long death of the muscleman action film, peaking with Sylvester Stallone and Arnold Schwarzenegger in the mid-1980s to the early 1990s, delayed the financial imperative for studios to invest in developing superhero films. What is clear, however, is that the sustained era of comic book cinema can be defined as having started with 2000's *X-Men*—produced by Richard Donner, who had delivered us the son of Krypton twenty-two years prior. Twentieth Century Fox's foray into the genre set off a continued burst, eventually leading to the creation of two distinct cinematic universes: those of Marvel and DC. What had been sporadic releases such as Reeve's Superman, the Tim Burton–directed *Batman* series, or even Wesley Snipes as Blade, cemented into a more consistent, viable genre with the release of *X-Men*.

What connects *X-Men* and Baudrillard? In short, two hypers: hyperreality and hypermasculinity. Hyperreality denotes the inability to distinguish reality from a simulation of reality—which, Baudrillard argues, leads us inexorably towards the simulacrum. Hypermasculinity, on the other hand, can be defined as the exaggeration of stereotypical male behavior, such as feting of physical strength and aggression over emotional intelligence and empathy. Part of this "macho" image is founded on being effortlessly muscular and imposing in stature. Comic books—from *Action Comics* #1 onwards—provide a clear intersection between hyperreality and hypermasculinity, given as they are to presenting dramatically masculine physicality. And yet, the intangibility of comics—that inevitable removal from reality caused by the need to represent rather than to replicate—presents a rather neat buffer to the issue of hyperreal culture, creating a need for something we do not have or want. A person may temporarily wish to fly like Superman or have his physical proportions—but, presented as they often are, this notion is fantastical rather than definable as actual longing. In the context of comic books, a person *cannot* become the physical iteration of the superhero. Where this becomes a fascinating prospect is when the medium shifts to that of film: here the superheroes are, by and large, represented as flesh and blood. The buffer is removed, and the audience can see (or perhaps might see the physical potential of) themselves within the source material. Now Baudrillard's Phases of the Image become important considerations:

> Such would be the successive phases of the image:
> It is the reflection of a profound reality;

It masks and denatures a profound reality;
It masks the absence of a profound reality;
It has no relation to any reality whatsoever:
it is its own pure simulacrum.[4]

This sequence is the journey into hyperreality, a space with no referentials, which is known as a simulacrum. In the evolution of comic book cinema, the physical manifestations of hypermasculinity have denatured a profound reality (male physicality in its average guise) and traveled through Baudrillard's phases as a natural evolution.

In view of this phased development, the boundaries of hyperreal hypermasculinity will be bookmarked by the first and purported last iteration of Hugh Jackman's Wolverine: *X-Men* in 2000 and *Logan* in 2017. In time, the nature of the genre is likely to become even more hyperreal. With this in mind, it is important to note the attempts—conscious or otherwise—of the earlier superhero films of the twenty-first century to ground themselves notionally in a form of realistic interpretation. This section will focus on the Fox and Marvel Studios films, as the DC Cinematic Universe will be discussed elsewhere in this volume. For the sake of brevity and clarity, this chapter will mostly avoid discussing large ensemble films—for example, the Avengers series or *Captain America: Civil War* (2016)—and will largely focus on the physical manifestations of hypermasculinity instead of on behavioral elements. The focus can thus remain on a key attribute which, as Erica Scharrer noted in *Experiment*, creates a scenario whereby "hypermasculine males exhibit extreme and exaggerated forms of masculinity, virility and physicality."[5] The journey from exaggeration to simulacrum is most potently examined through the representation of masculine physicality.

BECOMING HYPERMASCULINE

When Jackman first appeared as the adamantium-augmented superhero Wolverine, he was thirty-one years old. Though tall at 6 ft. 3 in. (1.9m), he lacked a particularly muscular physique—in direct contrast to the comic-based, 5 ft. 3 in. (1.6m), burly character he was hired to play.

In this initial iteration, Jackman bears all the hallmarks of a heteronormative, idealized Western Everyman: tall, slim, fit, conventionally good looking. The animalistic and brutal nature of his character are presented through mannerisms rather than raw physical presence. He does not provide a truly

Hugh Jackman as Wolverine in X-Men (2000) © 20th Century Fox

realized corporeal manifestation of the comic book figure. What is fascinating about this image—and a hallmark of the genre's relationship with physical hypermasculinity—is that somehow, seeing the transformative journey Jackman has taken and the subsequent popularity of the extreme muscular look, Jackman does not look quite right in this picture. He has not truly *become* Wolverine—which is bizarre when one considers that *X-Men* is his first and one of his most successful outings as Logan.

This Everyman physical quality already begins to distort in the early 2000s. *Spider-Man* (2002) stars Tobey Maguire as the eponymous hero. There is a famous scene where, having been bitten by the radioactive spider, a gaunt Peter Parker slumps into a feverish sleep, only to wake empowered and bulked up. He stares at himself in the mirror, visibly confused at the overnight appearance of a six pack. What is fascinating about this transformation is that it represents the actual (what actors have to go through to complete these roles) and the virtual (a clearer iteration of the comic book original). In a 2007 *E!News* article, Maguire reveals that he received the role only after stripping down to reveal his physique—which suggests that the super-skinny Parker was an effect enhanced either by visual tricks or CGI.[6] The genre is set on a hypermasculine path: actors need to prepare for their roles to substantiate the dimensions their characters inhabit on the page. This trend instigates an era of quasi-hypermasculinity, signified by Jackman's increasing muscularity in the same role for 2003's *X2*, and the hiring of younger, fitter men in roles such as Superman (Brandon Routh) in 2006's *Superman Returns* or the Human Torch (Chris Evans) in 2005's *Fantastic Four*.

"SOMETIMES, YOU GOTTA RUN BEFORE YOU CAN WALK"

What Maguire's transformation scene also sets in motion is the standard requirement in the genre to show, usually in topless scenes, the effortless hypermasculinity of the characters. In some films this is not a surprise. Chris Hemsworth's Norse god Thor, for example, would be expected to have a suitably classical heroic physique. Henry Cavill's Superman should probably look like he can hold up an oil rig if that is what he is doing in the film. However, the pattern becomes odd when it does not seem to even correlate with the nature of the character. Take, for example, Benedict Cumberbatch's Dr. Strange, who has magical powers, or Paul Rudd's Ant Man, who is a master thief with a special suit that makes him microscopic. Even Robert Downey Jr.'s Iron Man seems to have bulked up by the time of 2010's *Iron Man 2*, even though his superheroism is derived from his intellect and from technology, with a robotic body that allows him to embody the heroic body without needing to physically possess muscularity. These developments indicate an acceleration through Baudrillard's phases of the image: though the genre may have, in small instances, suggested a reflection of a profound reality (that the Everyman could, perhaps, become a superhero), it very quickly moves on to the second phase—the masking and denaturing of a profound reality. These men, edging into the hypermasculine realm, represent an Everyman that does not truly exist. The slim, injured Tony Stark of 2008 came to resemble more the physique of someone with superpowers in 2010—all while still devoting most of his time to refining his reactor technology. Stark's Everyman quality is masked by his new physique and denatured by the very fact that he seems to maintain it with no effort at all.[7] This perversion is driven by the innate conflict between the two desirable drivers of the genre: to get as close as possible to the source material and to appear relatable to its core audience, which has consistently been men aged 18–35.[8] There is a sense of impossibility when it comes to balancing these two conflicts: one cannot have the wondrous, transformative nature of the comics while also presenting these heroes as merely above average.

There is also the question, once the pattern of actors hiring specialists to condition their physiques is established, of professional pride: to be a superhero, post–Maguire Spider-Man and Jackman Wolverine, actors have the pressure of knowing they need to look the part. What this presents is homogenous athletic hypermasculinity, where even characters who do not rely on physical strength look like they work out. Paradoxically, scenes showing any of these characters working out are quite rare—though it could be argued that due to his corporate responsibilities, philanthropy, playboy lifestyle, and crime-fighting duties, moviemakers need to show audiences how Batman maintains his physique. Hence, we see him work out in both the Christian Bale and Ben Affleck iterations. Yet he is very much an isolated figure among the current representations of film superheroes.

Where this masking and denaturing of a profound reality takes root is in its lack of care for what it presents: actual humans as effortless comic book characters. It is no surprise that, when one searches online for "Hugh Jackman Wolverine workout," pages and pages of hits show up. It is an ephemeral ideal presented on screen, so tantalizing, since we know this person is real, he exists, and he did something to make himself look this way. The profound reality—the tenet that the Everyman in each character reflects a more universal possibility of heroism—has been denatured into a quest to replicate this hypermasculine totem of heroism: the physical intertwined with the moral. Never mind that these actors are *paid* to look like these heroes. Never mind that they have months, and hours per day, and teams of experts supporting them, to create what is largely a temporary result. Millions of people across the globe want to be like the Wolverine they see on screen, even if Hugh Jackman himself does not look like that six months after filming has wrapped.

ABSENCE OF A PROFOUND REALITY

Of course, one would have to believe in the innate ability of the Everyman to be heroic to even think such a thing could be denatured. It certainly seems as though the genre itself believes so: perhaps because the comics industry was born out of an audience's desire to see transformative goodness in its heroes, which creators assume to be a desired reflection of potential in oneself. But, if that is not true and there is no profound reality of potential good, the image comes to reflect this absence. Take what Mike Ryan, Jackman's trainer for *The Wolverine*, had to say about their preparations:

> When we were building Hugh up for the Wolverine movie, we got a call from Baz Luhrmann who was directing Hugh in the movie *Australia*. Baz said, "Come on, guys, back it off! He's getting too big." And you can see Hugh getting bigger in the film. In *Wolverine*, Hugh looks big onscreen, but really he's just ripped. That's the secret to looking good. It's not just about getting big, it's about getting ripped.[9]

The Simulacrum of Hypermasculinity in Comic Book Cinema   25

Hugh Jackman as Wolverine in The Wolverine (2013) © 20th Century Fox

The fantasy of one film is ruined by the construction of another. This discrepancy belies the lack of profundity in outcome or result. Luhrmann and the film he is trying to create is irrelevant, because the dividing line has now dissipated. The image is now for, and only of itself: Jackman *has* to look like this because he *is* the Wolverine. His complete integration with the character now means that not only is there no Everyman within, but the suggestive connection between source material and audience is also lost. To think one could be Wolverine from the comics is fantasy; to think you could be Jackman, by the time *X-Men Origins: Wolverine* (2009) and *The Wolverine* (2013) were released, is nigh impossible.

"I'M DISTRACTING YOU, YOU TURD-BLOSSOM!"

It is almost too tempting to list and categorize every actor who has undergone a comic book metamorphosis, but one stands out as particularly notable in the context of visualised hypermasculinity: Chris Pratt's representation of Peter Quill/Starlord in the *Guardians of the Galaxy* series. This transformation illuminates the absurdity of the denaturing process, based as it is on

Chris Pratt as Andy Dwyer in Parks and Recreation (2009–15) © NBC Studios

referentials, which ultimately are ephemeral—leading us inexorably to the final phases of the image.

Before *Guardians of the Galaxy* (2014), Pratt was most famous for portraying Andy Dwyer in television series *Parks and Recreation* (2009–15). Dwyer is a stereotypical Everyman figure in the series—constantly down on his luck, bumbling through success and misfortune with equal pluck, his constant positivity both a source of annoyance for other characters but also a source of much sympathy and love. He is out of shape physically, unkempt for the most part, and tends to keep favor with others by living on the merits of his charm.

Then came Pratt's turn as Peter Quill, arguably making him a household name. Quill shares many attributes with Dwyer. He often reacts to situations rather than planning ahead, and he spent his adult life as a chancer who has survived rather than thrived. He is plucky and charming, but he is also muscular, athletic, and heroic. At the beginning of the film, his attempt to be known as "Starlord" is laughed at. By its conclusion, he is not only justly called that, but he has also become a Guardian of the Galaxy. In this film, the Everyman has been clearly denatured. It is as though they constructed a proxy of Andy Dwyer—albeit in perfect physical form—only to reduce

Chris Pratt as Peter Quill in Guardians of the Galaxy (2014)

these characteristics to actual barriers preventing Quill from ascending to true Starlord-dom.

In this process, the denaturing of a profound reality occurs on several levels. One, it remodels the essence of the Everyman physically: in the sixth season of *Parks and Recreation*, an explanation for Andy Dwyer's obvious physical transformation was included in the plot. What could account for Dwyer's shift to athletic physique? He loses fifty pounds after giving up beer. Though such a brief explanation adroitly sidesteps the many questions raised by his dramatic change, it perpetuates an illusion of ease: cut out one thing, and such a physique is achievable and effortless. The imperfections of the Dwyer Everyman can be shed like a snake's skin, but in doing so, the image inhabits a place where that physical Everyman is completely different.

Two, it denatures the context of the Everyman so that the positives at the beginning of the film become barriers (and later quirks) that Quill must transcend to become his "better" self. Three, it mutates Pratt's performance as Dwyer, leaving the notional Everyman in a quasi state of flux between being and nonbeing; either iteration warped by the other's existence to the point where the actuality of what constitutes averagely male is strained to breaking point. Four, it denatures the notion of an Everyman as even being profound. With the shifting sands of impossible physicality and stratification of priorities in terms of what constitutes a "good" man, the things that make an Everyman become toxic to the image. The characteristics (generalized flaws in masculinity, such as a beer belly) become the porcupine's needles, bursting the bubble of an imperfect contender for that of the ultimately brave (to the point of self-annihilation) model of machismo. If something can be erased so easily, how can it be profound?

Five, the obsession with Chris Pratt's transformation for the film denatured the profound reality of make-believe. Now that an Everyman had become an action hero, it was subsequently incumbent upon all masculinity to follow suit. Much as how the Amell/Arrow reality became blurred via social media, as will be discussed later, so too did the Pratt/Dwyer/Starlord character merge through a flurry of memes. The link between real and unreal was itself denatured. Andy Dwyer now had not only the desire but the overwhelming impetus to become the Starlord.

ONWARDS TO THE HYPERMASCULINE SIMULACRUM

When placed in context with one another, these transformative moments in each comic book film present the next phase: masking the absence of a profound reality. What these scenes intend is to say that the impossible is not only real but that it is also actualized in physical form. The summation of six months or more of intense physical work and dietary restriction, all for a matter of seconds on screen, ferments the idea that all men can be this, or in fact, are this. If we glance above the convex lens of presented masculinity, we uncover the mask. Not only is this hypermasculinity absent in daily life or the everyman's reality, it also masks the profundity itself.

Six pack? No big deal. Bowling ball shoulders? Yeah, that is just the way it is. By suggesting an innate physical power with a near-perfect manifestation, these representations disempower those fulfilling the role. Their sacrifices become nothing, a mere trifle, so that their fictional alternatives have it simply as a state of "being." This robs the reality side of the equation from any sort of profound meaning in this state by denying it even happens. And in the real world, where actors have trainers to help and months to train and chefs to cook and hours per day to work out, they are also marginalized away into superficiality. These men become a model for being men, even though everyone knows that it is likely only they who can be these transformative vessels.

This lack is masked not only by the near-obligatory "reveal" shot, but also by the processes that propel it into prominence. Actors work out just before the cameras roll, forcing glycogen into their muscles (known as "the pump") to make them even bigger. They go through a period of dehydration so that the skin around the muscles shrinks, making the muscles more pronounced. The use of CGI enhancement to extend these features further is never overly revealed (because it would expose the masking process). Finally, factor in the possibility of steroids—and there is now an environment driven into a dangerous simulacral underworld.[10] While never quite distorting masculinity to the realms seen in the extremes of bodybuilding, it is caught in a loop of tweaking, enhancing, presenting as real something which is in actuality unnatural, fleeting, and impossible to maintain for even the actors over the duration of the film shoot.

This hypermasculinity steps outside and beyond the fantasy of cinema, its boundaries purely delineating referentials within its own bubble. Transformations are compared to others, the hierarchy of masculinity a comparison network where the more hyper, the better. Nowhere is this one-upping better illustrated than in *The Avengers* (2012) where, when the effete Loki has a showdown with the gigantic Hulk, Loki is interrupted mid-monologue and smashed like a ragdoll into the ground. Having put Loki in his hypomasculine place, Hulk walks away muttering the famous line: "Puny god."[11] In the simulacra, even immortality plays second fiddle to the hypermasculine ideal.

As scholars have noted, we can see the clearly destructive path hypermasculinity (or machismo) takes, where the unwavering narrative is to be "not just male, not just masculine, the macho must be hypermasculine in ideology and action."[12] In any genre, medium, or occupation—from being in the army to producing hip-hop music—the evidence points to the presentation of hypermasculinity having an inherently negative impact on impressionable young men. As Fancher, Knudson, and Rosen observed, "hypermasculinity is more likely to develop in an environment that is male-only or male predominant. In addition, we propose that the more opportunities men have to reinforce one another's behavior (sic), the higher the levels of hypermasculinity will be."[13] This visual reinforcement in turn bleeds unrealistic behaviors and modes of being into the real world, creating mental health issues and contributing to the increased levels of violence and abuse within society.

OLD MAN LOGAN

The looming endpoint of the hypermasculine simulacrum in superhero cinema can be no better typified than Hugh Jackman's final outing as Wolverine in *Logan* (2017). Much like Miller's comic *Old Man Logan* (2008–9),

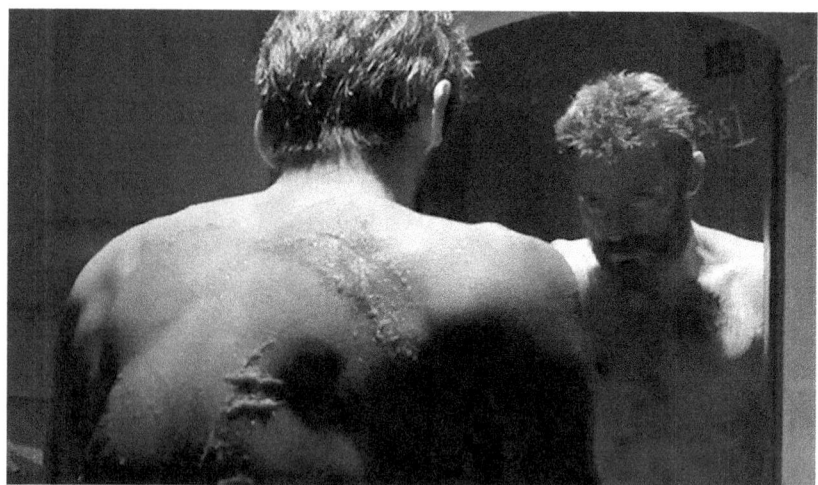

Chris Pratt as Peter Quill in Guardians of the Galaxy (2014)

we witness a failing, ageing character, still ferocious but shorn of much of his potency and physicality. *Logan*—which, in true hypermasculine fashion, cannot bring itself to label its hero an old man—pits this grey-bearded version against the ultimate enemy: his younger self, in the form of X-24.

It is vitally important to remember that the endpoint of the simulacrum is an image shorn of all referentials; it is its own reference. And so *Logan* stands. It teases connections to other films, other stories, but nothing is overt. Someone could watch the film without ever having seen Jackman as Logan previously and understand the pathos of a man facing the younger version of himself. We even get a scene where Logan looks at himself in the mirror, still muscular but clearly diminished—a clear nod to the near-obligatory shirtless "reveal" scene which is now a trope of male-dominated superhero movies.

The extreme physicality of X-24—itself a seemingly hyped version of previous Jackman outings—is a constant reminder that Logan has become *less*. This decline is all the more ironic, because the toxic element degrading our hero is the adamantium—the metal core which represents his power, his ferocity, and his image. In true toxic masculinity terms, Logan must choose: walk away, or sacrifice himself to save a different version of his attributes: the young mutant Laura, created from Logan's DNA. The referentials in this imagery *feel* meaningful—the old man confronts his dangerous younger self to save his genetic offspring. Yet, the relevance is internalized in a circular loop. That it is Laura who kills X-24, and not Logan, denotes a changing of the guard, a move away from the hypermasculine extremes of previous outings. The trouble with this notion is that this is a bubble: there is no series, no sequel, and no actual change. The audience is supposed to mourn *and* celebrate the hypermasculine hero and his sacrifice, content in the knowledge the future will be different, better, yet somehow the same through Laura. The potency of doubling becomes, as Baudrillard suggests:

> Of all the prostheses that mark the history of the body, the double is doubtless the oldest. But the double is precisely not a prosthesis: it is an imaginary figure, which, just like the soul, the shadow, the mirror image, haunts the subject like his other, which makes it so that the subject is simultaneously itself and never resembles itself again, which haunts the subject like a subtle and always averted death. This is not always the case, however: when the double materializes, when it becomes visible, it signifies imminent death.[14]

While pursuing a laudable attempt to critique the hypermasculine excess and the power abuses of the past, Mangold's film cannot reach out and grasp beyond the critical juncture of its own finality. It fulfils what Mosher and Tompkins suggested was the end point, " . . . the pride of masculine ascendancy—the hubris of 'masculine superiority'—precedes a fall into death," but not in a connected, broader way.[15] Jackman's Logan dies in the only way he can, as he cannot avoid the hypermasculine conflict that will resolve his violent cycle. Instead of embedding a character's end in a fuller narrative, it can and does only deal with the end of the end within the end itself, not a continuation or beginning of anything. The critique loses its sting in this way. Logan is still killed by X-24, the old man bested by his hypermasculine self. That the thing which kills him is a CGI-generated, hyperreal version of himself that cannot possibly exist is patently simulacral. Neither version of Logan is seen anywhere else and probably will not be again, yet the image instills pathos in its narrative, the cycle of Wolverine's journey borne back ceaselessly into the past. It has become its own simulacrum, and there is every chance we might not see Laura—our true change in the environment—again.

With the advent of the modern superhero movie came a portal into the real world: a reflection of reality, as Baudrillard noted. Yet as technology developed, budgets increased, and the number of films proliferated, so too did the image of masculinity move along the phases. Hints of the hypermasculine became key tenets, overpowering any sense of nuance. That key connection—image as reflection—was removed and what emerged was a denatured hyperreality, whose mere existence undercuts any idea of a profound reality that might be found in the notional Everyman.

Perhaps the step into the final phase, the simulacral unreality, will actually save us from the excesses hypermasculinity brings into society, aligning the films more with the inherent fantasy of their print originators. There is a sense—with Hulk, Thanos, the giant former wrestler Dave Bautista—that perhaps we are slowly edging away from the pressurizing representation of "normal" men transforming themselves into godlike beings with apparent ease. Then again, just look at the shape 46-year-old Paul Rudd got into for *Ant-Man* (2015). In a world where hegemonic patriarchy is still going strong, a paradigm shift in gender politics is required if we are ever to achieve the goal of equality. With this in mind, how healthy is it that the first quarter-century of the new millennium is (at least in cinematic terms) dominated by a genre that dictates masculine identity in almost exclusively impossible hypermasculine terms?

When a man who requires a suit to fight for him—Robert Downey Jr.'s Iron Man—how can it possibly make sense that he is in such fantastic shape? And yet, in the simulacra, even this combination of technology and physicality is not good enough. Consider *Avengers: Age of Ultron* (2013) and *Civil War* (2016) to see Stark's inherent villainy leading to his hamartia in *Endgame* (2019): having a bigger brain than his muscles. It is not a solution to suggest these transformations need not occur. What is vitally important is that we explore ways of uncoupling heroism and hypermasculinity.

NOTES

1. "Christopher Reeve," *IMDb*, accessed June 10, 2019, https://www.imdb.com/name/nm0001659/bio?ref_=nm_ov_bio_sm.

"Harry Rulon-Miller '51 Invitational," *Princeton Day School*, December 8, 2017, https://issuu.com/princetondayschool/docs/hrm_program_17_for_issuu.

2. Orrin E Klapp, "Heroes, Villains and Fools, as Agents of Social Control," *American Sociological Review* 19, no. 1 (February 1954): 60.

3. It is interesting to note, given Reeve's hallowed position as a progenitor of the superhero physique, that his later disability saw a transformation from physical manifestation of heroism into one of heroic spirit, as discussed by José Alaniz, who briefly examines Reeve's conscious cultivation of an inspirational and hopeful narrative following his injury. For instance, the Foundation for a Better Life's billboard advertisement featured Reeve's headshot and the words "Superman. Strength *Pass It On*." As Alaniz points out, the use of this headshot conveniently hides his (injured) body from view while invoking the heroic body through the reference to Superman. Combined with the 2000 Super Bowl add that featured a walking Reeve through

the use of CGI, it is clear that the heroic spirit cultivated by Reeve required the elimination of his disabled body in favor of a plastic, digitally animated, or even referenced-only heroic body.

4. Jean Baudrillard, *Simulacra and Simulation*, trans. Sheila Faria Glaser (Michigan: The University of Michigan Press, 2000), 6.

5. Erica Scharrer, "Hypermasculinity, Aggression, and Television Violence: An Experiment," *Media Psychology* 7, no. 4 (2005): 353–76.

6. Marc Malkin, "Spider-Man's Shirtless Audition," *E!News*, May 7, 2007, https://www.eonline.com/news/59203/spider-man-s-shirtless-audition.

7. It is worth noting that Tony Stark is an Everyman in a strictly "wish fulfillment" way: a rich, quick-talking playboy who gets to play hero. He is not an Everyman alter ego, such as Clark Kent or Peter Parker.

8. Victoria McNally, "Why 2016 is the Year We Need to Stop Pretending Women Aren't Geeks," *MTV*, December 22, 2015, http://www.mtv.com/news/2683640/geek-media-numbers-breakdown/. Joanna Piacenza, "Superhero Movies Possess Staying Power with Viewers, but Moviegoers Say They Want to See More Diverse Characters," *Morning Consult*, April 26, 2018, https://morningconsult.com/2018/04/26/superhero-movies-possess-staying-power-with-viewers/.

9. Joel Snape, "Hugh Jackman Workout: How He Got Ripped for Wolverine," *Coach Mag*, March 31, 2016, accessed September 6, 2016, http://www.coachmag.co.uk/exercises/celebrity-workouts/146/exclusive-hugh-jackman-wolverine-workout.

10. Steroids are simply synthetic testosterone, mimicking the hormone that predominantly drives masculine traits. Steroids are taken in order to become more masculine.

11. *Avengers Assemble,* directed by Joss Whedon (2012; Burbank: Marvel Studios).

12. Donald L. Mosher and Silvan S. Tomkins, "Scripting the Macho Man: Hypermasculine Socialization and Encultration," *Journal of Sex Research* 25, no. 1 (February 1988): 64.

13. Peggy Fancher, Kathryn K. Knudson, and Leora N. Rosen. "Cohesion and the Culture of Hypermasculinity in U. S. Army Units," *Armed Forces and Society* 29, no. 3 (Spring 2003): 328.

14. Baudrillard, *Simulacra and Simulation*, 95.

15. Mosher, "Scripting the Macho Man," 82

RENEWING HEGEMONIC MASCULINITY EVERY WEDNESDAY

Arrow and Television Form

JAMES C. TAYLOR

In this chapter, I explore how the specificities of television form combine with conventions of the superhero genre to facilitate or inflect the perpetuation of hegemonic masculinity. I first examine the ways in which televisual seriality is gendered and consider if these impact the gendering of live-action superhero television. A short overview of key superhero television shows outlines how their representations of masculinity are in dialogue with television form. Using Jason Mittell's concept of "complex television," I frame developments in television in the last few decades that pose challenges to restrictive understandings of gender, in particular, the increasing use of this mode in *Lois and Clark: The New Adventures of Superman* (1993–1997) and *Smallville* (2001–2011).[1] In proceeding to focus on *Arrow* (2012–), I am not proposing a clean trajectory for gender representation in superhero television. *Arrow* is an interesting case study for examining how modes of television narration that can destabilize normative masculinity are deployed in a show in which the superhero protagonist and lead actor's (Stephen Amell) persona enforce a particularly rigid model of hegemonic masculinity. Through analysis of *Arrow*'s narrative structure, story, and stylistic motifs, I identify and interrogate strategies through which hegemonic masculinity is affirmed.[2] I proceed to explore how these strategies are developed in intertexts and paratexts that Amell generates through his participation in professional wrestling and use of social media.

Superhero narratives typically celebrate physically strong, white, heterosexual masculinity, contributing to the inscription of this as the hegemonic model of masculinity in Western culture. However, it is crucial to note that hegemony is not a set constant. Raewyn Connell explains that "'[h]egemonic masculinity' is not a fixed character type, always and everywhere the same. It is, rather, the masculinity that occupies the hegemonic position in a given pattern of gender relations, a position always contestable."[3] This contestability is elucidated by Connell's assertion that masculinity is not a system but rather "a configuration of practice *within* a system of gender relations" (original emphasis).[4] As a configuration, hegemonic masculinity can be *reconfigured*. Alterations occur in the process of renewal that Raymond Williams stresses is inherent to hegemony. Its internal structures "have continually to be renewed, recreated and defended; and by the same token . . . they can be continually challenged and in certain respects modified."[5]

The serialization of *Arrow*, which airs for twenty-three weeks a year, provides a regular structure for the renewal, and potential modification, of hegemony. The show's intertexts and paratexts weave into this structure. My understanding of intertextuality and paratextuality follows Gérard Genette's formulation of these concepts and Johnathan Gray's development of them in relation to film and television.[6] If we consider a text to be a work such as a novel or television show, its intertexts and paratexts form explicit or indirect relationships with the work, framing and shaping the work's meanings. As Gray explains, "intertextuality often refers to the instance wherein one or more bona fide shows frame another show, whereas paratextuality refers to the instance wherein a textual fragment or 'peripheral' frames a show."[7] An intertext is another whole work in dialogue with the work at hand. Genette suggests quotation as the most literal kind of declared intertextuality.[8] Intertextuality also takes more implicit forms, such as previous works in a genre, setting audience expectations for a new work. "Textual fragments" deemed paratexts include officially circulated materials such as trailers, merchandise, and DVD covers, alongside unauthorized audience creations such as fan sites, internet memes, and cosplay. The intertexts and paratexts encountered vary among audience members, allowing for divergent frameworks through which audiences can approach a text, yet officially circulated intertexts and paratexts seek to steer audience engagement. The *Arrow* intertexts and paratexts that Amell generates provide creator-sanctioned frameworks. In this chapter, after observing the serialized renewal of hegemonic masculinity in *Arrow* (the text), I pay particular attention to its wrestling intertexts and Amell's social media paratexts, since these are prominent and distinctive ways in which *Arrow*'s discourses on masculinity are furthered.

SERIALITY, GENDER, AND SUPERHEROES

Seriality is inherent to the superhero genre, which began in monthly comic books and rapidly spread to other serialized forms. Broadly speaking, we can define two modes of seriality: *series*, in which the diegetic world is continuous but storytelling is episodic, with no character or plot development occurring between installments, and *serial*, in which plots cumulatively develop across multiple installments.[9] In his pioneering study of television, John Fiske enumerates distinctions between masculine and feminine televisual forms, with mode of seriality being a key factor.[10] As summarized by Mittell, "Fiske contrasts the feminine facets of open narrative deferment, emotional expressiveness, domestic settings, and character complexity against masculine norms of exclusively male professional spheres, rational actions, and narrative closure."[11] Fiske's feminine category is exemplified by soap operas, which feature ongoing melodramatic storylines about interpersonal relationships. Pre-1990s superhero television shows, such as *The Adventures of Superman* (1952–1958), *Batman* (1966–1968), and *The Incredible Hulk* (1978–1982), follow a series structure and largely adhere to Fiske's masculine category. *Lois and Clark* represents a significant shift. Like earlier Superman television shows, *Lois and Clark* is set in the professional sphere of newspaper journalism and stages episodic encounters between Superman (Dean Cain) and villains. However, much emphasis is also placed on romantic tension between Lois Lane (Teri Hatcher), Superman, and his civilian identity, Clark Kent. The romance develops in serial form across four seasons, from courtship to engagement to marriage. *Lois and Clark*'s blending of masculine and feminine conventions reflects Mittell's claims. While Mittell accepts Fiske's distinctions for television contemporaneous to Fiske's writing, in the 1980s, he argues that, since then, gendered qualities are interlaced in "complex television," a dominant mode of prime-time drama. Complex television exhibits "interplay between the demands of episodic and serial storytelling" that correspondingly elicits interplay between the gendered logics ascribed to these modes of serialization.[12]

This blending, and its potential to impact representations of masculinity, is pointedly evident in *Smallville* and *Arrow*. Over ten seasons, *Smallville* depicts a teenage Clark Kent (Tom Welling) slowly becoming Superman. The first season uses an episodic "monster of the week" format, while characters' relationships develop across the season. Later seasons place greater emphasis on storylines that span multiple episodes. *Arrow* exhibits heightened narrative complexity, using the development of two interconnected stories set five years apart as a structuring device for the first five seasons. These stories each have arcs which span a season, while many episodes feature weekly villains. The story set five years in the past depicts the physical and emotional trials that Oliver endured after being stranded on a remote island. These experiences make Oliver, upon returning to his native Starling City at the beginning of season one, emotionally closed off while highly proficient in combat, skills he puts to use as violent vigilante Arrow in a campaign to eliminate corrupt businessmen.[13] Oliver's mission as Arrow provides the primary story, in which he is well equipped to defeat criminals but ill prepared for reconnecting with loved ones, which is an ongoing narrative concern.

The protagonists of *Smallville* and *Arrow*'s distinct masculinities are interwoven with the shows' structures, narrative concerns, and approaches to the superhero genre. *Smallville*'s coming-of-age story explores Clark's emotional and moral development, alongside bodily changes as his superpowers develop. Rebecca Feasey considers Clark representative of a recurring model of masculinity for teen science-fiction television, in which male leads "are seen to be entirely comfortable with their emotional, thoughtful and considerate feminine side."[14] Clark's caring nature and involvement in the domestic issues of family and friends is also akin to the characterization of many other teenage superheroes, such as Peter Parker/Spider-Man and Kamala Khan/Ms. Marvel. Meanwhile, in *Arrow*, Oliver's repression of feeling is in keeping with the brooding male superhero archetype exemplified by Bruce Wayne/Batman, whose civilian identity inhabits the professional world while his superhero identity fights crime. This archetype is comparable to the model of television masculinity that Feasey identifies in crime dramas, in which the male detective "has to sacrifice domestic duties and family commitments for the good of his professional career and for the greater good of society."[15] Appropriately, Batman is often called the "world's greatest detective." In *Arrow*, an established superhero archetype and model of television masculinity interlock to compound Oliver's emotional withdrawal, although the ongoing exploration of Oliver's need to emotionally reassimilate into Starling City prevents a simple affirmation of this attitude. Rather than the more harmonious fusion of masculine and feminine qualities found in *Smallville*'s protagonist, Oliver's arc dramatizes tension between masculine and feminine traits, laying bare the emotionally withdrawn male superhero archetype for examination.

THE POLITICS OF SERIALITY

Umberto Eco calls superhero comic books "iterative" narratives, observing that they repeat storylines over and over.[16] He finds their stories and series structure inherently ideologically conservative: in each installment, superheroes fight forces that threaten to upend the status quo and their victories reaffirm the established order.[17] Federico Pagello extends Eco's examination of seriality to superhero texts in other media and finds that, subsequent to Eco's writing in 1972, many of these texts exhibit an enhanced commitment to serial narration, although still ultimately reiterate the same stories.[18] In season one of *Arrow*, Oliver seeks to be proactive, harnessing postrecession sentiments by hunting the corporate elite. Favoring an ongoing serial mission to overturn the establishment suggests that the potential for reforming social norms is built into *Arrow*'s design.

Oliver's efforts in Starling City are counterplotted by an extended origin story. Pagello outlines a temporal paradox in superhero origin stories: the origin is the part in a superhero's adventures where development actually happens—where civilian transforms into superhero—yet also builds toward the point at which development ceases and the narrative assumes an iterative cycle.[19] Furthermore, the constant retelling of origins itself becomes a form of iteration. In his analysis of contemporary superhero films, Jeffrey A. Brown argues that the "obsessional focus in the films on the moment that the regular man becomes the superhero is a ritualized presentation of masculinization."[20] As superhero texts retell stories of men gaining physical strength and taking on the duty of enforcing order, hegemonic masculinity is entrenched through iteration. Whereas in cinema, a superhero's origin often spans a film's duration, the process through which Oliver becomes Arrow is protracted by flashback sequences, dispersed through five seasons. This structuring device prompts narrative strategies that avoid simple repetition. In *Arrow*'s flashbacks Oliver gains physical strength, combat skills and the resolve to command his and others' destinies, offering a sustained presentation of the construction of hegemonic masculinity. Counterplotting this construction against the interpersonal challenges Oliver faces in Starling City, and the gradual thawing of his emotions, further illuminates the process of construction by outlining an inverse deconstruction. As season one progresses, the present-day Oliver develops a capacity for empathy, increasingly giving enemies a chance at redemption before, at the beginning of season two, he renounces killing. The contrasting changes Oliver goes through on the island and in the city draw attention to each other, revealing hegemonic masculinity as unfixed.

As Oliver lets people into his vigilante life, the part of him that is most closed off is prized open. The first recruit to "Team Arrow," John Diggle (David Ramsey), joins with the rationale of preventing Oliver from losing his humanity. John, readjusting to civilian life after military service, empathizes with Oliver's struggle to negotiate the emotional battlefield of interpersonal relationships. Like many of the team's subsequent members, including Roy Harper (Colton Haynes), Rene Ramirez (Rick Gonzalez), and Dinah Drake (Juliana Harkavy), John struggles with emotional expression. The influx of emotionally wounded characters to Team Arrow ensures that, after Oliver becomes more emotionally literate following season one, the dismantling of hardened exteriors is repeatedly dramatized. Members of Team Arrow help one another connect with their emotions and with other humans. The masculinization that Brown locates in the superhero origin story is therefore destabilized when this narrative is combined with another genre trope, the superhero team. A common feature of superhero team narratives is a focus on friendship, conflict, and romance among teammates, prompting comparisons to soap operas.[21] This quality is ideally suited to complex television's concern with interpersonal relationships. The team dynamic provides a framework for restaging the accommodation of conventionally feminine traits in masculinized identities.

Oliver's development in the past and present do not just occur along inverse lines. There is also a shared trajectory for Oliver's sociopolitical awakening, as he transitions from self-absorbed beneficiary of the patriarchy to socially aware citizen who sees inequality. While Oliver learns of his father's misdeeds and becomes embroiled in various nefarious organizations during his five years away, his awakening intensifies upon returning to the city, as he realizes the extent of his family and friends' participation in upholding social hierarchies. Furthermore, by performing as the oblivious trust-fund brat that he used to be, "Oliver is forced to face the realities of his privileged lifestyle" and reflect on his complicity in the system he now seeks to topple.[22] This theme is enforced through other young characters, namely Oliver's sister Thea Queen (Willa Holland) and best friend Tommy Merlyn (Colin Donnell), similarly being prompted to assess the wider impact of their privilege.

Despite Oliver's crusade for social change, his actions also reinscribe hegemonic masculinity. The conservative function of Oliver's seemingly subversive mission becomes apparent when understood as a manifestation of a trope that Brown identifies in which having privileged white men as villains valorizes "the superhero's version of white heterosexual masculinity."[23] The difference in degree, rather than kind, between Oliver and his establishment villains is evident in how he commands authority over the city, his family, and his teammates. In the absence of an assertive father figure, Thea is presented as spiraling into delinquency: taking drugs, crashing cars, and being sexually promiscuous. Oliver steers her back to respectability and she eventually joins Team Arrow. Despite bringing a diverse range of people into Team Arrow—including lower class criminals (Roy), people of color (John, Dinah, Rene), and LGBTQIA+ identities (Sara Lance [Caity Lotz] and Curtis Holt [Echo Kellum])—Oliver repeatedly exercises authority over them. This is exemplified in the training Oliver imposes on new recruits in season five, which entails repeatedly, and brutally, taking them down. Thus, *Arrow* conveys the idea that the heterosexual white male needs to enforce order.

Arrow reiterates a range of elements that simultaneously enshrine and modify hegemonic masculinity. The fraught interaction of these elements facilitates shifts in the cycle of repetition. In some cases, these shifts repress more radical elements. For instance, after season one, Oliver ends his proactive crusade against the wealthy elite and adopts the more conventional reactive approach, while integrating into the system by becoming involved in managing his family's company and then running for mayor, albeit with a very vague political agenda. In other cases, the shifts reframe Oliver's authority. Though having his capacity for empathy nurtured by teammates who are marginalized by the hegemonic order, Oliver is prompted at least to acknowledge their social situation. At times, the destabilization of Oliver's dominance is even a central narrative concern, such as during brief periods when Team Arrow operates without Oliver—in season three when Oliver is thought dead and in season six when Oliver passes the Arrow mantle to John—and when his teammates quit in rejection of Oliver's leadership in season six.

SERIALIZED MUSCLES

Scott Bukatman discusses the centrality of the body in superhero comics, asserting that "[t]he superhero body is everything—a *corporeal*, rather than a *cognitive*, mapping of the subject into a cultural system." (original emphasis)[24] While superhero bodies, like the mutant bodies of the X-Men, can express marginality, the hyper-muscular bodies of many male superheroes declare social dominance through physical strength. A crucial difference between representations of the body in comics and live-action television and film is the presence of a performer. The temporality of the performance is distinct from television to film. A film actor returning for a sequel typically has at least a year to enhance their physique. For example, in the *X-Men* film franchise, Hugh Jackman's appearances as Wolverine showcase significant leaps in the star's musculature from installment to installment.[25] Meanwhile, television actors give "ongoing serial performances," reprising their roles on a weekly basis, with prime-time dramas generally shot in continuous seasonal blocks.[26]

The temporality of Amell's musculature in *Arrow* is interwoven with the show's structure and weekly broadcast schedule. A promotional poster for season one maps the structure on Oliver's body. Oliver is presented head-on and shirtless, Starling City behind him. His musculature exemplifies the hegemonic ideal, blemished only by an assortment of pronounced scars and tattoos. Here is Oliver in the present, physically marked by the trials he overcame in the past. The image encapsulates Brown's claim that the male superhero "requires suffering as evidence of his superiority."[27] Due to the weekly broadcast schedule and largely continuous filming, Amell's body does not noticeably grow between episodes, creating a sense of Oliver's masculinity being a secure constant. Yet it is emphasized that he has to work to maintain his physique. Regular scenes feature Oliver working out, often on a salmon ladder: a vertical apparatus that requires its user to perform pull ups while lifting the handrail into the next set of brackets. Oliver performs this task shirtless, showcasing his musculature in unedited takes that make clear that Amell himself is ascending the ladder. The regularity of this workout is underscored when Team Arrow's technology expert Felicity Smoak (Emily Bett Rickards) informs another character that Oliver uses the ladder "every Wednesday," the day *Arrow* initially aired on North American television network The CW, thus reflexively acknowledging how *Arrow* harnesses weekly scheduling to ritualize the maintenance of masculine power.[28] By inscribing suffering and physical strength into the show's structure and Oliver's body, then exhibiting this body in promotional materials and episodes, the seriality of Oliver's body becomes a tool for renewing hegemonic masculinity.

The workout scenes enforce the assertion of hegemonic masculinity, but also undermine some narrative conventions that inscribe male dominance. Juan Llamas-Rodriguez analyzes how working out serves as a structuring device in *Arrow* and situates it within the network-specific context of The CW's branding, summarized as "sexiness and self-reflexivity."[29] Seminaked bodies offered up for erotic display are a trope of CW shows: "[t]hese scenes

Arrow Promotional Poster © 2012 CW

are explicitly presented to be looked at, often with little or no reference to plot or character development."[30] Following Llamas-Rodriguez, such scenes showcasing male bodies outside of narrative progression present them as objects, temporarily revoking the role of active subject, and possessor of the gaze, that Laura Mulvey famously ascribes to male characters in Hollywood cinema.[31] Helen Wheatley discusses how Mulvey's theory of the male gaze is problematized significantly by television, due to the medium's heterogeneous nature and history of catering to female desire.[32] Wheatley analyzes television shows that accommodate the (heterosexual) female gaze by exhibiting male bodies and featuring female characters gazing at them, "show[ing] the viewers what they should be looking at and how."[33]

Felicity gazing at Oliver in 'Salvation' © 2012 CW

Once Felicity joins Team Arrow, the "to-be-looked-at-ness" of Oliver's body is underscored. A scene in "Salvation" opens with Felicity and John watching a news report about a real estate developer failing to be indicted following a fire at one of his properties.[34] Felicity turns to look upward, prompting a cut to a low-angle shot of a shirtless Oliver doing pull ups on a ceiling-mounted bar. The proceeding cut takes us to the top of the room, looking down at Oliver, whose torso is presented in mid-shot while Felicity is out of focus below. The next shot is closer to Oliver but changes the focal length so that Felicity, and her admiring gaze, are in sharp focus. The progression of these shots first direct the audience to what they should be looking at (Oliver), exhibit it, then demonstrate how they should be looking. Importantly, this desiring look is gendered. While Felicity gazes at Oliver, John's eyes are directed at the monitors. Oliver's body is authorized as eroticized object solely for women. In commonality with many other CW series, such as *Smallville* and *Supernatural* (2005–present), the self-reflective sexiness of *Arrow*, while accommodating female desire, reinforces heterosexuality as the norm.

It is crucial to recognize, contrary to Llamas-Rodriguez's claim, that this scene, and others like it, do not pause plot or character development. Felicity's expression when she turns from the monitor is initially one of curiosity. Directing her gaze toward Oliver sets in motion the episode's story by raising the question of how Oliver will respond to the news report. In a literal sense, Oliver's elevated position represents authority, a power affirmed through his exhibition of physical strength. By the end of the scene, Oliver has determined that Team Arrow will punish the real estate developer. The presentation of Oliver's body and development of the scene situate Oliver as both eroticized object and commanding subject, affirming these hegemonic qualities. Female characters' consistent acknowledgement of Oliver's attractiveness ensures that his desirability is implicit even in workout scenes that do not feature a diegetic female gaze, while these scenes foreground expression of authority through physical strength. For example, in "Vendetta," John tries to convince Oliver that Helena Bertinelli (Jessica De Gouw), a dangerous vigilante with whom Oliver is romantically involved, is beyond redemption. Throughout the conversation, Oliver performs an elaborate workout, beginning with handstand pushups and progressing to the salmon ladder, each activity presented in long takes that underscore Oliver's strength. Staging the discussion this way positions Oliver as superior and exemplifies how power dynamics are often negotiated in *Arrow*'s workout and training scenes.

As with iterative plot elements, the repetition of workout and training scenes in *Arrow* makes hegemonic masculinity's constant renewal apparent. In this process of renewal and its intersections with television form, modification is again facilitated. Not only is the male body positioned as an object of the scopophilic female gaze, but as bodily exhibitions dovetail with serial plot developments, namely the expansion of Team Arrow, the nature of these exhibitions shifts. Evan Hayes Gledhill discusses the comparable display of male and female heroic bodies in *Arrow*, arguing that female teammates, like Oliver, are at once sexualized objects and active subjects.[35] In later seasons, the accumulation of diverse new teammates complements a phasing out of Oliver's workout scenes. While we still see characters working out from time to time, a related motif emerges in the show's increasing proclivity for long Steadicam takes during fight sequences. These roaming shots follow individual team members or shift from one to another. The sustained takes, following the logic of the shots of Oliver working out, showcase the physical ability required. This motif distributes the power assigned to physical strength more democratically among teammates. Therefore, the team dynamic dislodges the heterosexual white male's superior command of physical strength.

SERIALIZING STEPHEN AMELL

In the last few decades, actors playing superhero roles have been required to cultivate superhero physiques. Will Brooker discusses how Christian Bale's intensive training regime for *Batman Begins* (2005) was narrated in paratexts that parallel his transformation with the journey his character takes to become Batman.³⁶ Amell, having already built his musculature prior to getting the lead role in *Arrow*, personally creates paratexts that narrate the maintenance of his physique.³⁷ On Facebook, Twitter, and YouTube he regularly shares photos, workout videos, and behind-the-scenes footage of *Arrow*'s fight choreography. These paratexts interlock Amell's persona with Oliver, ensuring that the actor and character's masculinities feed into each other.

Amell's social media activity has also spawned intertexts that further entwine Amell and Oliver. In 2015, an antagonistic exchange between Amell and wrestler Stardust (Corey Rhodes) on Twitter constructed a narrative that developed into Amell attending and participating in World Wrestling Entertainment (WWE) events. When we examine the nature of wrestling, and analyze Amell's WWE appearances, it becomes apparent that the resulting intertexts do not simply stabilize Amell's masculinity but also reveal it as a performance. Henry Jenkins discusses WWE wrestling as "masculine melodrama," another form of serialized storytelling that blends masculine and feminine qualities:

> its characteristic subject matter (the homosocial relations between men, the professional sphere rather than the domestic sphere, the focus on physical means to resolve conflicts) draws upon generic traditions that critics have identified as characteristically masculine; its mode of presentation (its seriality, its focus on multiple characters and their relationship, its refusal of closure, its appeal to viewer speculation and gossip) suggests genres often labeled (sic) feminine.³⁸

The extent to which this blend of qualities mirrors what Mittell identifies in complex television is salient. Jenkins demonstrates that WWE wrestling harnesses this combination of elements to express, and offer a remedy for, threats to masculinity, observing the dramatization of restrictions placed on working class masculinity.

Amell's conflict with Stardust dramatizes a different affront to his masculinity. Following the Twitter animosity, Amell supposedly attended the *WWE Raw* event as a spectator on August 10, 2015, and was attacked by Stardust, only to retaliate by leaping into the wresting ring, tackling then pummeling his assailant. In the ensuing backstage exchange, Triple H (Paul Michael Levesque) brands Amell an "actor," a term Stardust wielded tauntingly on Twitter.³⁹ Amell impassionedly retorts "I'm an actor, I'm also a man," foregrounding Amell's anxiety at his profession being situated as feminized. Upon agreeing to let the "actor" wrestle Stardust in a tag team match, Triple H refers to Amell as "the Green Arrow" with a condescending sneer and warns him not to bring a stuntman. Triple H's tone positions Arrow as a fictional character whose most masculine feats are not even performed by Amell. While there is an implicit, self-reflexive acknowledgement that wrestlers are also actors, their masculinity is salvaged through a mode of performance that is "intensely physical," requiring great physical strength and agility.[40]

In the match, which featured on 23 August 2015's *Summerslam*, Amell proves that he possesses such abilities. The match's promotion presents it as a comic-book showdown. Amell enters the arena wearing his Arrow costume and the commentators frequently refer to him as the Green Arrow. On the one hand, these strategies hold Amell and Arrow apart from wrestling conventions. On the other hand, they underscore parallels between superhero texts and professional wrestling, namely hyperbolic characters and clashes between heroes and villains. In the match's climactic move, Amell leaps off the top rope, out of the ring, onto both of his opponents. As he rises to celebrate, large bruises are clearly visible on his shoulder. After the match, he posted a photo of his bruise-ridden back on Twitter, the accompanying text proclaiming "Worth it."[41] The photo pointedly recalls the *Arrow* poster showcasing Oliver's scarred torso. Amell's wrestling victory certifies his masculine authority by demonstrating that he has the physical strength and capacity to endure pain akin to professional wrestlers and his character in *Arrow*.

Amell's collaboration with WWE, which was effectively serialized across social media and television, asserted his physical capabilities while being tacitly, and in some ways explicitly, acknowledged as a performance. The various self-reflexive strategies, combined with the overt mode of emotional expression that Amell adopts in keeping with the theatrical conventions of wrestling (in contrast to his restrained performance style as Oliver), present his masculinity as something that must be performed, earned, and defended. Hegemonic masculinity's construction and renewal is dramatized via WWE wrestling's hyperbolic mode of melodramatic address.

The serialized (re)construction of Amell's masculinity continues in social media activities that invite fans to participate in this process. Hosted on Amell's Facebook account, "Meme Monday" and "Fan Art Friday" maintain regular weekly engagement between star and fans and complement *Arrow*'s broadcast schedule. Meme Monday in particular implicates fans in the construction of masculinity, due to the memes, created by fans, often expressing Amell's masculinity. For example, after posting a photo of himself with a morose expression and injured nose after shooting a fight sequence, Amell later shared memes fans created using the photo. One adds the text "you

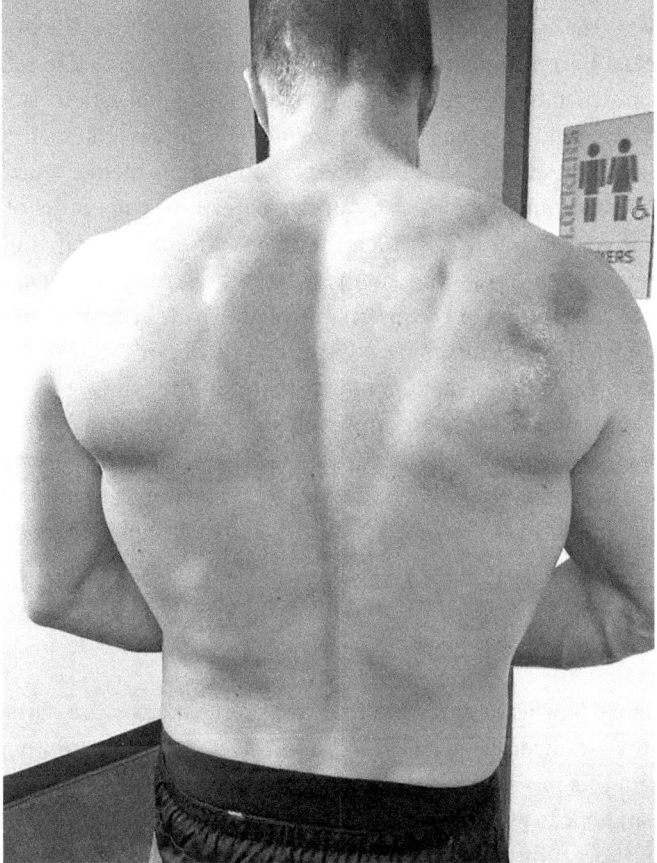

Stephen Amell on Twitter after Summerslam © 2015 Stephen Amell

should see the other guy," supplementing Amell's endurance of pain with the suggestion that he inflicted greater pain, thus enforcing Amell's physical superiority.[42] Other responses are more reflexive about the interaction of reality and fiction in Amell's persona. In reference to Barry Allen (Grant Gustin) altering *Arrow*'s diegetic timeline following events in *The Flash* (2014–), one of the memes features the caption, "When you go through 3 seasons of hell to bring justice and Barry reverses the timeline."[43] This resituates the image's expression of suffering within the fictional universe of *Arrow*, recognizing that Amell's endurance is intrinsically linked Oliver's.

Other memes are even more nimble in playfully interweaving different facets of Amell's persona. One includes a photo of Stardust about to throw water at Amell above a frame from *Arrow* in which Oliver and Barry mourn at a grave.[44] The caption reads "he should of [sic] thought twice before picking up the glass Barry." The implication is that Stardust was killed in retaliation, but in the switch from Amell's wrestling persona to Oliver, these two identities are compounded as the killer. The meme's creator has built their own narrative by fusing Amell's roles. The interplay among the meme's story, Amell's wrestling story, and *Arrow*'s story underscores how the model of strong, authoritative masculinity to which they all contribute is itself constructed through narration. By sharing memes like this one, Amell cultivates in his fans an understanding of the process through which hegemonic masculinity is renewed. The feedback loop in which one of *Arrow*'s central creative agents authorizes fan-created paratexts that reinforce the show's model of hegemonic masculinity exposes this model as a construction. Yet despite the significant degree of self-reflexivity that Amell's selections accommodate, it is important to acknowledge that he decides which memes to sanction, policing how his masculinity is presented. Memes that Amell approves are permitted to reflexively reconstruct his and Oliver's brand of hegemonic masculinity, but not present oppositional masculinities, thus strengthening hegemonic masculinity's privileged position.

The serialized forms of *Arrow*, its intertexts and paratexts, are harnessed by the show's producers and star to reiterate hegemonic masculinity, yet also illuminate this process of renewal and facilitate a degree of modification. Not all audiences will engage with the intertexts and paratexts discussed, but even those only encountering *Arrow* can observe the process of renewal through the dramatization of tension between masculine and feminine qualities. Qualities of complex television unpick gendered logics that underpin the superhero genre, while the ways in which superhero and televisual conventions interlock engender strategies for both, entrenching and dislodging masculine ideals which are stubbornly rooted in contemporary culture. Amell's wrestling simultaneously amplifies the physically superior and performative dimensions of his masculinity while complementing the melodramatic qualities of *Arrow* and furthering the enmeshment of Amell and Oliver. His regular engagement with fans on social media then invites them to partake in hegemony's renewal, their creative activities constructing hegemonic masculinity in a quite literal sense that demonstrates acute awareness of the layers of performance and narration that comprise Amell/Oliver's masculinity.

Superhero conventions continue to both suppress and facilitate the modification of hegemonic masculinity as *Arrow*, and the diegetic universe it initiated, evolve. The expansion of the universe in *The Flash* and *Legends of Tomorrow* (2016–) and its subsequent resituation as a multiverse that incorporates *Supergirl* (2015–), pursues the model of multiseries seriality that has been refined in superhero comics over decades. One principle of this model is that each series should be distinct. This requirement prompts a range of identities and approaches, from *The Flash*'s emotionally attuned male protagonist and *Supergirl*'s cheery while physically strong eponymous superheroine (Melissa Benoist), to *Legends of Tomorrow*'s diverse time-traveling team who often contend with historical gender and racial discrimination. As with Team Arrow, when characters from these shows meet in "crossover" episodes, their interactions can challenge one another's attitudes. Yet the imperative for differentiation fixes *Arrow* as the multiverse's "dark and gritty" masculinized space, its storylines replete with torture, organized crime, and brooding. The multiversal expansion pluralizes, and provides opportunities for interrogating masculinities, while fixing limitations on the extent to which Oliver's masculinity can be reconfigured. Opening up Oliver, and the social space he inhabits, to other identities and ideas via *Arrow*'s serial development prompts reassertions of Oliver's hegemonic masculinity that allow us to see it destabilized but protect it from being upended.

NOTES

1. Jason Mittell, *Complex TV: The Poetics of Contemporary Television Storytelling* (New York: New York University Press, 2015).

2. My analysis of *Arrow* focuses on, but is not limited to, season one, since it sets into motion key dynamics for the show. At the time of writing, there have been six seasons of *Arrow*.

3. Raewyn Conell, *Masculinities* (Cambridge: Polity, 1995), 77.

4. Connell, 84.

5. Raymond Williams, *Problems in Materialism and Culture* (London: Verso, 1980), 38.

6. Gérard Genette, *Palimpsests: Literature in the Second Degree*, trans. Channa Newman and Claude Doubinsky (Lincoln: University of Nebraska Press, 1997).

Jonathan Gray, *Show Sold Separately: Promos, Spoilers, and Other Media Paratexts* (New York: New York University Press, 2010).

7. Gray, *Show Sold Separately*, 117.

8. Genette, *Palimpsests*, 2.

9. Mittell, *Complex TV*, 235.

10. John Fiske, *Television Culture* (London and New York: Routledge, 1987).

11. Mittell, *Complex TV*, 251.

12. Mittell, 19.

13. Initially called the Hood, Oliver's superhero identity subsequently becomes Arrow and then Green Arrow. For the sake of simplicity, throughout this chapter I refer to him as Arrow.

14. Rebecca Feasey, *Masculinity and Popular Television* (Edinburgh: Edinburgh University Press, 2008), 50.

15. Feasey, 5.

16. Umberto Eco, "The Myth of Superman," *Diacritics* 2, no. 1 (1972).

17. Eco, 21–22.

18. Federico Pagello, "'The Origin Story' is the Only Story: Seriality and Temporality in Superhero Fiction from Comics to Post-Television," *Quarterly Review of Film and Video* 34, no. 8 (2017): 725–45.

19. Pagello, 729–31.

20. Jeffrey A. Brown, *The Modern Superhero in Film and Television: Popular Genre and American Culture* (London and New York: Routledge, 2017), 39.

21. For example, Grant Morrison discusses 1980s *Justice League* comics as "a witty soap opera" in *Supergods: Our World in the Age of the Superhero* (London: Jonathan Cape, 2011), 290.

22. Evan Hayles Gledhill, "Twenty Percent of His Body: Scar Tissue, Masculinity and Identity in *Arrow*," in *Arrow and Superhero Television*, ed. James F. Iaccino et al (Jefferson: McFarland and Company, 2017), 82.

23. Brown, *The Modern Superhero*, 119.

24. Scott Bukatman, *Matters of Gravity: Special Effects and Supermen in the 20th Century* (Durham: Duke University Press, 2003), 49.

25. See Daniel J. Connell's chapter in this volume.

26. Mittell, *Complex Television*, 119.

27. Brown, *The Modern Superhero*, 47.

28. *Arrow*, Episode 8, "The Brave and the Bold," directed by Jesse Warn, aired December 3, 2014, on The CW.

29. Juan Llamas-Rodriguez, "Working Out as Creative Labor, or the Building of the Male Superhero's Body," in *Arrow and Superhero Television*, ed. James F. Iaccino et al (Jefferson: McFarland and Company, 2017), 67.

30. Llamas-Rodriguez, 66.

31. Laura Mulvey, "Visual Pleasure and Narrative Cinema," *Screen* 16, no. 3 (1975): 6–18. Analysis of male bodies exhibited to be gazed at often supports Mulvey's framework. Richard Dyer demonstrates that male pin-ups are posed in ways that express power and activity in "Don't Look Now," *Screen* 23, no. 3–4 (1982): 61–73. Similarly, when examining scenes from Hollywood cinema in which the male body provides spectacle, Steve Neale identifies strategies that repress erotic contemplation and maintain the characters' roles as subjects, in "Masculinity as Spectacle: Reflections on Men and Mainstream Cinema," *Screen* 24, no. 6 (1983): 2–16.

32. Helen Wheatley, *Spectacular Television: Exploring Televisual Pleasure* (London: I. B. Tauris, 2016), 208.

33. Wheatley, 214.

34. *Arrow*, Episode 18, "Salvation," directed by Nick Copus, aired March 27, 2013, on The CW.

35. Gledhill, "Twenty Percent of His Body," 84–89.

36. Will Brooker, *Hunting the Dark Knight: Twenty-First Century Batman* (London: IB Tauris, 2012), 97–101.

37. Llamas-Rodrigues uses Amell to explore the unpaid labor that actors in contemporary Hollywood are pressured to undertake to make themselves attractive candidates for roles in "Working Out as Creative Labor."

38. Henry Jenkins, *The Wow Climax: Tracing the Emotional Impact of Popular Culture* (New York: New York University Press, 2006), 77. Jenkins refers to the company as World Wrestling Federation (WWF), which was its name prior to 2002.

39. *WWE Raw*, Event RAW #1159, USA Network, August 10, 2015.

40. Broderick Chow et al "Introduction: Hamlet Doesn't Blade: Professional Wrestling, Theatre, and Performance," in *Performance and Professional Wrestling*, ed. Broderick Chow et al (London and New York: Routledge, 2017), 2.

41. Stephen Amell, "Worth It," *Twitter*, posted August 23, 2015, https://twitter.com/StephenAmell/status/635620041317318656.

42. Stephen Amell, "You Should See the Other Guy," *Facebook*, posted August 15, 2016, https://www.facebook.com/stephenamell/photos/a.976747499077184.1073741842.1469219 75393078/1118510381567561.

43. Stephen Amell, "When You Go Through 3 Seasons of Hell," *Facebook*, posted August 15, 2016, https://www.facebook.com/stephenamell/photos/a.976747499077184.1073741842.1469219 75393078/1118510348234231.

44. Stephen Amell, "He Should of Thought Twice, *Facebook*," posted February 15, 2016. https://www.facebook.com/stephenamell/photos/a.976747499077184.1073741842.1469219 75393078/999420560143211.

"I'LL SHOW YOU WHAT IT MEANS TO BE A MAN"

Hegemonic Masculinity of *Batman v Superman: Dawn of Justice*

JANNE SALMINEN

BATMAN RETURNS AGAIN

Superhero movies of the 2010s operate on a highly metaphorical level, even when they try to convey realism. They rarely articulate their ideologies explicitly. Nevertheless, within the increasingly inclusive representational context of contemporary blockbusters, the conservative and even antifeminist attitude of *Batman v Superman* stands out. While the film's attitude by no means suggests that comparable films are somehow unproblematic, the film in question arguably provides a strong example of a film dealing with gender—and masculinity, particularly—in a way that narrows the possibilities for gender rather than expands them.

Batman has been a staple of popular culture since 1939.[1] One of the defining iterations of the character was the 1960s television series, *Batman*, starring Adam West as the caped crusader. Adam West's portrayal of Batman is perhaps best described as a parody of the square and rigid masculinity of the time, but it is also the version that most cinematic incarnations of the character have tried to suppress. Will Brooker argues that the 1960s television series is viewed as a deviation from the "truth" of Batman by those currently responsible for the films and the audience they are aiming to address.[2] Specifically, Brooker refers to the colorful and campy tone of the television series, which in turn made the entire concept of Batman encapsulating masculine ideals seem laughable, potentially ridiculing hegemonic masculinity itself.

Batman v Superman: Dawn of Justice (2016) introduced audiences to yet another cinematic incarnation of Batman. Christopher Nolan's "realistic" version of Batman (portrayed by Christian Bale) was laid to rest in *The Dark Knight Rises* (2012), but under the direction of Zack Snyder, Ben Affleck's portrayal offers no dramatic change in the continuing narrative of the caped crusader. If anything, *Batman v Superman* shifts into an even deeper state of hypermasculinity.[3] The film ostensibly has two main characters, but since in the theatrical version of the film Superman has only forty-three lines of dialogue, it is not entirely unreasonable to state that Batman is the main character of the film.[4]

The Batman/Bruce Wayne of *Batman v Superman* is a grizzled, cynical, middle-aged man, who has fought his own personal war on crime for some twenty-odd years. Even though Batman's origin story has been told a few times in previous Bat films, *Batman v Superman* retells it during the opening credits. Young Bruce (Brandon Spink) is walking out of a movie theatre with his mother and father, and they are mugged by a robber, who shoots both of Bruce's parents. The film adds a small but thematically significant new element: Bruce's father Thomas (Jeffrey Dean Morgan) prepares to punch the mugger in defense and utters the name of his wife, Martha (Lauren Cohan), as his last words. From this early scene, the film establishes a theme of men protecting women, and women in the film are often in a vulnerable position when compared to the male-identified characters. This opening scene is a nightmare that adult Bruce is having, focusing on his father's inability to save Bruce's mother. Thomas Wayne's failure is referred to again during a later scene where Batman and Superman hash out their differences.

WHEN CLARK MET BRUCE

The plot of *Batman v Superman* is set in motion in a scene that takes place during the climactic battle of the previous Superman film, *Man of Steel* (2013). Superman is battling his nemesis General Zod (Michael Shannon) in the city of Metropolis, and their superpowered exchange of punches causes entire skyscrapers to collapse. Bruce Wayne, as his civilian self, is racing to save the employees of Wayne enterprises while the city is crumbling around them. This precredits sequence establishes Bruce Wayne as an action hero with or without a Bat costume, while at the same time showing how Superman's presence undermines Batman's masculinity. This new type of man, one who comes from another world, becomes the embodiment of every significant change or upheaval taking place. The film eventually elaborates on why Batman and Superman dislike one another, but no line of dialogue manages to displace the message this first scene expresses: the world is changing at a rapid pace and the person who was once the paragon of masculine ideals is being lowered to the status of a mere mortal.

Batman's mistrust of Superman has shades of xenophobia: an illegal alien arrives to displace someone whose status in society had been guaranteed by his vast inherited wealth. Bruce Wayne as Batman can operate without anyone interfering with his affairs, but when Superman does the same, he is described as the enemy.[5] The extremely fragile nature of Batman's masculinity does not allow him to accept Superman—not because of the latter's power but because of his Otherness. According to Julien Chambliss, Superman has been historically associated with immigrant narratives. The character has often represented the ideal immigrant narrative, in which his alien traits combine with American values and allow him to improve society.[6] *Batman v Superman* does not specifically show Superman improving society and he seems bored with rescuing people, but the immigrant element remains and frames Batman's mistrust as being at least partially similar to the crisis of (white) masculinity that has been brewing for quite a while.[7] Batman's worries are somewhat understandable since Superman possesses such immense powers, but his role as a nonhuman Other and the immigrant metanarrative seem to be at the core of Batman's disproportionate reaction.

Batman/Bruce Wayne seems to represent aspects of the anxiety felt by groups of men, particularly in the United States, who feel that social advances have left them powerless. In *Stiffed: The Betrayal of the American Man*, Susan Faludi outlines how economic changes of the early 1990s contributed to a perceived crisis of masculinity, as the role of men as breadwinners began to diminish. Faludi argues that while the economy eventually recovered, the postwar generation of men, raised on images of self-reliant white men who take charge of society, sensed that the connection between men and the public domain was being severed and that in some way, they had been betrayed.[8] During the twenty-odd years between Faludi's work and the 2016 US presidential election, this sense of betrayal seems to have only increased. The continuing advances made by feminism and the repercussions of the 2008 financial crisis allowed Donald Trump to evoke similar feelings of victimhood. He also suggested that his form of white masculinity, coming outside of the "feminized Washington establishment," would lead the way back to "real" America.[9] Since *Batman v Superman* came out in 2016, it is difficult not to see it being tangential with the societal discourses that took place in the United States during (and since) the 2016 election. While Batman/Bruce Wayne is not exactly a surrogate for Trump, there are some striking similarities: both produce their own form of hypermasculinity, argue that the changes taking place in society (apparently caused by unreliable immigrants and ineffective politicians) demand drastic actions, and both were born into great wealth and privilege. Batman's hypermasculinity is made explicit in scenes where he exercises aggressively (dragging tyres and lifting large weights). Trump's hypermasculinity is constructed mainly through his talk of vitality and threatening to cause bodily harm to protesters.[10] In both cases, hypermasculinity is associated with physical ability and aggressiveness.

CANONIZED BAT-GENDER NARRATIVE

Hegemonic masculinity, a concept popularized by Raewyn Connell, is the idea that certain forms of masculinity are most legitimate when trying to maintain the dominant position of men in society. This legitimacy is not established by individuals but is a collective product of cultural ideals reacting with institutionalized power or great wealth.[11] These preferred forms of masculinity can favor elements like competitiveness, physical toughness, sports skills, heterosexuality, and conformity. Hegemonic masculinity could be described as a canonized gender narrative for men.[12] When understanding the hegemonic masculinity of *Batman v Superman*, it is necessary to view the Batman as a part of a continuum of representations. The film initially hints that the hegemonic masculinity represented by Batman is in crisis and that formulating a hybrid masculinity is the solution. According to Tristan Bridges and C. J. Pascoe, hybrid masculinity does not necessarily mean the formulation of an inclusive masculinity, but a process in which hegemonic masculinity appropriates practices from subaltern masculinities or femininity.[13] In *Batman v Superman*, this hypothetical hybrid masculinity would have jettisoned or at least problematized Batman's intensely aggressive and hostile, xenophobic behavior. In the end, any adjustments Batman makes to his masculine identity remain so minimal that they barely register as changes. Initially, he wants to kill Superman, then he befriends him. Once Superman dies, Batman decides that he needs to gather other superpowered individuals around him so that together, they can protect Earth from destruction. He merely adds a dash of camaraderie to his militaristic version of masculinity.

Batman films in the past have varied in their construction of masculinity. Some of them have portrayed Batman's masculinity as artificial and added

Previous Batmen. Left to right: Michael Keaton (Batman, 1989), Val Kilmer (Batman Forever, 1995), George Clooney (Batman and Robin, 1997) and Christian Bale (The Dark Knight Rises, 2012) © 1995 Warner Bros. Pictures

layers of complexity to his sexuality, while others have made him explicitly heterosexual, with masculinity as an inherent quality of the character. *Batman* (1989), directed by Tim Burton and starring Michael Keaton, sketched Batman as a performance of masculinity, devised by Bruce Wayne as a reaction to cope with his inability to conform to the masculine ideals of his society. In her book *Hard Bodies*, Susan Jeffords argues that the film explores how conservative bio-essentialist masculine ideals were running out of steam during the tail end of the Reagan era.[14] Jeffords also adds that in *Batman* masculinity is literally treated as an artificial costume, designed to make Wayne more physically intimidating.[15] While similar elements were present in the subsequent sequels, it would appear that the recent live-action Bat-films have settled on a Batman whose mode of masculinity is rather static and conservative, allowing little or no room for fluidity. Along with the physical change in Batman's appearance, the Bat-costumes have become more utilitarian while abandoning the idea that the person wearing the suit is using the suit as a part of a masculine performance.

Brooker notes that the Christopher Nolan cycle of Batman films (2008–12) focused on undermining the colorful history of the character in favor of a "one-note militarized pillar of heterosexuality."[16] Nolan's Bat-films also favored a color scheme and an aesthetic which, as noted by Martin Fradley, worked to distance the films from camp, homoeroticism, and brightness under the guise of "realism" and "political seriousness."[17] While *Batman v Superman* is far from realistic (albeit so grim and dark that it borders on parody), it continues on the same trajectory as the Nolan films, retaining the militaristic aspects of Batman. He refers to being at war with Superman and uses an arsenal that gives him the destructive power of a small army, and the gender representations which focus on dispassionate heterosexual masculinity are at the center of the main narrative.[18] Whereas the Nolan films featured Bruce Wayne as a monogamous heterosexual, in *Batman v Superman*, his heterosexuality is made explicit by showing him waking up next to a person who is at least suggested to be a woman, cyphering from the shot of her naked backside and from Alfred's wry comments on how Bruce refuses to settle down and start a family. When Bruce interacts with Diana Prince (Wonder Woman's civilian persona), this portrayal of him as a philandering playboy is brought to focus as he appears to be trying to seduce her as much as he is trying to find out why she is in Gotham. Portraying Bruce Wayne as a heterosexual playboy also distances *Batman v Superman* even further from the homosexual fantasy of the early 1940s comics and the camp 1960s *Batman* television series. Beth A. Eck notes that heterosexuality has been an integral part of American masculinity since the early twentieth century. The need to link heterosexuality with masculinity was essentially a homophobic reaction to what little visibility the homosexual population of the United States had managed to claim for themselves. Eck also contends that this reaction eventually resulted in increased media representations of men who have multiple but mostly inconsequential sexual relationships with women.[19]

Literary critic Glen Weldon argues that while the "definitely not gay," humorless, dark, and hyperrealistic narrative of Batman has permeated American (and perhaps Western) culture with great success, a counter-narrative which parodies all the aforementioned qualities has also emerged. In Weldon's view, this counter narrative has arisen mostly due to social media and has on a smaller scale been embraced by some recent official incarnations of the character (in LEGO-based films and video games and in the cartoon series *The Brave and The Bold*).[20] These counter-narratives and their performativity of masculinity stand so far away from the rigidity of *Batman v Superman* that, even if considered a form of parody, they leave Snyder's work isolated in its outlook. The film constructs a world in which the masculinity represented by Batman is the dominant and preferred mode of masculinity and defines what constitutes a "real man."

Throughout the film, Batman and other characters refer to humanity as "men" consistently, an archaic descriptor, given that the film was released in 2016.[21] What makes it particularly interesting is how Batman angrily declares that Superman is not a "real man."[22] He is referring to Superman's extraterrestrial origins but also creating the boundaries which formulate which kind of men are "real" and which are not. The film's consistent use of "man" as the basic unit of society results in othering everyone who fails to meet the standards for the hegemonic masculinity constructed in the film. In a trailer leading up to the release of *Batman v Superman*, Batman tells Superman, "It's time you learned what it means to be a man," but the line was cut from the theatrical release.[23] Even without this particular line of dialogue, Batman still articulates the same sentiment throughout the film. While Batman does not have the innate abilities of Superman, *Batman v Superman* spends a lengthy amount of time showcasing the arduous physical exercise that Bruce needs to go through in order to maintain his crime-fighting abilities. During these exercise scenes, we are also shown the scars he has acquired during his career as a vigilante. Susan Jeffords notes that films which focus on the hero as a pain-resistant fighting machine also tend to view vulnerability and "softness" as a betrayal of national safety as if it is up to these masculine bodies to protect society from harm.[24] Jeffords refers to action films of the 1980s, but the thematic similarities between *Batman v Superman* and the films she mentions are too striking to ignore. Jeffords's analysis proposes that one of the key themes of these conservatively aligned films was centering on a white male hero who aggressively fights to restore society to the state it was in before becoming "feminized." A similar theme is present in *Batman v Superman*, as Bruce contemplates how "men" can still be saved and that he, as a white straight man with great wealth, can restore society to what it once was.[25]

NONDISRUPTIVE WONDER WOMAN

In the gender hierarchy of *Batman v Superman*, women can be equal to men, but they need to be goddesses with superhuman abilities. If Wonder Woman is to fight alongside Batman and Superman, she must still be able to retain her femininity, allowing her to be an action hero without destabilizing the heterosexual hegemony. Wonder Woman is shown to have superpowers that are comparable to those of Superman, but she still looks slender next to the hulking physiques of Superman and Batman. Nicola Rehling argues that muscular female lead characters crystallize the idea that muscular physique is not an exclusive trait of biological men and disrupt the patriarchal definitions of femininity.[26] Without this disruptive quality, Wonder Woman becomes a representation of neoliberal femininity or what is sometimes identified as post feminism. According to Yeal D. Sherman, partial equality produces conditions in which neoliberalism and feminism assemble a new form of

Batman V Superman: Dawn of Justice (2016). Top: Superman (Henry Cavill), Wonder Woman (Gal Gadot), and Batman (Ben Affleck) face Doomsday. Bottom: Ben Affleck as Batman is noticeably bulkier than previous cinematic iterations of the character. © 2016 Warner Bros. Pictures

femininity, which does not liberate women from objectifying themselves. The project of self-care implies self-management and announces a willingness to compete in both the private and public spheres. Sherman also notes that this process erases structural inequality and focuses on the individual's responsibility in finding success.[27] Catherine Rottenberg argues that the neoliberal colonization of feminism erodes the emancipatory impetus of feminism.[28] Wonder Woman does not pose a threat to the hegemonic masculinity of *Batman v Superman* but provides rather a complementary neoliberal variation on feminism. She is allowed to enter the realm of men since she has no real destabilizing power and does not represent true change in the gender structures of their world.

Raewyn Connell and James W. Messerschmidt note that gender is defined relationally and that patterns of masculinity and femininity are formed in contrast to one another, even if that contrast is imaginary. They also note that the counterpart to hegemonic masculinity is emphasized femininity, which complies with the patriarchal gender order and maintains the asymmetrical relationship between masculinities and femininities.[29] If Wonder Woman predominantly represents tamed feminism that works within the oppressive structures rather than dismantling them, the other female characters' purpose is to, in one way or another, emphasize the dominant masculinity of the male heroes. Lois Lane (Amy Adams) repeatedly needs to be rescued, Superman's adoptive mother Martha Kent (Diane Lane) needs to be protected, and Senator Finch (Holly Hunter) plays into Lex Luthor's (Jesse Eisenberg) hands at every turn until she finally meets her explosive demise. Wonder Woman's role in propping up the hegemonic masculinity of the film stands out so glaringly precisely because she is capable of the same things as the male heroes but still fails to have any real impact on the eventual outcome of the film. By not giving the female characters any real agency in the story, *Batman v Superman* seems to anticipate a similar backlash against feminism to the one that took place in the 1980s, as identified by Faludi.[30]

Batman v Superman is not only a direct sequel to *Man of Steel*, but it also continues to address the perceived crisis of masculinity which that film dealt with in a particular way. James Mulder describes *Man of Steel* as an articulation of the crisis of white masculinity in America, which works to restabilize masculine identities through nonflamboyant realism and melancholy.[31] Mulder's interpretation would allow us to see the conflict between Batman and Superman as two forms of masculinity crises in conflict but eventually realizing that the real enemy (and victim) is that which lies outside their gender performances. They do not synthesize a new type of masculinity but negotiate masculinity, setting aside their insignificant differences to battle those who could genuinely disrupt the gender order which allows them to maintain their dominant status.

QUEER LUTHOR

Fanning the flames of the feud between Batman and Superman is Luthor, who is one of the principal characters in defining the hegemonic masculinity of the film. Eisenberg portrays Luthor as a hyperactive billionaire, who has the youthful energy of a startup whiz kid from Silicon Valley. While Silicon Valley is hardly a beacon of egalitarianism, it seems fitting that the main villain of the film is so strongly associated with an area that is known for its liberal leanings. Nick Serpe notes that the tech sector of California views itself as having a worldview that is almost antithetical to that of Trump supporters, with some notable exceptions.[32] Luthor also has some brief, sexually ambiguous moments; in particular, a scene where he licks his fingers after pushing a candy into another man's mouth. The scene conveys how Luthor is someone who enjoys abusing power, but it also carries significant metaphorical weight simply by being the sole representation of anything non-heterosexual in a movie that is so adamantly gray and straight. The manner in which Luthor is portrayed in the *Batman v Superman* is close to Cesar Romero's Joker from the 1966 *Batman* television series, deviating somewhat from the usual tradition of portraying Superman's nemesis as a calculating intellectual, with megalomaniacal tendencies and the occasional outburst of rage.[33] This playful, colorful, and queer version of Luthor in *Batman v Superman* is, for all intents and purposes, a "jokerized" version of Luthor, who represents a queer disruption which galvanizes the masculine identities of Batman and Superman by contrasting their hegemonic masculinity with the subaltern masculinity of Luthor. Brooker argues that Joker traditionally has represented queerness when placed alongside Batman's stoic presence.[34] He also adds that by making Batman fight off a queer villain, the potentially queer readings of the hero can be deflected, coinciding with the idea that the dominant narrative for the character does not allow for him to be anything except brooding and masculine.

Luthor's ambiguous sexuality, physical shortcomings (he is considerably slimmer than either of the heroes, and shorter), combined with his unclear methods of amassing billions of dollars, make him the embodiment of certain groups that have subverted or "perverted" normative masculinity and as such threaten "correct" masculinity, which in the film is signified through Batman and Superman. Rehling points out that films which vilify queerness or, more specifically, portray it as a threat to white masculinity, tend to suggest that straight white men have somehow unjustly been losing ground to women, people of color, and generally anyone who does not look like them.[35] The ultimate goal of Luthor's convoluted plan is never made entirely clear. He seems to be setting the stage for some massive global disruption, either by using Batman and Superman's conflict or by eliminating them. Once Luthor's plan shifts into its final phase, his motivations remain vague, but his role as a disruptor of heterosexual hegemony becomes clearer.

"MARTHA, MARTHA, MARTHA"

Batman and Superman eventually wind up fighting each other, as the title suggests. After pummeling each other for a while, Batman gains the upper hand by utilizing various gadgets that weaken the Man of Steel. Just as Batman is about to impale Superman with a homemade kryptonite spear, he hears Superman's pleas to rescue his mother, Martha, who has been captured by Luthor's goons. Batman is confounded to hear his opponent mention a name that happens to be the name of his own deceased mother. Lois runs to the scene, begging a confused Batman not to kill Superman. In a mere few seconds, the conflict dissolves, and Batman vows to rescue Martha, while

Superman goes to apprehend Luthor. The anticlimactic resolution of the driving conflict in the film serves mainly to reiterate how women (other than Wonder Woman) are helpless and defined by what they mean to the male main characters. It also recalls the moment during the opening credits of the film, when Thomas Wayne failed to protect his wife which then led Bruce Wayne to formulate his Bat persona. Claire Duncanson contends that military masculinities often define a vulnerable feminized "Other" as being in the immediate need of protection.[36] By the time this scene takes place, femininity has been firmly established as being an attribute of those who are the Other, as humanity is referred to as being formed of "men." This abrupt and surprising resolution to the conflict also points to the idea that Batman's crisis of masculinity can be resolved by seeing women as helpless victims in the machinations of queer villains. Judith Butler notes that heterosexual privilege operates by naturalizing and normalizing itself, which then also requires it to constantly police itself and its boundaries against queerness.[37] A similar line of reasoning seems to be behind the sudden unification of Batman and Superman's interests.

Luthor's backup plan is to reanimate the dead body of General Zod, utilizing Kryptonian technology. He also mixes his own blood into the reanimation matrix, suggesting that the resulting creature is at least partially Luthor's offspring. Through this creature, which is called Doomsday in this article, as it closely resembles the creature which famously killed Superman in the comic books in 1992–1993, the lingering theme of procreation is brought to the forefront. Batman and Superman uniting to fight Luthor and the monster he has created points towards the idea that the overlapping crises of masculinity are resolved by banding together against a common enemy, one that represents the larger societal changes taking place in a postmodern society by simply existing. Rosi Braidotti argues that monstrous creatures and monstrous bodies serve as a counterpoint to the construction of clean, healthy fit, white, decent, law-abiding, and heterosexual bodies, which postindustrial culture emphasizes. As such, they also express the anxieties the majority has over minorities emerging as possible patterns of becoming.[38] Doomsday is not only a creature that looks monstrous, with bony protrusions and dark gray skin tone, but he/it was not "born" in any conventional sense of the word. He/it emerged from a pool of regenerative fluid. The film implies that it is some kind of human/Kryptonian hybrid, which can be read as a metaphor for new forms of families and kinship being destructive to the normative gender order present in the film. The heroes have traditional familial origins, even if they have been orphaned, and strive towards forming their own nuclear families (or should be striving according to those close to them), but Luthor and his "child" Doomsday threaten to tear down the prevailing society.

Wonder Woman makes her appearance in her full battle regalia after Batman and Superman have become friends, arriving to join in the fight against Doomsday. It is as if the resolution of the conflict between the heroes has now fortified hegemonic masculinity to such an extent that a woman with superpowers has permission to step forward and join in on the fight to protect society. Prior to Wonder Woman's arrival, Superman and Batman have great difficulty stopping Doomsday. She appears to be more than capable of handling the monster, but for the purposes of proving that Superman is indeed a "real man," Superman takes the kryptonite spear and drives it through the monster's chest. Weakened by the kryptonite radiation, which Wonder Woman would have been immune to, Doomsday manages to penetrate Superman's chest with one of his/its bone protrusions. Superman's sacrifice now allows him to prove that he too is willing to sacrifice his body, just like Batman, and that the most important tasks in society are handled by men, even if a more competent woman is standing right next to them. This robs Wonder Woman of any real impact she might have had on the outcome of the final battle. In the last scenes of the film, Superman's body is cared for by Lois and Wonder Woman as Batman watches from the shadows, once again reminding the viewer how a clear separation of roles exists in the world of this film.

Raewyn Connell and Rebecca Pearse argue that a character dichotomy in which men and women are supposed to have specific character traits that define gender is primarily based on cultural bias.[39] *Batman v Superman* enforces the idea that excursions outside the established gender dichotomy are possible but anomalous at best. Lois is shown to be a competent reporter, which the film presents as being anomalous and worthy of ridicule. While doing her job as an investigative reporter, Lois confronts an army general (Harry Lennix) in the men's room. "You're in the wrong bathroom, miss," the general says while washing his hands. Lois's persistent questioning prompts the general to say, "with balls like that, maybe you're in the right bathroom after all."[40] This transmisogynistic line tries to find humor in Lois's behavior, framing it as uncommon for women and linking gender with biological attributes. Rosemary R. Philips sees legal struggles over who can use which bathrooms being one of the key issues of LGBTQ rights in the United States as it sets the parameters for how transgender people can participate safely in public life.[41] This one line of dialogue keeps the film firmly in a mode which insists that there are certain gender categories that should remain consistent.

BATMAN AND SUPERMAN VERSUS AUDIENCES

Perhaps not surprisingly, the hypermasculine fantasy of Batman and Superman punching their way to resolve a crisis of masculinity did not resonate terribly well with contemporary audiences. Only 27 percent of professional critics viewed the film favorably.[42] Metacritic, on the other hand, gives *Batman V Superman* a score of 44 out of 100, indicating mixed or average reviews.[43] Anthony Lane, a film critic for the *New Yorker*, noted that Wonder Woman is one of the few positive elements of the film and she is hardly in it.[44] Similarly, the *New York Times* critic Anthony Oliver Scott noted that Superman and Batman both seem to be motivated by narcissism rather than civic duty.[45] Sam Riedel of Bitch Media took a decidedly feminist approach towards critiquing *Batman v Superman* and claimed that Wonder Woman was one of the very few things in the film that attempted to subvert the otherwise "blatantly misogynistic" worldview on display.[46] This lackluster reception was reflected at the box office. It might seem improbable that a film that made $872 million worldwide could be considered a financial disappointment.[47] However, considering the production budget, marketing, and merchandise agreements, the movie barely made the king's ransom it was expected to make.[48] Box office, audience scores, or critical reception does not necessarily indicate how influential a film might eventually be, but it is worth noting that they contribute to a narrative of disappointment associated with the film.

Michael Ryan and Douglass Kellner identify the "crisis films" of the 1970s (such as *Jaws*, *Exorcist*, *The Godfather*) as functioning metaphorically when dealing with pressing societal concerns which were emerging at the time. Ryan and Kellner argue that these "crisis films" were reacting to feminism in particular, since it had the potential to displace "male paternalist power" from its dominant position.[49] Instead of dealing with these issues openly, these films addressed the challenging of societal ideals through giant sharks and demons.[50] While those films were reacting to social movements of the 1960s, it is possible to see *Batman v Superman* adopting a similar strategy of using metaphors to address perceived crisis of the 2010s. *Batman v Superman* positions itself as a continuation of the canonized gender narrative for Batman, further marginalizing alternative readings of the character. Batman's gender narrative is also presented as being the culmination of the hegemonic masculinity proposed by the film. The same masculinity experiences a crisis as Superman (an illegal alien with superpowers) arrives and partially undermines Batman's "hard won" masculinity. Eventually, this crisis is resolved by first reaffirming a dichotomy in which men with noticeably masculine features are the ones in charge of what direction society takes. Second, women with masculine characteristics are anomalous in this dichotomy, but these digressions are tolerated if they manage to otherwise maintain a form of femininity that complements the hegemonic masculinity. Similarly, any changes that take place in society, represented by Wonder Woman, are palatable if they do not represent or demand any drastic changes to the status quo. If any dramatic changes were to appear, the status quo would be defended by all those capable of performing at the same level as the dominant males. Luthor, a stand-in for the liberal tech industry, queerness, and subaltern masculinities in general, is shown to be the true threat to society, not the internal struggles which initially pitted Batman and Superman against each other. The film ends with the idea that women are allowed to be a part of large societal projects but that these projects are started by men, and they aim to maintain the prevailing gender order or even reverse the changes that have taken place in a postindustrial society, implying that an altered dynamic would be unpalatable, as would further advances in equality.

The film constructs its hegemonic masculinity through bursts of exposition and action. The film presents several narratives that include transgressions to the conservative gender order of the film; some of them eventually come together, but others do not. Much like the plot of the film itself, these transgressions and narrative arcs build toward a general sense of malaise towards any changes that would disrupt the patriarchal gender order and/or how (white) men are no longer appreciated as much as they feel they should be. It is completely possible, albeit unlikely, that *Batman v Superman: Dawn of Justice* proves to be a key film when understanding how popular culture influenced and was influenced by the discourse on the merits of feminism and broadening understanding on gender categories.

NOTES

1. Glen Weldon, *The Caped Crusade: Batman and the Rise of Nerd Culture* (New York: Simon and Schuster, 2016), 11–12.

2. Will Brooker, *Hunting the Dark Knight: Twenty-First Century Batman* (London: I. B. Tauris: 2012), 116–17.

3. In this article I will be referring to the theatrical version of the film unless otherwise noted.

4. Charles Bromesco, "Superman Only Has 43 Lines of Dialogue in *Batman VS. Superman*," *Screencrush*, April 18, 2016, http://screencrush.com/batman-vs-superman-dialogue/.

5. In the film, Bruce explains his reasoning to his butler Alfred Pennyworth (Jeremy Irons) as follows: "Jesus, Alfred, count the dead. Thousands of people. What's next? Millions? He has

the power to wipe out the entire human race, and if we believe there's a one percent chance that he is our enemy we have to take it as an absolute certainty . . . and we have to destroy him." *Batman v Superman: Dawn of Justice,* directed by Zack Snyder (2016; Burbank: Warner Bros.).

6. Julian C. Chambliss, "Superhero Comics: Artifacts of the U.S. Experience," *Juniata Voices* 12 (2012): 147.

7. Judith A. Allen hypothesizes that perhaps maintaining the patriarchy is so stressful to those benefiting from it that masculinity resides in a perpetual state of crisis. Judith A. Allen, "Men Interminably in Crisis? Historians on Masculinity, Sexual Boundaries, and Manhood," *Radical History Review* 82 (2002): 202.

8. Susan Faludi, *Stiffed: Betrayal of the American Man* (New York: William Morrow and Company, 1999), 595–98.

9. Paul Elliott Johnson, "The Art of Masculine Victimhood: Donald Trump's Demagoguery," *Women's Studies in Communication* 40, no. 3 (2017): 230–34.

10. Ben Schreckinger, "Trump on protester: 'I'd like to punch him in the face,'" *Politico*, February 23, 2016, https://www.politico.com/story/2016/02/donald-trump-punch-protester-219655.

11. Raewyn Connell, *Masculinities*, 2nd ed. (Cambridge: Polity, 2005), 77.

12. Raewyn Connell and Rebecca Pearse, *Gender in the World Perspective: Third Edition* (Cambridge: Polity, 2015), 91–100.

13. Tristan Bridges and C. J. Pascoe, "Hybrid Masculinities: New Direction in the Sociology of Men and Masculinities," *Sociology Compass* 8, no. 3 (2014): 247–49.

14. Susan Jeffords, *Hard Bodies: Hollywood Masculinity in the Reagan Era* (New Brunswick: Rutgers University Press, 1994), Kindle ed., Loc. 1212–20.

15. Jeffords, Loc. 1226–30.

16. Brooker, *Hunting the Dark Knight*, 176–77.

17. Martin Fradley, "What Do You Believe In? Film Scholarship and the Cultural Politics of the Dark Knight Franchise," *Film Quarterly* 66, no. 3 (2013): 26.

18. These militaristic elements are most apparent in the conversations between Bruce Wayne and his butler Alfred Pennyworth (Jeremy Irons) and how the majority of Batman's weapons are attached to the vehicles he uses.

19. Beth A. Eck, "Compromising Positions: Unmarried Men, Heterosexuality, and Two-Phase Masculinity," *Men and Masculinities* 17, no. 2 (2014): 151–52.

20. Weldon, *The Caped Crusade*, 280–82.

21. *Batman v Superman*, Snyder.

22. *Batman v Superman*.

23. "Batman v Superman: Dawn of Justice—Official Trailer 2," Warner Bros. Pictures, *Youtube*, December 2, 2015, http://www.youtube.com/watch?v=fis-9Zqu2Ro.

24. Jeffords, *Hard Bodies*, Loc. 510–19.

25. Eventually, Superman is accepted by Batman as a real man, which coincides with them realizing that the status quo of society is threatened by disruptive and possibly queer forces.

26. Nicola Rehling, *Extra-Ordinary Men: White Heterosexual Masculinity in Contemporary Popular Cinema* (Plymouth: Lexington Books, 2009), 105.

27. Yael D. Sherman, "Miss Congeniality," in *Feminism at the Movies: Understanding Gender in Contemporary Popular Cinema*, ed. Hilary Radner and Rebecca Stringer (London and New York: Routledge, 2011), 82–83.

28. Catherine Rottenberg, "Neoliberal Feminism and the Future of Human Capital," *Signs: Journal of Women in Culture and Society* 42, no. 2 (2017): 329–48.

29. Raewyn Connell and James W. Messerschmidt, "Hegemonic Masculinity: Rethinking the Concept," *Gender and Society* 19, no. 6 (2005): 848.

30. Susan Faludi, "Reagan's America: The Backlash Against Women and Men," in *Movies and American Society*, ed. Steven J. Ross (Oxford: Blackwell, 2002), 326–30.

31. James Mulder, "'Believe It or Not, This is Power': Embodied Crisis and the Superhero Film," *Journal of Popular Culture* 50, no. 5 (2017): 1062.

32. Nick Serpe, "Trump Disrupts the Valley," *Dissent* 64, no. 4 (2017): 76–81.

33. An example of Cesar Romero's portrayal of the Joker is "The Joker is Wild" episode from the 1966 *Batman* television series which features the Joker's first appearance in said television series. Its twenty-five-minute run time introduces all the elements that would define this version of the Joker: convoluted plots, over-the-top reactions, and the desire to make Batman seem ridiculous. *Batman*, Episode 5, "The Joker is Wild," directed by Don Weis, aired January 26, 1966, on ABC.

34. Brooker, *Hunting the Dark Knight*, 127–28.

35. Rehling, *Extra-Ordinary Men*, 252.

36. Claire Duncanson, "Forces for Good? Narratives of Military Masculinity in Peacekeeping Operations," *International Feminist Journal of Politics* 11, no. 1 (2009): 67–68.

37. Judith Butler, "Gender is Burning," in *Feminist Film Theory*, ed. Sue Thornham (Edinburgh: Edinburgh University Press, 1999), 339.

38. Rosi Braidotti, *Metamorphosis: Towards a Materialist Theory of Becoming* (Cambridge: Polity, 2002), 199–200.

39. Connell and Pearse, *Gender*, 42–43.

40. *Batman v Superman*, Snyder.

41. Rosemary R. Philips, "The Battle over Bathrooms: Schools, Courts, and Transgender Rights," *Theory in Action* 10, no. 4 (2017): 100–104.

42. "Batman v Superman: Dawn of Justice," *Rotten Tomatoes*, April 28, 2018, https://www.rottentomatoes.com/m/batman_v_superman_dawn_of_justice/?search=Batman V Superman.

43. "Batman v Superman: Dawn of Justice," *Metacritic*, July 4, 2018, http://www.metacritic.com/movie/batman-v-superman-dawn-of-justice.

44. Anthony Lane, "Duels and Rules," *The New Yorker*, April 4, 2016, http://www.newyorker.com/magazine/2016/04/04/batman-v-superman-and-francofonia.

45. Anthony Oliver Scott, "Review: 'Batman v Superman' . . . v Fun?" *The New York Times*, March 23, 2016, http://www.nytimes.com/2016/03/25/movies/review-batman-v-superman-dawn-of-justice-when-super-friends-fight.html?_r=0.

46. Sam Riedel, "Batman v Superman v Misogyny: The Antifeminism of 'Dawn of Justice,'" *Bitch Media*, March 31, 2016, https://bitchmedia.org/article/batman-v-superman-v-misogyny-antifeminism-dawn-justice.

47. "Batman v Superman: Dawn of Justice (2016)," *Box Office Mojo*, March 14, 2018, http://www.boxofficemojo.com/movies/?id=superman2015.htm.

48. The estimations on how much *Batman v Superman* actually cost to produce and market vary, but $800 million would appear to be the amount the film needed to make in order to break even. For more see Russ Burlingame, "What *Batman v Superman* Needs to

Gross to Break Even," *Comicbook.com*, March 3, 2016, http://comicbook.com/2016/03/16/what-batman-v-superman-needs-to-gross-to-break-even/.

49. Michael Ryan and Douglass Kellner, *Camera Politica: The Politics and Ideology of Contemporary Hollywood Film* (Bloomington: Indiana University Press, 1988), 49–52.

50. Ryan and Kellner.

PART II

THE MONSTROUS OTHER

THE MONSTROUS IN *BATWOMAN*

Military Masculinity and Domestic Spaces

ESTHER DE DAUW

In the *Batwoman: Elegy* graphic novel (2010) and the 2010–15 *Batwoman* comics, the American military remains a space reserved for and productive of hegemonic masculinity. The Kane family's investment in military masculinity influences their construction of the domestic sphere and, with the eventual elimination of two characters who embody feminine identities, the familial relationship between Kate and her father Jacob reconfigures itself as a military unit. This chapter explores military masculinity's culturally exalted, hegemonic status and its impact on feminine identities through the analysis of Batwoman's performance of military masculinity in light of her feminine villains and their monstrosity. These female villains are cast as an invasive force with Gotham functioning as a complex analogy, embodying both the (violated) homeland that needs to be protected and the breeding ground for a hostile force that needs to be repelled and destroyed. When Batwoman inevitably fails to fulfil the demands of military masculinity and operates outside of it, she is recast as a foreign threat that needs to be contained or destroyed.

THE BINARY: MALE AND FEMALE SOLDIERS

The *Batwoman: Elegy* graphic novel covers Batwoman's origin story, touching on Kate's childhood and early family life. Her family consists of herself, her twin sister, Beth, and her parents: Gabi and Jacob Kane. Both Gabi and Jacob have military careers and wear formal uniforms and fatigues. However, the family is depicted as setting aside their own personal (or professional) desires to accommodate Jacob's career while Gabi's representation of the female soldier contains old-fashioned stereotypes. The concept of the female soldier often, paradoxically, reinscribes traditional gender roles as first constructed through World War II military propaganda. To preserve the ideal soldier identity as a male warrior, female soldiers were purposefully marketed as naturally feminine women doing naturally feminine work. The Women's Army Corps (WAC) consciously crafted women's place in the war as natural, with the work requiring essentially feminine skills, as Michaela Hampf discusses: "The flip side of this new recognition of women's place in the war was that the special skills that made Wacs so valuable were often precisely those nurturing and caring skills that were traditionally assigned to women. To accept Wacs as fellow soldiers now, to give them their proper credit and support, would make them better wives when the war was over."[1] In other words, serving in the military would strengthen and develop women's feminine qualities, which would help them in their future duties as wives and mothers, because their role within the military was essentially feminine.

The origin of the female soldier as serving a quintessentially feminine purpose has stuck, with the debate over women's suitability to serve in the armed forces often focusing on their (masculine) combat abilities. Initially, women's military service was set to end after World War II, with cultural propaganda promoting the idea that women would return to the home. However, the Women's Armed Services Integration Act in 1948 secured women's right to participate in the armed forces even while it heavily restricted the number of women that could be recruited or promoted. According to Hampf, the act "permanently fixed the basis for ethnic and gendered discrimination within the armed forces during the next two decades."[2] With the rise of second wave feminism in the 1960s, women's place in the military again became hotly debated. *Rowland vs Tarr* (1971) challenged the draft in an increasingly anti–Vietnam War atmosphere, partially based on its gender discrimination against women. The idea that women could not maintain similar levels of fitness as men was challenged in 1979 when the enlistment qualifications for men and women were made the same. However, women remained barred from active combat zones and were assigned to support units only. While this rule did not mean that women never saw combat, the legalization of this rule in 1994 enshrined the idea that female soldiers should be protected from violence, which remained the sphere of men. This stratification intensified in the wake of 9/11, as America's mass media machine began to reproduce the fears, anxieties, and coping mechanisms of 1950s' Cold War America.[3] Following the terrorist attack on the World Trade Center, American mass media began to reiterate traditional gender roles, relegating women to the domestic sphere where they would be protected by men who could engage in violence without hesitation or fear. As Susan Faludi writes, popular culture and mass media obsessively engaged in "the denigration of capable women, the magnification of manly men, the heightened call for domesticity, [and] the search for and sanctification of helpless girls."[4] As evidenced by Faludi's analysis of the media discourse surrounding Jessica Lynch, a female American soldier injured in Iraq in 2003, female soldiers were infantilized and framed as innocent, pure, feminine women who needed male heroes to protect and save them from the consequences of combat. Paradoxically, this resulted in the actual deaths of female soldiers being largely ignored in order to sustain the myth that manly soldiers (and by extension, the paternal and patriarchal US military machine) are capable of protecting women.[5]

From conception to modern-day iteration, the question of the female soldier's place in combat remains at the forefront of the debate, focusing specifically on women's ability to participate in violence. The possibility of military femininity incorporating a female warrior identity threatens both the male soldier's monopoly on combat and traditional ideas of femininity as soft and gentle. Military masculinity is culturally framed as entirely masculine, invested in the elimination of the feminine from masculine spaces and bodies. Traditionally, women's "soft" bodies are considered weaker than men's, whose capacity for muscularity makes them the more suitable soldier. Helena Carreiras and Gerhard Kümmel discuss how debates on military capability frames the ideal attributes of soldiers, such as "aggressiveness, physical strength, action orientation, boldness, stamina, willingness to endure exposure to extreme physical danger and readiness to taking lives" as fundamentally, biologically masculine.[6] The female soldier, on the other hand, is burdened with "the myth of the genuinely peace-loving, passive, gentle and squeamish woman which denies these attributes to women and the female body and psyche."[7] The cult of the body maintains that male and female bodies have essentially differing roles biologically. In this coda, male bodies are strong and muscular, serving the natural function of the warrior, the protector and the conqueror, but women are mothers and wives. The female body is fundamentally constructed around the uterus and this makes the female soldier unsuitable for combat. Carreiras and Kümmel reveal the fallacy behind these traditional ideas surrounding muscular bodies and pinpoint how, given similar levels of training, male and female bodies attain similar levels of fitness. The gender roles infusing female and male soldier identities are outdated but remain in effect in popular culture's understanding and representation of military culture, as evidenced by *Elegy*'s portrayal of Kate's family life.

The Kane children are raised on military bases, and some of the tension within the family revolves around their relocation from one military base to another as Jacob Kane climbs the career ladder. The repercussions of this relocation on Gabi's career are never mentioned. In fact, it is unclear what role or rank she has. Instead, the scenes focusing on Gabi and her relationship with the twins are domestic, scenes in which Jacob does not make an appearance. For instance, the first time the reader sees Gabi she is dressed in army fatigues; but she has also just made the twins their dinner, reminds them about their homework, and ends up scolding them for lying to one of their teachers. She tells them they have to take "**responsibility** for your actions. And when you act **wrongly,** you have to **answer** for it. Without hiding, without complaint. That's **integrity** and it is the foundation of **honor,** and that's something your father and I both **believe** in" (original emphasis).[8] In this scene, Gabi combines the military's ethics with the traditional roles of housewife and mother. Wearing fatigues and lecturing her children on behavior stereotypically associated with and fostered by the military, Gabi represents the female soldier's role as being fundamentally feminine: the rearing of children and instilling the correct code of behavior. It also indicates the family's exaltation of the military code of conduct as even children are expected to maintain honor and discipline. This scene is directly contrasted with the scenes of Jacob being a soldier actively engaged in combat on the next page.

Jacob's identity as a soldier is clearly the physical, front-line warrior role. He is fighting the enemy, in a distant place that can only be vaguely identified as Middle-Eastern, while coordinating assault strikes. This panel series is laid over an image of the American flag to highlight the patriotism of military combat and, by extension, military masculinity. Belkin writes how the American military and its "masculinity [are] often portrayed as a central element of the American melting pot, a site where citizens come together, become soldiers, and defend the nation so as to minimise foreign threat."[9] The cultural understanding of military service as fundamentally American and masculine is perpetuated by *Elegy* with the male soldier framed as a quintessentially American warrior ideal. This further presents the military's gender roles as fundamentally American and essential to preserving the American way of life. To safeguard America, and the domesticity only just witnessed in the comic, male soldiers have to be warriors and female soldiers have to be mothers, caretakers, and teachers. Despite being a military professional,

Jacob the Soldier © 2010 DC Comics

Gabi's primary identifier is motherhood, to the extent that the reader never sees her perform any military duties, does not understand her military work, or even knows her rank. Simultaneously, Jacob never seems to inhabit a domestic, fatherly role. The family maintains a traditional nuclear structure, with the mother staying at home and the father advancing his career. Combined with the family's consistent deference to Jacob's professional needs, it is clear the male soldier has an elevated status within this family model.

The family's perpetuation of traditional gender roles aligns Gabi with femininity and Jacob with masculinity. The twins embody a similar split, with Kate being consistently depicted as masculine and Beth as feminine. During the flashbacks to Kate's early family life, Kate often functions as Beth's protector and is considered tomboyish. The twins are also often dressed in either the same outfit or in contrasting colors, with Beth in white and pink and Kate in black and red. Beth's colors are very dainty and feminine, while Kate's colors are harsher and more masculine.[10] The *Batwoman* comics (2010–15) maintain this gendered split that frames Kate as aligned with the masculine. In *Batwoman #7* (2012), Jacob recounts how Beth resembled their mother, while Kate was more like him.[11] In *Batwoman #10* (2012), Jacob elaborates with a story from the twin's childhood when their cat became very ill and

Jacob took her behind the house to put her down humanely. He realized too late that the twins had been watching and while Beth cried, Kate did not and helped him bury the corpse. He highlights how this moment solidified Kate's masculine attributes. She was just like him, "[u]nsentimental. Stubborn. Capable of closing off the part of herself that lets a little girl cry over her dead cat."[12] In contrast, Beth was nothing like him: "I saw only that she was patient enough to play with the younger kids on the base. Sweet enough to paint me birthday cards. So selfless she let Kate score every goal . . . And for all the ways she **wasn't** like me, I think I secretly loved **Beth** more" (original emphasis).[13] In this monologue, Jacob reveals that even from early childhood, Kate possessed those qualities that Carreiras and Kümmel have identified as exalted masculine traits. Yet, at the same time, the feminine traits exhibited by Beth, the kindness and softness, are romanticized as more worthy of being the object of (masculine) love. Beth is cast as a feminine signifier who needed to be protected. The romanticization of soft femininity does not prevent the exaltation of masculinity, as femininity is fetishized as the Other that needs to be possessed and controlled by signifiers of the masculine. Within military masculinity, the feminine is a romanticized ideal that needs to be protected within the feminine signifier but destroyed within the masculine signifier. It can be the object of love, but it exists within the civilian, the victim, and not the soldier. The Kane family is split alongside a traditional binary: the masculine and the feminine, but with the aggrandizement of the male soldier and military masculinity, this split cannot be maintained.

ELIMINATION OF THE FEMALE AND MILITARY MASCULINITY CONSTRUCTION

Within dominant American culture, military masculinity enjoys an exalted status that is validated through combat, discipline, and authority. Within all levels of American mass media, military masculinity is often interpreted or represented as the uncomplicated cultivation of masculinity in its purest, most direct, and fetishized form.[14] As the warrior ideal, the soldier must protect signifiers of the feminine while destroying those feminine elements within himself that could weaken his hard masculinity. Paradoxically, the male soldier's ability to protect the feminine *depends* on his ability to destroy it. Femininity's destruction becomes inevitable as masculinity's privileged status demands that its survival be prioritized over femininity. The *Batwoman* comics, as well as the *Elegy* graphic novel, maintain this split, perpetuate the idea of the combat soldier as exclusively masculine and, inevitably, destroy their feminine signifiers.

The Kane nuclear family, with its traditional military gender roles and glorification of military masculinity, is a microcosmic example of the protection/destruction duality and, eventually, this leads to the death and destruction of the two family members that signify femininity. When Kate is twelve years old, she, her sister and her mother are kidnapped. Kate is the only survivor to return home with her father. The feminine signifiers' "softness" is their downfall and Kate, who is stubborn, unemotional, and unsentimental, survives. The masculinity of the soldier, cultivated and honored, protects her. Following the loss of the feminine (and through them, the domestic), the familial relationship becomes even more focused on reproducing the dynamics of the military unit. From this point on, Kate and Jacob's relationship is marked via her loyalty and obedience to him. As a child, she resisted and expressed disagreement with the way the family navigated the needs of Jacob's military career. With the loss of the domestic, the family has also lost a space that is marked by characteristics of the civilian sphere—the ability to question authority, engage in debate, and form a political identity. The military unit, on the other hand, is marked by the need to defer to authority and obey orders without question.[15] Jacob and Kate's relationship becomes characterized by discipline, with Kate calling her father "sir" and "colonel," but only occasionally "pops."[16] In *Batwoman #13* (2012), Kate says, "my father didn't train a bystander. He trained a **soldier**" (original emphasis).[17] Jacob grooms his daughter as the ideal soldier, with her childhood as basic training, ready to construct her life around her own military career. Their relationship is not domestic or indeed parental.

Halfway through *Elegy*, Kate's relationship with the military takes center stage. As soon as she can, Kate joins the United States Military Academy, also known as West Point. Kate explicitly frames this decision as following in her father's footsteps and the result of her childhood trauma. She wants to prevent what happened to her mother and sister from happening to other signifiers of the feminine. This cements her parallelization with her father and their shared commitment to the performance of military masculinity. Kate's soldier identity is heavily enmeshed with the male soldier role and the masculine warrior ideal. The comic highlights how Kate excels in the physical requirements and was even appointed to be her brigade's XO.[18] Her performance can be read as a challenge to the cult of the body and the way the concepts of the female and male soldier are defined within American culture. However, Kate's desire to become a soldier and her ability as a soldier are framed in masculine terms. Instead of constructing a new female soldier concept that embodies a new female warriorhood, Kate maintains the gender divide that constructs the alignments of combat soldier = male and domestic soldier = female through her adherence to the military code of conduct that denies her a place in the military.

While at West Point, Kate enters into a romantic relationship with another cadet, Sophie Moore, which results in charges of homosexual conduct. Her superior officer, Colonel Reyes, tells Kate that he is duty bound to investigate the charges but that he can avoid suspending her if she promises that it was a misunderstanding and that it will not happen again. Instead, Kate admits that she is gay because "a cadet shall not lie, cheat or steal, nor suffer others to do."[19] While Kate remains true to her personal identity and does not compromise her integrity, the use of the cadet code of conduct to justify her decision to do so frames this moment as exemplary of Kate's adherence to military masculinity, which the comic has consistently defined as unemotional, selfless, and obedient to a commanding officer. Her loyalty is presented as uncomplicated and does not allow for any identities that stray from the preconceptualized roles of female and male soldier. Kate never discusses the use of DADT as discriminatory, hypocritical, or unconstitutional. This failure to engage with the wider institutionalized forces that construct military values and the idealization of the male soldier hints at an inability to imagine a female warriorhood and reconfigure the concept of the female soldier. Kate's lack of engagement with these structural inequalities demonstrates how Kate, having been raised in idolization of the military, is incapable of voicing the critique necessary to embody a new female soldier. Instead, she is trapped in her attempt to embody the male soldier as the only combat option available to her. Knowing that she will be expelled, she remains true to the code of ethics that prohibits a new conceptualization of soldier identity, making her complicit with its discrimination and her own dehumanization.

A WAY TO SERVE: VIGILANTISM AS MILITARY SERVICE

Kate's discharge from the military affects her deeply on a personal level and causes her to become directionless. Conditioned to obedience to a superior officer both through her relationship with her father and her time at West Point, Kate experiences freedom as a destructive force. She becomes unmoored instead of liberated. For the first time in her adult life, Kate is homed in a domestic setting (her stepmother's house), outside the bounds of the military and her militaristic relationship with her father. This domestic setting is heavily contrasted with her time in the military. Even the line art, which was straightforward and traditional during her time at West Point, becomes less linear. During this time, Kate drinks too much and parties too hard. Her existence in the domestic space is marked by chaos, self-indulgence, recklessness and luxury. It is the very opposite of the military tenets of discipline, (self)control and integrity that Kate and the comic itself exalt. This frames domestic spaces as toxic; something that infects and destroys the hardness necessary to maintain military masculinity. Kate does not pull herself out of her self-destructive spiral until she is attacked late at night on her own. As the man takes a swing at her, Kate ducks out of the way and says "Think I'm some **victim**. You don't know. I'm a **soldier**" (original emphasis).[20] The contrast between the two bold words: "victim" and "soldier" is telling: Kate has defined her identity through the masculine warrior ideal of the soldier. The "soldier" and "victim" are two ends of the spectrum or, each other's double. Similar to how the superhero inevitably exists as a double of its alter ego, the secret identity, the soldier exists in relation to its civilian or domestic double. This civilian double is both the romanticized signifier of soft femininity and the embodiment of toxic luxury and self-indulgence that is infectious to hard masculinity. To maintain her military masculinity, Kate must eradicate her status as a civilian and return to her soldier identity.

During this speech, Kate successfully fights off her would-be mugger and comes face-to-face with Batman. Their brief, wordless confrontation results in Kate staring up into the rain at the bat chevron being projected onto the sky. The lack of dialogue or any sound effects clearly mark the incident's importance, pinpointing it as the formative moment in which Kate decides to become a vigilante. At first, she strikes out on her own, without telling anyone, but once she leaves the domestic sphere, Jacob returns as a notable presence in her life. Their militaristic commander/soldier relationship crystalizes further when he confronts her about being a vigilante. Her body language becomes wooden and stiff, like a soldier at parade, and her answers are monosyllabic, either "no" or "sir."[21] Jacob's angry monologue, as demonstrated below, is punctuated by hand gestures and shouting, mirroring popular images of drill sergeants shouting at enlisted men.

Eventually, Kate breaks away from her stance and attempts to explain herself, saying "you've **got** your **uniform**, your answer to your **duty**. That **bat** they shine in the sky . . . civilians think it's a call for **help**" (original emphasis).[22] Kate draws a line between herself and the civilian. Even though expulsion from the military would release her from duty, Kate continues to

Drill Sergeant 1 © 2010 DC Comics

feel its burden. The fetishization of military service and its selflessness, honor and integrity make it impossible for Kate to live within the civilian sphere. She continues, "It's a **call** to arms ... I've found my way to **serve**" (original emphasis).[23] Kate explicitly identifies vigilantism as a way to inhabit the masculine soldier role outside of the military. The exaltation of military masculinity prevents Kate from conceptualizing life as a (feminine) civilian and becomes the root of her vigilantism. In doing so, Kate marks the civilian population as victims, the double haunting the soldier.

At this point, Jacob takes over Kate's training. He calls in several favors other military personnel owe him in order to get Kate into international training programmes. His voice is the one that narrates Kate's training montage: "Make no mistake: you do this, you're going to **war**" (original emphasis).[24] Instead of conceptualizing vigilantism as the protection of a civilian population, it is framed as going into battle with an enemy force. Kate's superhero role as the Batwoman is firmly aligned with that of the soldier who functions within a military unit. While Batman struck out on his own to look for teachers and often trains by himself, Kate remains under the watchful eye of her father/commander. Batman's training was used to mark his independence; for Kate, it becomes a road to "service." Batman makes his own code and is the master of his universe, but Batwoman is a foot soldier going through basic training. Even when her training is finished and she begins working, it is her father who (using his new wife's fortune) builds her a hideout and provides her with all her equipment. He is the one who places the bat chevron on her chest, like a rank or insignia, so everyone will know that she is "one of the good guys."[25] Compared to the Batman, who has his own (inherited) fortune and often builds/designs his own gear, Batwoman is completely dependent on Jacob for supplies and, presumably, an income. Kate (and the Batwoman) remain tied to a superior (and male) officer.

Their relationship dynamic does not change until their militaristic sphere is penetrated by a toxic and destructive feminine signifier as Beth returns to Gotham and reveals she is still alive. The revelation that Jacob had known all along about Beth's survival causes a rupture in Jacob and Kate's relationship. Jacob explains his decision to keep Beth a secret as a way to protect Kate and let her move on with her life. Without the added trauma of knowing her sister might have been alive and being tortured somewhere, Kate would not have been distracted from her own life or her pursuit of military service. Maintaining the illusion that Beth was dead sustained the elimination of the feminine within their military unit. The reintroduction of the feminine destroys their relationship, as the revelation of Jacob's *abandonment* of the female signifier causes Kate to question his ability as a superior officer and to reject his leadership. Her separation from Jacob marks the start of Kate's true attempt at independence, turning away from military masculinity and attempting to create a new soldier/superhero identity. However, the cultural fetishization of military service and Gotham's function as an unstable feminine space sabotage any attempts at conceptualizing a new female soldier or superhero identity.

GOTHAM AS AN ANALOGY

Within the DC universe, Gotham is presented as a gothic feminine space and functions as its own double. Within the Batman comics specifically, Gotham is considered, in turns, a city that allows for untold opportunities (like New York) and an urban hellscape where monsters are real. In *Batwoman #14* (2012), Gotham is described as "the dark heart of the world" and *Batwoman #16* (2013) refers to it as the "Kingdom of lunatics."[26] Metaphorically, Gotham functions as the heartland of America itself. In *The Terror Dream*, Faludi writes about the fundamental myth at the foundation of America's obsession with passive femininity and violent masculinity: the domestic homestead as surrounded and constantly under threat by a violent wilderness that can overwhelm the homestead at any time. Faludi tracked this original myth to the days of initial colonial settlement, when the Puritans lived under the terror of attack from a native population (that they had originally brutalized). Among colonial settlers, there existed a widespread fear of the kidnapping of white women and their inevitable rape by Native Americans, despite the available evidence that rape was exceedingly uncommon. Furthermore, many women who were kidnapped by Native Americans refused to return to white society and often sought to escape their white family members if they were ransomed back.[27] Not only does this national myth focus on the vulnerability of white women (as property that could be stolen) and the need for powerful white men to protect them, it also incorporates fears of "the enemy among us" as there is a constant, sneaking suspicion that the enemy exists at home in the shape of a woman. The national myth of America's homeland requires both the protection and control of white women by white men in order to safeguard the homeland.[28] Following 9/11, this national myth returned in the collective media consciousness through its denigration of female soldiers and its focus on domesticity. Mass media consistently reiterated the national myth: in order for the domestic homestead (the feminine sphere) to survive the threat of invasion, it requires the masculine institution of nationhood to protect it. As Jason Dittmer writes, in "gendered reading of national security culture, it is the 'soft' feminine nation that is to be protected by the 'hard' masculine state."[29] As a result, American culture remains fearful of the nation becoming feminized, of women having too much control and destroying the hardness required to protect the homestead from invasion or even from leaving and abandoning the homestead and male protection (i.e., control). Women and female spaces need protection but also haunt hard masculinity through the possibility of contaminating and destroying it.

Gotham is the representation of that post-9/11 homeland and functions as a liminal space where doubles exist side by side. It is the homestead that is simultaneously preserved as a civilian safe space in a world or landscape (the presettled American wilderness) that seeks to invade the homestead and the homestead that has already been invaded, whose inhabitants reject white patriarchy and join their captors, becoming the enemy: the villain hiding within the civilian. Gotham is a place of seepages where the domestic becomes monstrous as the native population includes both innocent civilians and Gotham's mad, underworld villains. In order to protect Gotham, its heroes need to constantly police its population, which can birth a new monstrosity any minute. In this space, hard masculinity is buffeted by both sides: the monstrous villains and the soft civilians. As its own double, Gotham is the invaded homeland struggling to be reclaimed (or the homeland-under-siege by invading forces) and the enemy's stronghold. In this land of seepages, the masculine heroes struggle to preserve the hard masculinity necessary to avoid contamination by toxic femininity and to protect the homestead.

The first line of defense against the invading forces rising out of the civilians/victims is the Gotham City Police Department (GCPD). But, in a place like Gotham, the GCPD functions as both ally and enemy. Widely considered as corrupt and exploitative, many police officers work as lackeys for villains or as spies for organized crime. Simultaneously, the GCPD are Batman's foot soldiers. A well-known feature of Gotham is the Bat-Signal housed at the top of the GCPD headquarters. The police use it when there is a crime they cannot solve or when they cannot withstand a villain's attack on the city. The chevron is a call for help and, as Kate says, a call to arms when Batman is summoned and, in turn, summons his army. The Bat-Signal aligns the police and the Batman as a military unit, with Batman as the superior officer.[30]

The bat chevron is a prominent insignia within the DC universe, and many characters use it, but there is only one who controls it: Batman. Within Gotham, he is the de facto head or general of a quasi-military group of superheroes, known as Batman Incorporated. Through her use of the bat chevron, Kate is (unofficially) part of the military group that Batman commands. After all, Jacob gave it to her because it signified her alignment with Batman, "the good guys." No matter how many times she claims that she is not officially affiliated with Batman, the symbol marks her as "one of Batman's shadow soldiers."[31] Gotham's military hierarchy does not allow Kate to function outside of it—as a female warrior soldier—and insists on reaffirming her place in the hierarchy when she rejects Jacob's authority. No matter how hard she works to establish a separate military space or soldier role, Gotham's seepages make this impossible. For instance, the *Batwoman* comics insist on vigilantism's connection to military hierarchy and explicitly frame the superhero costume as a military uniform that needs to be earned. In *Batwoman #1* (2011), Kate's cousin Bette becomes her sidekick. Although Bette was once a member of the Teen Titans and is known as Flamebird, Kate considers Bette to be an amateur and burns the Flamebird outfit. To earn a uniform, Bette has to go through the training Kate sets out for her while wearing a pair of grey coveralls clear of any identifying markers that might denote a rank or organization, and is called "plebe," the same word used for first-year military cadets.[32] Despite her rejection of Jacob, Kate maintains the quasi-military structure of Batman Incorporated, with clear hierarchies of authority, and enforces this structure on other vigilantes even when she attempts to reject her place in the Batman Incorporated hierarchy.

> **FLAMEBIRD:** I still can't believe you turned down Batman to partner with those tools. I mean, you wear his **symbol.**
> **BATWOMAN:** It's **my** bat. And I'm not a member of his cult.
> **FLAMEBIRD:** Sure, **Bat**woman.
> (original emphasis)[33]

In this exchange, Kate attempts to take ownership of the bat, but Flamebird's response highlights that this is both ridiculous and impossible. In many Batman comics, various members of Batman Incorporated are referred to as "a bat" but "the bat" is always Batman. It cannot be Kate's bat because it always has been the Batman's Bat and that was the reason Jacob gave it to Kate. Wearing the bat chevron and working in Gotham (where no vigilantes work without Batman's approval) puts Batwoman automatically under Batman's authority.

Kate simultaneously exists within and reproduces a hierarchical structure, and sets out to escape it. This breaking away from a direct, quasi-militaristic superior officer is the first attempt Kate makes to separate herself from the male soldier role and to create a new, female warrior identity where she functions as more than just the foot soldier. However, the cultural worship of the military industrial complex—and with it, the extolling of the male soldier—that consumed her early childhood years and nuclear family is inescapable. As she considers vigilantism a form of military service, her choice to be a superhero limits her ability to break free from the military's gender roles. Her use of the bat chevron continually identifies her as a soldier from Batman's army to outsiders, no matter how much she denies it. Her own dynamic with Flamebird is a hierarchy instead of an equal partnership, dressed up in the accoutrements of military service. Gotham, as a complex homestead, both domestic and dangerous, contaminates its heroes. Without a strict militaristic masculinity to protect them, its heroes become the monsters they set out to fight. Breaking away from her (male) superior officers places Kate beyond the protection of the gender binary. Without a military unit, Kate becomes vulnerable to the toxic feminine influences of the villain and the civilian.

THE MASCULINE SOLDIER AND ITS FEMININE DOUBLE

Kate's performance of the Batwoman role is marked by her desire to inhabit the realm of the male soldier, and her costume is respected and exalted the same way members of the military respect their uniforms as symbols of

Batwoman © 2010 DC Comics

sacrifice and duty. However, Kate's appearance could not be further from that of a military soldier. Instead of masculine signifiers, Batwoman uses femininity as a weapon in her fight against Gotham's criminals.

Within this traditionally male gender role, Batwoman performs a heightened femininity. She has long, red hair, and her red lipstick stands out against her incredibly pale skin. Batwoman purposefully plays with monstrous femininity in order to "strike fear into the heart of criminals," a goal that is the origin of all Bat-heroes in Gotham. *Elegy* especially has many panels focusing on close-ups of Batwoman's mouth, often stretched into a terrifying grin. While the comics also depict Kate sweating and grunting in her workouts, the Batwoman herself remains femininely pristine in combat. Her injuries, obvious on Kate, are covered up in the Batwoman costume and only instances of spurting blood are visible. This conscious performance of monstrous femininity, while inhabiting the male soldier role, cannot stand.

Performing monstrous femininity within her new soldier role and eventually rejecting any male authority figure as a commanding officer is not possible in Gotham. Kate's performance of monstrous femininity becomes all too real. Seduced by the villainous Natalia Mitternacht, Kate's control over her Batwoman persona is shattered. She becomes plagued by nightmares, while Batwoman experiences moments of excessive aggression. Kate does not remember these episodes, but they are clear to the reader as she has sharp canines, is incredibly violent, and uses a strange, purple speech bubble with a gothic font. The focus on her teeth and her mouth, blood-red, invokes images of the female vampire, whose bloodthirsty and lustful nature threatens the established order. While initially only an illusion brought on by hypnosis, *Batwoman Future's End #1* (2014) solidifies this transformation and makes it real. Having succumbed to monstrous femininity, Kate is murdered by a stake through the heart. Her blending of monstrous femininity and the male soldier role, as a way towards female warriorhood, only brings about the toxic femininity that military masculinity must destroy. In places like Gotham, where monstrously feminine spaces and populations must be controlled by a military hierarchy, female warriorhood cannot be brought into existence. The comic's exaltation of military masculinity traps Kate in a double bind: adherence to military masculinity is impossible, as she is continually expelled from its male spaces, but the creation of a new female warriorhood is monstrous and must be destroyed. She becomes her own double: the villain to her superhero, who is also the civilian and the victim.

Superheroes often exist as part of a double: the superhero and their secret, civilian identity. This doubling is complicated by the other double haunting the narrative: the superhero and the villain. For the masculine soldier who needs to both protect and destroy the feminine, the supervillain and the civilian identity are closely linked through femininity. In Gotham, all these identities become blurred. Within this environment, doubles cannot maintain their barriers and seep into each other, just as Gotham functions as its own double. As its protector and its soldier, Batwoman meets her doubles: all her villains who function as monstrous women. It is also the place where she becomes unmoored, free from the constraints of military masculinity. Kate's increasingly desperate struggles against her own doubles—the fragile civilian and the monstrously feminine villains—slowly infect her own hard military masculinity.

The *Batwoman* comics and *Elegy* graphic novel exalt military masculinity and consistently reproduce its (gender) dynamics. At first, this places Kate in the position of the foot soldier, whose attempts to embody military masculinity are sabotaged. But when Kate seeks to escape or resist the perpetuation of the military industrial complex and attempts to reconceptualize the female soldier as a combatant, she is cast in the role of the villain and her femininity becomes monstrous. For female combatants in the Gothic Batwoman universe, there is only one option: the villain or the civilian. The existence of the rigid gender roles maintained by the exaltation of military masculinity (which is sustained through feminine vulnerability) prohibit the existence of the female soldier as combatant and the female combatant as heroic, maintaining hegemonic masculinity and fragile femininity.

NOTES

1. M. Michaela Hampf, *Release a Man For Combat: The Women's Army Corps during World War II* (Köln: Böhlau Verlag, 2010), 147.
2. Hampf, *Release a Man For Combat*, 90.
3. Susan Faludi, *The Terror Dream: Fear and Fantasy in Post-9/11 America* (New York: Metropolitan Books, 2007).
4. Faludi, *The Terror Dream*, 14.
5. It took until 2015 to lift official restrictions on the roles and positions female soldiers could fill, and it was not until 2019 that the men-only draft was ruled unconstitutional on the basis of gender discrimination. Jim Miklaszewski and Halimah Abdullah, "All Combat Roles Now Open to Women, Pentagon Says," *NBC News*, December 3, 2015, https://www.nbcnews.com/news/us-news/pentagon-nbc-news-all-combat-roles-now-open-women-n473581. Gregory Korte, "Military Draft: Judge Rules Male-Only Draft is Unconstitutional," *USA Today*, February 24, 2019, https://eu.usatoday.com/story/news/nation/2019/02/24/military-draft-judge-rules-male-only-registration-unconstitutional/2968872002/.
6. Helen Carreiras and Gerhard Kümmel, "Off Limits: The Cults of the Body and Social Homogeniety as Discursive Weapons in Targeting Gender Integration in the Military," in *Women in the Military and in Armed Conflict*, ed. Helen Carreiras and Gerhard Kümmel (Berlin: Springer, 2008), 31.
7. Carreiras and Kümmel.
8. Greg Rucka et al., *Batwoman: Elegy* (Burbank: DC Comics, 2010).
9. Aaron Belkin, *Bring Me Men: Military Masculinity and the Benign Façade of American Empire 1898–2001* (London: Hurst and Company, 2012), 3.
10. These colors are also practical; they help the audience identify Kate as she is wearing the Batwoman colors. They also foreshadow Beth's future role in the comic.
11. W. Haden Blackman et al., *Batwoman #7* (Burbank: DC Comics, 2012).
12. W. Haden Blackman et al., *Batwoman #10* (Burbank: DC Comics, 2012).
13. Blackman.
14. Belkin, *Bring Me Men*, 1–17.
15. Belkin, 40–41.
16. Rucka, *Elegy*.
17. W. Haden Blackman et al., *Batwoman #13* (Burbank: DC Comics, 2012).
18. The brigade XO, or executive officer, is usually the second-in-command who manages the daily activities and administration of any company, battalion, regiment, or brigade.
19. Rucka, *Elegy*.
20. Rucka.
21. Rucka.

22. Rucka.

23. Rucka.

24. Rucka.

25. Rucka.

26. W. Haden Blackman et al., *Batwoman #14* (Burbank: DC Comics, 2012). W. Haden Blackman et al., *Batwoman #16* (Burbank: DC Comics, 2013).

27. Faludi, *The Terror Dream*, 199–263.

28. Of course, this national myth also functioned to justify the ongoing and systematic genocide of Native Americans by colonial leadership and later, the US government.

29. Dittmer Jason, *Captain America and the Nationalist Superhero: Metaphor, Narrative and Geopolitics* (Philadelphia: Temple University Press, 2013), 28.

30. This is not to say that this position of Batman as the superior officer remains unquestioned. For instance, *Gotham Central* (2002–6) often showcased the open rebellion against and resentment of the use of the Bat-Signal by police officers. In these critiques, Batman is framed as an interloper outside of the established order. Furthermore, Gordon's obedience to Batman's orders and his reliance on Batman instead of his own troops frames him as a "bad" or nonmasculine superior officer. Instead of modeling superior and authoritative masculinity, Gordon is only another foot soldier. As he is the highest ranking officer in Gotham, this robs the police department of a suitable superior officer who exists within the chain of command proper. This debate locks two entrenched interpretations of masculinity into a self-perpetuating conflict.

31. W. Haden Blackman et al., *Batwoman #4* (Burbank: DC Comics, 2011).

32. W. Haden Blackman et al., *Batwoman #1* (Burbank: DC Comics, 2011).

33. W. Haden Blackman et al., *Batwoman #19* (Burbank: DC Comics, 2013).

DAYS OF FUTURE PAST

Queer Identities and the X-Men

DREW MURPHY

Within the Marvel Universe, the X-Men are a unique kind of superhero team. Conceived during the Silver Age of comic books in 1963, the X-Men are mutants: a subspecies of humans who are born with superhuman abilities that are carried and activated within the X-gene, largely during puberty. These heroes were born during the early stages of a social revolution that started in the early 1960s and carried on well into the 1980s. Institutions were facing significant pressure from a generation of young people who were becoming increasingly disenfranchised by rigid beliefs about normality, power structures, and interpretations of equality.

During this time, Marvel's most popular comic books very clearly reflected the social and political issues of their readers.[1] In particular, the themes and experiences of the X-Men were often read as representations of the lived experiences of marginalized groups who were targeted because of their "otherness"; a sentiment further developed in the 1970s under prolific contributor, Chris Claremont.[2] Mutants as a race face constant oppression, and leaders like Professor Xavier and Magneto seek to carve out safe spaces for their peers. Initially, the X-Men were interpreted as an allegory for the civil rights movement in the United States. Stan Lee addressed this himself, stating in a 2000 interview that the X-Men were "a good metaphor for what was happening with the civil rights movement in the country at the time."[3] However, later readings of the X-Men have argued that the prejudice faced by mutants can also be linked to the experiences of minority groups who experience isolation and alienation because of their sexuality.[4] For example, the search for safe spaces for mutants can be broadly linked to the aims of the Gay Liberation movement and the heightened attention paid to this as a result of the Stonewall Riots in 1969. The storylines that define one of Marvel's greatest teams consistently focus on the lasting impacts of prejudice and otherness.[5] We, as readers, are reminded that even though they defend the world and possess prodigious powers and skills, they fight for a world that fears and hates them.[6] This chapter will focus specifically on the ways in which the X-Men can be read as representative of the negotiations undertaken by queer people in society, focusing firstly on the negotiations of mutantism and how this manifests itself through acts of "passing." It will further examine the mortality of mutant characters in the Marvel Universe in comparison to other superheroes and how this relates to a sense (or lack) of safety for LGBTQIA members of society. Finally, it will explore the journey of the mutant leader Cyclops and draw comparisons to the negotiation of othered masculinities for mutants to the negotiation of queer identities in our culture.

In selecting a corpus in which to explore these themes, the term "text" has been used in a literary sense to include both comic book and live action sources that can be interpreted to determine a message or meaning. The aim of this chapter is to illustrate the ways in which the experiences of mutantkind can be read as metaphors for the lived experiences of LGBTQIA members of society; to highlight how nonmasculine characters are barred from accessing status and prestige; and to examine the performance of masculinity itself. I chose texts from across the X-Men canon, including storylines which are considered seminal to the Marvel Universe in general and which indicate the X-Men's status within that universe. I selected "The Days of Future Past" storyline, chronicled in *Uncanny X-Men #141–142* (1981), and the subsequent 2014 film, alongside *Extraordinary X-Men #1–5* (2016) to explore the concept of passing as a means to evade oppression. The positions of the X-Men in a crowded landscape of superpowered beings will be discussed through the *Avengers vs. X-Men* (2012) and the *Inhumans vs. X-Men* (2016–17) comic book events. I use *Avengers vs. X-Men* in conjunction with *All New X-Men #1–5* (2013) to explore the journey of the mutant Cyclops over time, and how his presentations of masculinity can be linked to research on queer identity negotiations.

PASSING AS HUMAN: NEGOTIATIONS OF DILEMMATIC IDENTITIES

In a world of heroes, mutants occupy a unique space among other powered beings. While superheroes like Captain America, Iron Man and Spiderman are largely celebrated for their heroic deeds by the public, the X-Men are subject to open acts of hatred and bigotry, with regular attempts to depower or kill them.[7] This is perhaps most famously explored in the *Days of Future Past* storyline that appeared in *Uncanny X-Men #141–142*. Considered to be a seminal storyline for the X-Men, *Days of Future Past* centers on a futuristic, dystopian world in which the X-Men have lost the battle for equality and mutants are placed in massive internment camps. In this future, Kitty Pryde uses her mutant ability, with the help of Rachel Summers, to travel back in time and stop the events that would lead to the deaths of millions of mutants and humans alike. The need for Kitty to change the course of history is shown earlier in the story when she is traveling back to the mutant internment camp guarded by Sentinels, walking past the gravestones of fallen X-Men and other superheroes who were killed in the fight against the rise of this dystopia, describing the segregation of mutants and humans:

> In the year 2013, there are three classes of people: "H," for baseline human—clean of mutant genes, allowed to breed. "A," for anomalous human—a normal person possessing mutant genetic material ... forbidden to breed. "M," for mutant. The bottom of the heap, made pariahs and outcasts by the Mutant Control Act of 1988. Hunted down and—with a few exceptions—killed without mercy. In the quarter-century since the acts passage, millions have died. They were the lucky ones.[8]

This quote in and of itself illustrates the ways in which mutants in the Marvel Universe represent the oppressed. The classifications described by Kitty indicate not only how mutants are treated in this dystopian future, but also how they are regarded throughout Marvel comic and cinematic history. The X-Men are often subject to ridicule and prejudice due to their mutant status and are not considered superheroes in the same way that groups like the Avengers, the Fantastic Four, and the Guardians of the Galaxy are. While heroes like Captain Marvel and Iron Man can be relatively secure in their safety when the public becomes aware of their identity, the X-Men rely on secrecy and codenames for protection.

The segregation and isolation of mutants has been explored from the outset of the X-Men canon. New mutants reflect on not having anywhere to belong, older mutants ponder why they continue to fight for a world that doesn't want or accept them, and other superheroes consider their role in facilitating this cycle.[9] Within these texts, we also see a number of attempts to fit in or "pass" as human to avoid persecution. In the movie version of *Days of Future Past*, both Professor Xavier and Hank McCoy use a specially developed serum which allows them to pass in different ways. For Xavier, it allows him to walk unaided, but using the serum means he must sacrifice the use of his telepathic abilities. For Hank, it allows him to control the presentation of his powers. In doing so, he is able to control when to appear as Hank McCoy (a seemingly regular human) and when to transform into Beast (an ape/feline-like being, with pointed ears, blue fur, fangs, and oversized hands and feet). Control over his powers effectively allows Xavier and Hank to "pass," one as abled and the other as human.

In the same way that mutants in the X-Men canon employ passing as a means to avoid discrimination, research suggests that gay and bisexual men employ similar methods in an attempt to be accepted. Like mutants, there is a coming-out process for LGBTQIA+ people in which they have to come to terms with that which makes them different. For mutants, this could mean a physical transformation or an internal awakening of psychic abilities. For LGBTQIA+ members of society, this means a realization that they do not fit prescribed social norms on sexuality and gender performance. Research that has explored this realization has discussed the links between homophobic language and masculine performativity.[10] C. J. Pascoe's research, in particular, went into great detail in determining the ways in which the use of the terms "fag," "queer," "no-homo," and "that's so gay" serve a number of purposes in the performance of heterosexual masculinities.[11] On one hand, they reaffirm the idea that masculinity is intrinsically linked to heterosexuality, with homosexuality being nonmasculine by default.[12] This in turn creates predetermined performative expectations that become the dominant masculinity available to gay and bisexual men to occupy: an Othered identity.[13] Like the new mutants in the X-Men Universe who are negotiating their place in the world while being called "muties," "gene freaks," and "part of the mutant problem," gay and bisexual men must also find a way of negotiating the othering of their sexuality through language.[14]

For the vast majority of mutants in the X-Men Universe, passing is relatively uncomplicated, as they cannot be identified as mutants until they use their powers. The rest of the time, they appear as regular humans and are therefore in a position to build an identity that allows them to pass as human.[15] Passing serves a number of purposes for mutants, as it allows them to move about in the world unmolested as long as they remain in the closet. It may allow them the opportunity to build an identity which is not openly stigmatized.[16] However, mutants like Angel, Nightcrawler, and Glob are unable to fit into the human world as easily and therefore must either adjust to life on the fringes or resort to the measures that Hank employs in *Days of Future Past* (2014 film) to appear "normal." The fact that Hank engineers a serum that allows him to control how he presents himself bears a robust resemblance to research on LGBTQIA+ identities and performativity, particularly research on gay and bisexual men and masculine hierarchies.[17]

Such negotiations are present throughout multiple X-Men storylines and are explored in a number of ways. In *Extraordinary X-Men*, Storm's team is on the verge of a drawn-out conflict with the Inhumans over the possibility that the Terrigen mists will kill all mutants on the planet.[18] The interactions between the X-Men and the Inhumans on these issues and the ways in which mutants and Inhumans are talked about within the Marvel Universe as a whole can be interpreted as metaphorically representative of the ways in which hierarchies are established and reaffirmed in our culture, and the complicity of wider society in supporting these power structures. Throughout the Terrigen crisis, popular heroes choose not to become involved in the conflict (with the exception of the Human Torch). Instead, the choice between destroying the Terrigen mists and therefore condemning the Inhuman race to extinction, or not destroying the mists and forcing mutants to die or evacuate the earth is left to these two groups to fight out. Mutants are forced to question their role not only in wider society but also among other powered beings.

This theme has been present throughout interactions between the X-Men and the Inhumans. Both groups are offshoots of humanity, created by other species. While there is debate within the Marvel Universe as to the origins of mutants, the most popular theory is that the mutant species is the next step in human evolution, with mutants being born with a gene that becomes active during puberty, resulting in the manifestation of their powers.[19] They live in a society that vilifies and oppresses them, targeted by antimutant groups and restricted under the law. They are told that their mutation is an accident and that they must be cured or seen as dangers to the future of humanity. The origin of the Inhumans is more concrete, coming about as a result of experimentation by the alien race, the Kree, in an attempt to create an army of superpowered beings. The Inhumans have their own well-established society that celebrates their powers and is almost entirely separate from the rest of humanity under an Inhuman royal family, living in the city of Attilan. They operate under a hierarchy very different to the rest of humanity, with powered Inhumans in the highest positions of power and demanding the most respect. They can choose to manifest powers, taking part in a ceremony that transforms them. They go through this ceremony fully aware that they will emerge changed on the other side. Both species have faced oppression and discrimination due to their abilities, but their reception by humanity and other superheroes is significantly different. The Inhumans are seen as heroes when they participate in the battles of Earth and are not subject to the same extinction level events that the X-Men have gone through time and again. The respect they command within their own society often carries over to their interactions with other superpowered beings, unlike most mutants who have to demand a seat at the table.[20]

The themes of oppression and marginalization of mutants in *Inhumans vs. X-Men* are still as resonant in this storyline as they were in the comics of *Days of Future Past* (1981 comic), thirty-five years prior.[21] As the understanding of LGBTQIA+ identities shifted in the 1970s, '80s, and '90s, so too did the understanding of mutants in the X-Men universe. In 1993, the X-Men faced the Legacy Virus, and the events of this story closely mirror the real-life AIDS crisis. Not only are the symptoms of the Legacy Virus similar to the onset of HIV and AIDS (including skin lesions, weakness and fatigue), but the disease targeted only the Othered mutants and not regular humans. The *House of M* (2005) and *Decimations* (2005) stories deal with the threat and real-life possibilities of erasure, and *Avengers vs. X-Men* (2012) addresses complicity with prejudice and what this means for existing power relations in society. The message is always clear: to be mutant is to be the Other and therefore, to be at risk. The allure of passing as a means to escape this risk is undeniable, especially when coupled with the negotiation of mutantism internally and coming to an understanding that the world will still fear mutants despite their best efforts. While this is representative of the experience of any number of marginalized groups in society, the similarities to queer experiences in particular resonates clearly.

MUTANT MORTALITY: OPPRESSION OF THE OTHERED

In *What Is A Superhero*, David Lewis argues that there is one common superpower throughout the comic book genre. If a hero reaches a level of fame in society (like Captain America, Iron Man, Professor Xavier, etc.), they will gain the ability to bypass certain death. Their characters may well be killed off within the pages of a particular storyline, but they always return in some form.[22] Within the X-Men Universe, the most notable example is Jean Grey and the Phoenix. In *The Dark Phoenix Saga* (1980), Jean Grey dies three times. Each time, she is resurrected before being killed again, and we, as readers, are reminded that her death has changed her.[23] Our favorite characters may die in the course of a storyline, but it is only a matter of time before they are back.[24] Lewis suggests that the immortality (or mortality) of superheroes is related to Western attitudes towards death itself and our unwillingness to accept this eventuality. We look to our superheroes for validation that if we do enough good in our lives, we will live on eternally in the minds of others.[25]

The possibility of death is never far away for the X-Men. For the most part, mutants work as superheroes for a world that does not want them, and they are constantly under attack from supervillains as well as the society they protect. In both the comic book and cinematic versions of *Days of Future Past*, we see a world in which the X-Men have lost the fight for equality and have been killed by Sentinels and the humans who created them. *All New X-Men* finds mutants on the brink of a mutant civil war, with antimutant sentiment rising. *Extraordinary X-Men* and *Inhumans vs. X-Men* find the team attempting to avoid permanent extinction due to exposure to a substance that gives the Inhumans their powers. The X-Men, more than any other superhero team, act as a metaphor for our own mortality, rather than the potential to live on forever. The constant resurrection of Jean Grey not only exemplifies how comic book storylines repeat, but the manner of her repeated death is also significant. Jean rarely dies in the same ways that other heroes (and even other X-Men) do.[26] She is most frequently killed by others or sacrifices herself to prevent the Phoenix Force from destroying the Earth. Her deaths are the result of her mutantism. As Smith describes, "[t]he greatest enemy the X-Men face doesn't wear a mask or a gaudy costume: their enemy is hate and their enemy is fear. Until the means of perpetuating hate and fear are dissolved, the X-Men can never fully achieve the victory that they seek."[27] This memento mori has been present throughout the histories of minority groups across the world, despite the progress that has been made. Queer people in particular have seen remarkable changes and leaps in the fight for equality worldwide.[28] Recent years have seen a major push in the battle for marriage equality. Popular culture has seen a renewed effort for adequate representation of members of the LGBTQIA+ community, and the world of competitive sport (once viewed as a thoroughly heterosexual space) is showing signs of increased diversity with the comings-out of athletes in football, rugby, and swimming.[29] The picture presented to us is one of hope, ongoing progress, and "the slow but steady dissolution of prejudice."[30] However, despite this progress, recent research has found that protection from hate crimes is still a crucial concern for members of the LGBTQIA+ community worldwide. A study conducted by the National LGBT Federation of Ireland in 2016 found that 90 percent of respondents listed the introduction of hate crime legislation to offer protection against bullying and violence as their top concern.[31] Reported hate crimes against members of the LGBTQIA+ community have risen in the United Kingdom and the larger cities in the United States in the past few years, with 84 percent of respondents to one survey reporting more than once occurrence of online abuse based on perceived LGBTQ status.[32] Another found that the number of reported LGBTQIA+ hate crimes had risen by 78 percent between 2016 and 2017 in the UK.[33] In the United States, all mention of LGBTQIA+ rights were removed from the White House website following the inauguration of Donald Trump in 2017, and legislation ensuring LGBTQIA+ rights is systematically being rolled back at the time of writing. Like the X-Men, the true obstruction faced by the LGBTQIA+ community is fear and discrimination from the population at large instead of a singular villain.

In exploring the nature of prejudice as faced by minority groups, the X-Men explore another issue faced by members of the LGBTQIA+ community; where do they belong? In the extended "Rogue Edition" of the *Days of Future Past* film, it is revealed that the X-Mansion has been taken over and is under the control of Sentinels and humans conducting experiments on mutants. In *Inhumans vs. X-Men*, the leaders of each major mutant group must decide whether to go to war with the Inhumans to destroy the Terrigen mist that is killing them or leave the planet. *Avengers vs. X-Men* finds Cyclops reflecting on the place of the X-Men among other superheroes, telling the X-Men that mutants have only ever been seen as ugly stepchildren to the other heroes and that is why they must fight for their survival.

There is a consistent exploration of the meaning of family, home, and belonging for the X-Men. Like mutants, queer people are also frequently in a position in which they are confronted with similar questions of belonging and place. Like the ideological dilemmas that come up between "the mutant" and "the X-Man," LGBTQIA+ people must negotiate gendered expectations that conflict with the stereotypes and assumptions that come with identifying as queer.[34] The mortality of the X-Men, fighting for a world that does not want them, and the search for acceptance, are mirrored in the journeys of members of the LGBTQIA+ community in a number of ways. Not only must the X-Men find a way to survive in a world that fears mutants, they must also find a way of surviving alongside another, more popular offshoot of humanity in the Inhumans. In doing so, mutants must consider their place in the world and are often forced to fight to be seen and defended. During the search for belonging, mutants also experience infighting as groups respond differently to the ongoing prejudice and discrimination they face. Similarly, LGBTQIA+ activist organizations have, at times, disagreed and implemented different strategies in response to bigotry. In the Marvel Universe, the X-Men are often interpreted as promoting a strategy of assimilation in search of belonging, with the Brotherhood of Evil Mutants promoting a violent approach to creating mutant-only spaces. If we, as readers, interpret the X-Men as assimilationist, the narrative asks us "can acting human save mutants from being the Other"? And, as a metaphor, can the X-Men show us if acting heteronormative or masculine can save LGTBQIA+ peoples from being the Other?

MUTANT MASCULINITIES: WOUNDED IDENTITIES

The study of masculinity has long considered the role of media representations of men and women and how these lend themselves to gendered ideologies.[35] Specific research on the impact of depictions of masculinity has focused largely on the prevalence of the superhero body type as a seemingly attainable goal, the contrast between the masculinities of white and black superheroes, masculinity as defined by its relationship to femininity, and the prevalence of hegemonic masculine archetypes within comic books.[36] Of particular interest for this final section of this chapter is the relationship between mutant masculinity in comic books and queer identity negotiation in the real world, using the mutant Cyclops as an exploratory example.

In *Avengers vs. X-Men*, Cyclops occupies a role that at first glance perfectly fits Connell's description of the hegemonic man.[37] He is a prominent leader among his peers, dominant among the mutants, and seemingly respected by other high-ranking superheroes like Captain America, Black Panther, and Iron Man. Storm, one of the only prominent black female leaders in the X-Men, defers to him on decisions. Once Cyclops becomes a host of the Phoenix Force, he arguably transcends the masculinity of all other male superheroes. He is entirely unemotional, with the exception of anger, independent of others, and yet the leader of the other Phoenix hosts. Magneto refers to him in this form as "the greatest of men committing the greatest of deeds."[38] Cyclops in *All New X-Men*, after the events of *Avengers vs. X-Men*, is forced to confront the demons of his past, both contemplatively and in the form of a time-displaced younger Cyclops who is shocked at what he has become. In these issues, Cyclops is still intelligent and gives the air of the confident leader, but he is also much more emotional and dependent on the support of others to help him through the loss of control of his powers and the fractures within his team of X-Men. He is seeking to maintain control and respect while also becoming a beacon of hope and resistance for the mutant race.[39]

Gerri Mahn in particular frames Cyclops's masculinity as representative of the alpha male, the unquestioned leader who demands respect, much in line with the idealized male.[40] However, it can also be interpreted as a metaphor for the negotiations of masculine archetypes undertaken by queer men. Developing Raewyn Connell's theoretical framework of hegemonic masculinity, Margaret Wetherell and Nigel Edley posit that the discursive work that goes into creating the identity of the ideal man is just as important as the discourse itself.[41] In particular, the ways in which marginalized masculinities (including queer masculinities) are appropriated by heterosexual men tie into a "hybrid hegemonic bloc," resulting in the reinforcement of gendered power and the policing of masculine identities through perceived acceptance.[42] This is the balance that Cyclops tries to achieve, both for himself and later for the mutant race. We see just how much this has affected him in first few issues of *All New X-Men*, when he is confronted by his younger self in the present. Young Cyclops and the rest of the first team of X-Men (Angel, Beast, Iceman, and Jean Grey) are taken from their time and brought to the present day to confront an adult Cyclops in an attempt to show him how far he has drifted from the dream of mutants and humans peacefully coexisting. Over the next few issues, the adult Cyclops reflects on how the loss of control over his powers indicates a failure on his part and how he is subsequently unable to be an effective leader the way he once was. Young Cyclops is similarly conflicted, having to reconcile how a lifetime of prejudice and hatred has led him so far down a path he never envisioned for himself. The feelings of inadequacy and failure felt by both versions of Cyclops is similar to the experiences of queer men who feel as though they will never be seen as an equal among heterosexual men because of their sexual orientation.

Research has consistently identified the lengths that some queer men go to in order to be seen as masculine by heterosexual men and to avoid being labeled as effeminate by wider society.[43] Commonly referred to as "Straight Acting" in literature, research argues that this performativity is in direct opposition to the stereotypes of femininity within the queer male culture.[44] If we consider that certain gay and bisexual men develop an identity performance based on culturally available discourses that reject perceived notions of effeminate or "unmasculine" behavior, then common perceptions of queer masculinity can present an ideological dilemma in these performances. It is appropriate therefore to suggest that these men come under considerable pressure to reaffirm their masculinity and develop what can be seen to be a hypermasculine identity that through its performance labels them as masculine and simultaneously others queer men who also perform in this manner.[45] In a similar way, Cyclops tries to be the best leader and tactician to be seen as beacon for what mutants can be, as opposed to what they currently are.

Throughout their publication history, the X-Men have been interpreted by scholars and readers as representing many marginalized groups. Initial concerns about the first mutant team (middle-class, all white, and mostly male) have been mitigated somewhat over the years, and the team has grown and developed a diverse roster that is always shifting and can be seen to represent minority groups in some form. This chapter does not intend to suggest that the X-Men are uniquely representative of the queer experience. In fact, mutants were first read as a metaphor for racial tensions and segregation in the United States. The texts referenced throughout this chapter can be interpreted as representative of political, racial, gendered, and religious metaphors. However, there are storylines that are clearly indicative of queer experience. It is in the interactions within the mutant community, as well as with other strains of humanity in the Inhumans and largely nonmutant superhero teams, that we can draw comparisons between the lived experiences of mutants and the lived experience of members of the LGBTQIA+ community. While all superheroes must consider how best to protect their private lives and loved ones when performing their heroic deeds, for mutants, the issue of secrecy is often linked to a basic desire for safety and security. The *Days of Future Past* movie is one of many X-Men storylines that illustrates the lengths that some mutants are willing to endure to pass as human and achieve this safety. This was further explored through the mortality of mutant heroes, drawing comparisons to the ongoing fight of mutantkind to the fight for equality and visibility for members of the LGBTQIA+ community. The final section of this chapter examined the pressures faced by queer men to perform identities that are seen as masculine in the eyes of both other queer men and their heterosexual peers through a comparison with the masculinity of the mutant Cyclops.

In a world where the struggle for equality and protection for members of the LGBTQIA+ community is both making strides and meeting setbacks almost simultaneously, it is important to consider the ways in which a medium that is experiencing massive popularity can be used not just as a form of entertainment but as a means through which societal norms are produced, challenged, and subverted.

NOTES

1. For example, Spiderman in the 1960s often dealt with financial issues (how to pay rent), Iron Man was largely focused on the fight against Communism, and Captain America struggled with being a symbol of American ideals and not the American government.

2. Clancy Smith, "Days of Future Past: Segregation, Oppression and Technology in X-Men and America," in *The Ages of the X-Men: Essays on the Children of the Atom in Changing Times*, ed. Joseph J. Darowski (Jefferson: McFarland and Company, 2014), 67.

3. Bob Strass, "Interview: Stan Lee," *The Guardian*, August 11, 2000, https://www.theguardian.com/film/2000/aug/12/features.

4. Kelley J. Hall and Betsy Lucal, "Tapping into Parallel Universes: Using Superhero Comic Books in Sociology Courses," *Teaching Sociology* 27, no.1 (1999): 60–66.

Andrew Wheeler, "House of Xavier: How the X-Men Represent Queer Togetherness [Mutant and Proud]," *Comics Alliance*, June 16, 2014, http://comicsalliance.com/mutant-proud-xmen-lgbt-rights-family-community-identity/.

5. From the cultural revolution in the 1960s, through the AIDS epidemic and nuclear crisis in the 1980s, racism and homophobia in the 2000s, and juggling progress with oppression in the 2010s.

6. Joseph J. Darowski, *X-Men and the Mutant Metaphor* (Lanham: Rowan and Littlefield, 2014), 37.

7. We see examples of this in *All New X-Men #1* (2013) and *Extraordinary X-men #1* (2016).

8. Chris Claremont et al., *Uncanny X-Men #141* (New York: Marvel Comics, 1981), 110.

9. *Avengers vs. X-Men* is a good example of all three of these. Over 12 issues, Beast voices concern that he does not belong among other superheroes while mutants are in crisis, Scott affirms that humans will always send superheroes to kill mutants, and Captain America is forced to recognize that he is complicit in the oppression of mutants.

10. Brian Lacey, *Terrible Queer Creatures: Homosexuality in Irish History* (Dublin: Wordwell, 2015). Jane Ward, *Not Gay: Sex Between Straight White Men* (New York: New York University Press, 2015). Amit Taneja, "From Oppressor to Activist: Reflections of a Feminist Journey," in *Men Speak Out: Views on Gender, Sex and Power*, ed. Shira Tarrant. (London and New York: Routledge, 2013)

11. C. J. Pascoe, *Dude, You're A Fag: Masculinity and Sexuality in High School*, (Berkley: University of California Press, 2007), 55–56.

12. Raewyn Connell, *Masculinities: Second Edition* (Cambridge: Polity, 2005), 145–47.

13. Margaret Wetherell and Nigel Edley, "A Discursive Framework for Analyzing Men and Masculinities," *Psychology of Men and Masculinity* 15, no. 4 (2014): 355–64.

14. Brian Michael Bendis et al., *All New X-Men #1* (New York: Marvel Comics, 2013), 10–11.

15. Joseph J. Darowski, "When Business Improved Art: The 1975 Relaunch of Marvel's Mutant Heroes," in *The Ages of the X-Men: Essays on the Children of the Atom in Changing Times*, ed. Joseph Darowski, (Jefferson: McFarland and Company, 2014), 38–39.

16. Kelby Harrison, *Deceit: The Ethics of Passing* (Plymouth: Lexington Books, 2013).
Daniel Renfrow, "A Cartography of Passing in Everyday Life," *Symbolic Interaction* 27, no. 4 (2011).

17. While there is significant research on all members of the LGBTQIA+ community that could apply here, in the interest of being concise, this section will only focus on the experiences of queer men.

18. The Inhumans are a strain of humanity that have the potential to acquire special abilities through a process known as Terrigenesis (exposure to a mutagenic mist). This mist is poisonous to mutants, causing infertility and eventual death.

19. Other theories include mutants being the result of military experimentation in the Ultimate Universe (*Ultimate Origins #1*) or the result of genetic manipulation by the Celestials in the Earth X universe (*Earth X #0*). Brian Michael Bendis et al., *Ultimate Origins #1* (New York: Marvel Comics, 2008). Jim Krueger et al., *Earth X #0* (New York: Marvel Comics, 1999).

20. Notable exceptions here include Beast, Charles Xavier, and Storm.

21. Jeff Lemire, *Extraordinary X-Men #1* (New York: Marvel Comics, 2016).

22. David A. Lewis, "Save the Day," in *What Is A Superhero?* ed. Robin S. Rosenberg (New York: Oxford University Press, 2013), 37.

23. Chris Claremont et al., *Uncanny X-Men #132–134* (New York: Marvel Comics, 1980).

24. Matthew Rosenberg recently resurrected Jean Grey again in *Phoenix: Resurrection #1* (New York: Marvel Comics, 2018).

25. It is worth noting that comics centerd on the non-Western world do not shirk from the eventuality of permanent death, as discussed by Lewis, "Save the Day."

26. Jean has sacrificed herself on a couple of occasions to save others, notably in *The Dark Phoenix Saga* and *Phoenix: End Song* storylines. Claremont, *Uncanny X-Men #132–134*. Greg Pak et al., *X-Men Phoenix Endsong #1–5* (New York: Marvel Comics, 2005).

27. Smith, "Days of Future Past," 66.

28. Ann P. Hans and Andrew Lane, "Collecting Sexual Orientation and Gender Identity Data in Suicide and Other Violent Deaths: A Step Toward Identifying and Addressing LGBT Morality Disparities," *LGBT Health* 2, no. 1, (2015): 84–87.

29. Maebh Harding, "Marriage Equality: A Seismic Shift for Family Law in Ireland," in *International Survey of Family Law: 2016 Edition*, ed. Bill Atkin (London: Family Law, 2016). Nigel Jarvis, "The Inclusive Masculinities of Heterosexual Men within UK Gay Sports Club," *International Review for the Sociology of Sport* 50, no. 3 (2015). Juno Obedin-Maliver, "Time for OBGYNs to Care for People of All Genders," *Journal of Women's Health* 24, no. 2 (2015).

30. Smith, "Days of Future Past," 73.

31. Ciarán Ó hUltacháin et al., *Burning Issues 2, Responses* (Dublin: National LGBT Federation, 2016), 25.

32. Chaka L. Bachmann and Becca Gooch, *LGBT in Britain: Hate Crime and Discrimination* (London: Stonewall, 2017). Melanie Stray, *Online Hate Crime Report 2017: Challenging Online Homophobia, Biphobia and Transphobia* (London: Galop, 2017). Emily Waters et al., *A Report on Lesbian, Gay, Bisexual and Queer Hate Violence Homicides in 2017* (New York: National Coalition of Anti-Violence Programs, 2017). Nick Antjoule, *The Hate Crime Report 2016: Homophobia, Biphobia and Transphobia in the UK* (London: Galop, 2016).

33. Bachmann and Gooch.

34. Ideological dilemmas in identity performance arise when two or more conflicting performative expectations come into play. Wetherell, "A Discursive Framework."

35. Steve Craig, *Men, Masculinity, and the Media: 2nd Volume* (Austin: SAGE Publications, 1992). Joke Hermes, "Father Knows Best? The Post-Feminist Male and Parenting in *24*," in *Reading 24: TV Against the Clock,* ed. Steven Peacock (London: I. B. Tauris, 2007).

36. Jeffrey A. Brown, "Comic Book Masculinity and the New Black Superhero," *African American Review* 33, no. 1 (1999). Aaron Taylor, "'He's Gotta Be Strong, and He's Gotta Be Fast, and He's Gotta Be Larger Than Life': Investigating the Engendered Superhero Body," *Journal of Popular Culture* 40, no. 2 (2007). Alan Klein, "Comic Book Masculinity," *Sport in Society* 10, no. 6 (2007). Trevor Matthew Lanier, "The Supermen of the Justice League and X-Men: Comic Book Representations of Masculinity for Today's Audience," Thesis (Cambridge: Emmanuel College, 2010).

37. Todd W. Reeser, *Masculinities in Theory: An Introduction* (Sussex: Wiley-Blackwell, 2010).

38. Jeff Lemire et al., *Inhumans vs. X-Men #6* (New York: Marvel Comics, 2017).

39. Brian Michael Bendis et al., *All New X-Men #3-4* (New York: Marvel Comics, 2013).

40. Gerri Mahn, "Fatal Attractions: Wolverine, the Hegemonic Male and the Crisis of Masculinity in the 1990s," in *The Ages of the X-Men: Essays on the Children of the Atom in Changing Times*, ed. Joseph J. Darowski (Jefferson: McFarland and Company, 2014), 117–18.

41. Margaret Wetherell and Nigel Edley, "Negotiating Hegemonic Masculinity: Imaginary Positions and Psycho-Discursive Practices," *Feminism and Psychology* 9, no. 2 (1999): 335–56.

42. Max Morris and Eric Anderson, "Charlie is So Cool Like: Authenticity, Popularity and Inclusive Masculinity on Youtube," *Sociology* 49, no. 6 (2015). Demetrakis Z. Demetriou, "Connell's Concept of Hegemonic Masculinity: A Critique," *Theory and Society* 30, no. 3 (2001). Steven L. Arxer, "Hybrid Masculine Power: Reconceptualizing the Relationship between Homosociality and Hegemonic Masculinity," *Humanity and Society* 35, no. 4 (2011).

43. Demetriou, "Connell's Concept."

44. Reeser, *Masculinities in Theory*, 125.

45. Janet Holland et al., *The Male in the Head: Young People, Heterosexuality and Power* (London: The Tufnell Press, 1998). John Pachankis, "Social Anxiety in Young Gay Men," *Journal of Anxiety Disorders* 20, no. 8 (2006).

TORCHWOOD'S SUPERMEN

Bisexuality as a Hypermasculine Superpower

CRAIG HASLOP

In recent years, superheroes have become a preoccupation on British and American television screens. Netflix has commissioned several new shows charting the stories of Marvel superheroes, while one of the BBC's most globally successful series, *Doctor Who*, features a time traveler whose mastery over time allows her to save the earth time and time again.[1] Although there are examples of texts which can and have been read as portraying homosocial relations with a gay connotation, including *Batman* and *Sherlock*, historically, television fantasy series have tended to either ignore gay or bi men or position them as threats.[2] However, the numbers of queer supermen on television seems to be increasing, despite a continuing dearth of gay superwomen.

These new representations have challenged stereotypes of queer men as camp, foregrounding the idea that they can occupy spaces of "traditional" masculinity, once predominantly associated with heterosexuality. These traditional masculine traits, including physical strength/control, bravery, and occupational mastery, have been prerequisites for the standard version of heterosexual superhero masculinity.[3] As new queer supermen have emerged, first in comics, and more latterly on our television screens, academics have shifted from asking, "Where are our queer supermen?" to interrogating the extent to which our new gay supermen are, in queer terms, politically radical.[4] For example, in the world of comics, Schott highlights the plight of the superhero Northstar who came out in Marvel's *Alpha Flight* comic in 1992.[5] His character did not become popular in the Marvel Universe and, subsequently, Marvel downplayed his queer status. In turn, many fans created more radically queer versions of the character in their own writing. Thus, Schott argues that fans might have more queer superheroes at their disposal, but the narratives associated with them are simply too conservative.[6]

In the world of television, *Torchwood*, the spin off from the BBC's revitalized *Doctor Who*, which aired in the UK from 2006–11, has been lauded as one of the most radically queer science fiction series to grace British television screens.[7] The show follows the adventures of a team of alien investigators operating under the leadership of Captain Jack Harkness—a character first introduced in *Doctor Who*. The series rarely shied away from explicit depictions of queer sex with every cast member depicted as bisexual.[8] However, it went further: firstly, by representing sexuality as fluid through the portrayal of queer sexual encounters, which were not narratively labeled with a sexual identity; and secondly, by holding a position of ambiguity around the sexual identities of two leading men, Captain Jack Harkness and Ianto Jones, both of whom either had flirtations or known relationships with both men and women. Thus, the series pioneered a taken-for-granted approach to bisexuality that foregrounded its fluidity. The overt representation of bisexuality alone was groundbreaking, given its absence in the British media until *Torchwood*, as was the attempt to resist classifying characters as gay or bisexual as soon as they have a nonheterosexual encounter.[9] Academics are, however, divided on how effectively the series represented LGBTQIA+ issues. Dee Amy-Chinn suggests that the series casts bisexuality as "alien," while Andy Medhurst has referred to the show as a "post queer, pansexual perv fest," and Frederic Dhaenens has suggested the series disrupted wider practices of heteronormativity by replacing the traditionally heterosexual male hero with a white, nonheterosexual male.[10]

In this chapter, I wish to enter the academic debate about *Torchwood* from the perspective of its depiction of queer superhero masculinity through the lens of homo/heteronormativity theory. Using analysis of audience research, I question the extent to which the series challenges hetero/homonormativity and wider gender norms that uphold the heterosexual matrix. Heteronormativity refers to the cultural norms that maintain the dominance of the heterosexual matrix, a structure that relies on fixed notions of sexual and gender identity to maintain its artificial construction through universality.[11] Those who do not wish to take part in the institutions that uphold this structure, i.e., marriage, reproduction, and the norms associated with them, are made to feel excluded. Homonormativity is the pressure to live up to and comply with new practices (that often borrow from heteronormativity, e.g., mirroring the institution of marriage or the pressure to be a traditionally masculine man), established as part of the development and opening out of queer cultures through the liberalization in many countries of laws for and attitudes toward LGBT lifestyles.[12]

METHODOLOGY

As part of a wider project about *Torchwood* in 2012, I conducted five focus groups (one pilot and four further groups) in London and Brighton, in the UK, each comprising five to six people who represented a range of class backgrounds, different races/ethnic origins, and sexual orientations, and an even split of cis men and cis women. I was unable to recruit anyone identifying as trans to attend the focus groups.[13] Each session lasted one and a half hours. I screened one episode of *Torchwood*, "Kiss Kiss, Bang Bang," based on the high concentration of scenes with sexual content in that episode, which I followed with a facilitated group discussion of around forty-five minutes.[14] If the series was pushing queer boundaries, I wanted to understand how audiences experienced and interpreted the representations of gendered sexual identities presented on screen, given that talk about television is often social, and meaning about television is often made through our discussions with others. As Tamar Liebes and Elihu Katz have argued, the focus group operationalizes "the assumption that the small-group following the broadcast is a key to understanding the mediating process via which a program . . . enters into the culture."[15]

To be clear, this was a small audience study, and my aim was not to make universal "truth" claims about *Torchwood*, but rather to gather other interpretations of the series alongside my own, to consider how meaning is made around gendered sexual identities in the series through various discourses on gendered sexual identity. Thus, I use discourse analysis and define it as investigating "an interrelated set of texts, and the practices of their production, dissemination, and reception, that brings an object into being."[16] In this chapter, I focus on responses related to the reception of the series and how bisexuality, fluidity of sexuality, and masculinities are represented in terms of the superhero, the discourses that shape those representations, and the way they are brought into being through social interaction. I refer to the focus groups as Pilot and Gr1 for the first groups conducted, through to Gr4, and so on.

Using the research results, I focus on leading male protagonists of the episode—Captain Jack Harkness and Captain John Hart. Jack first appeared in the *Doctor Who* episode "The Empty Child" as a rogue time agent from the fifty-first century Time Agency, masquerading as an American army officer in World War II.[17] As Lee Barron highlights, by the time the audience meets Jack in *Torchwood*, he has already been elevated to hero status.[18] Now immortal, following the events of the *Doctor Who* episode, "The Parting of the Ways," and flung back in time, he has been living on Earth for centuries, helping to lead the new, governmental "Torchwood" organization.[19] In the episode, Hart, a new supervillain, arrives on Earth by way of a time- and space-traveling device. We discover that Hart is Jack's past lover and ex-colleague from the Time Agency and that he has other, more sinister motives beyond just visiting Jack. In the rest of this chapter, I want to explore audience reactions to these two characters as superbeings, the episode's portrayal of queer masculinity, and the implications of the interconnection between these two facets of their characters on wider arguments about the series' potential for queer liberation and debates about queer male superheroes.

TORCHWOOD'S SUPERMEN

Most of us think we know what we mean by the term "superhero." We instantly imagine a costume, a secret identity, and a mission to protect people. However, once we try to articulate what a superhero is, we stumble into definitional difficulties. Peter Coogan, in his analysis of what defines a superhero, suggests this is an issue of genre identification.[20] The superhero metagenre, if we can call it that, shares much of its characteristics, including secret identities, superpowers, and earth saving missions, with other genres, particularly those of fantasy or adventure. For example, the classic features of a comic book superhero such as Superman include having a costume and a secret identity, but there are a number of science fiction and fantasy shows that include characters with secret missions and superpowers who are not costume-wearing superheroes with a secret identity in the classical sense. A good example of this can be seen in Tim Kring's television series, *Heroes*.[21] In its first season, we are introduced to Claire Bennett, the cheerleader. She lives an everyday life as a teenage school girl, but is slowly discovering she has some sort of special power. She does not conform to the superhero formula of keeping a secret identity alongside a superhero identity. Instead, she must negotiate her powers as part of her everyday life. In this chapter, I am not arguing that Jack and John are the archetypal comic book superheroes, given that neither has a secret identity or a costume. Instead, I am suggesting that they represent a wider emerging category of superheroes, who are an integral part of science fiction and fantasy television (and film) and that the signification in the text that their superhero status confers upon them, gives them a special status in the text, worthy of close analysis, in relation to gendered sexual politics.

If we analyze the narrative of "Kiss, Kiss, Bang, Bang," Jack and John stand out from the rest of the cast as super heroes.[22] The entire Torchwood team are heroes, in the sense that they take part in the action to prevent alien incursions on Earth. However, Jack is immortal and understands time travel better than the others in the team. Hart is from the fifty-first century and has access to time traveling technology. In addition, Hart demonstrates super-strength early in the episode by throwing Jack with ease from the top of a building. He too demonstrates an understanding of time traveling technology beyond the human "heroes." Moreover, the respondents from my audience research also identified traits in the two leading men that set them apart from the rest of the Torchwood team. For example, Chris said, "it seemed to be related to them being superhuman as well because one is immortal and the other one is able to come and go through time."[23] Jenny said, "The two lead boys were just like gods of different religions . . . they were up there and everyone else was down there, there was a huge power gap between them."[24] Other participants, including Jenny above, highlighted the way they were different from the rest of the characters, "godlike" through a "huge power gap."

Given that my respondents classified Hart and Harkness as superheroes in the text, I wanted to understand how my respondents interpreted the character's queer masculinities. Their responses reveal a complex interplay of meanings between the two identities of queer masculinity and superhero. I have broken these down into several discourses that emerged from the group.

PLURAL MASCULINITIES

I started each session by asking broadly what the groups thought of the depiction of masculinities in the episode screened. The talk in each meeting quickly turned to the leading men and, for many participants, the problematic representation of masculinity in the episode. (It is important to note many also praised the series for offering different versions of masculinity.) Nick responded that, "I felt [it] did represent different types of masculinity . . . the one scene that really stood out for me in the whole of this episode was the one in the elevator . . . with the older man really saying "actually you're quite pretty and actually I'm much harder than you . . ."[25] Here, Nick draws attention to the idea of plural masculinities in the episode screened—he refers to Hart, who represents a "harder" version of masculinity and Ianto, who is portrayed as soft, gentle, and even vulnerable compared to other men in the series. Moreover, the participants not only noted different versions of masculinity but also that the portrayal of queer men in the series worked to reject stereotypes of gay men as camp. The respondent below highlights this about the scene reuniting Jack with his ex-colleague Hart. In the scene, the pair have a stand-off in the style of a w duel, a pastiche of the Western film genre, and instead start kissing, then fighting, and finally drinking together. Rosie said, "I like the scene where Captain Jack and John nearly fight then kiss then fight then kiss again ... in a way they're still like traditional manly men in that sense ... I like the way their sexuality isn't reduced to a stereotype."[26] Rosie noted that the episode challenged gay male stereotypes by presenting men who have sex with men as potentially both "traditional manly men" who fight but who are also able to show physical love for a man through kissing. This, in turn, challenges assumptions that ostensibly traditional masculine traits such as fighting are the preserve of heterosexual masculinity and positions *Torchwood*'s queer superheroes alongside other masculine heterosexual superheroes.

In terms of the respondents' own discursive constructions of masculinity, while many foregrounded their liberal views in terms of sexuality, some reiterated a binary notion of gender in their responses. It has been argued for some time now that gender is not the same as biological sex but is a social construct that has developed based on our biological sex.[27] Biological sex is often male or female (but not always in the case of intersex people); thus, gender has been socially constructed around a (false) male/female sex binary.[28] The reality of gender, one that some of my respondents were keen to highlight, is that it exists on a spectrum or as part of a gender matrix, with some biological men being more masculine and/or feminine than others. Analysis of two respondent's comments in particular reveals how traditional ideas of "masculinity" and "femininity" were privileged by some group members, even if more conservative notions of sexuality were, on the whole, challenged by my participants. Rosie said, "It's different to how gay people are often portrayed as camp; here they still have guns and everything. ... and actually the women are action heroes as well." Gillian followed Rosie's comment by noting, "But without being kind of butch."[29] Rosie highlights that there is a plurality of masculinity in the series and frames this as positive in terms of representation of gay men. However, she still discursively highlights the importance of men being "manly" despite being conscious of it (linking masculinity to power through guns), and her fellow participant further reifies the male/female gender binary by suggesting that the female representations are positive by maintaining femininity. This highlights the power of discourses of gender, whereby the focus group member draws on a language of gender as binary. While in the context of gay male representation, the groups welcomed the challenge to heteromasculinity that a gay but "traditional" form of masculinity offered, but many found it "stereotypical" in the context of traditional masculinity and superheroes.

STEREOTYPICAL MASCULINITY

While the screened episode challenges stereotypes of sexuality, it also reinforces gendered stereotypes. For example, Hart demonstrates an exaggerated version of masculinity numerous times in the text, through his ability to throw a man from a roof and his wide-ranging, continual sexual appetite. Jack's immortality signifies strength by surviving Hart throwing him from a building. Participants in various groups raised concerns about how reductive these qualities seem in relation to masculinity. Julie from Gr1 said, "I thought the portrayal of masculinity was in some ways quite stereotypical, these beautiful immortal strong men."[30] Chris from Gr2 went further than Julie and suggested that Hart's masculinity is extreme. Chris said, "there was the relationship between the two male leads, and one plays this kind of arrogant assholish masculinity all the way through, which I couldn't stand."[31] The exaggerated nature of the masculinity was also noted by other groups. Louise from Gr4 highlighted the inconsistency of the gender politics against the series' sexual politics, sparking a discussion about how it compares to other, similar television series:

> **LOUISE:** Yes but I think like, you know, considering that the sexuality is so fluid, you know, they're all quite kind of guns and punching each other and (laughs) sort of getting stuffed around by one another.
> **ROSEANNE:** But it's not always like that though is it? I'm just thinking, I'm trying to recall....
> **DANNY:** I think it was an extreme....
> **ROSEANNE:** Yeah.
> **DANNY:** That was fairly extreme and I think that's tied in with what we were saying about it being a metaphor or an alternative for the sex thing but I think even that is being set up actually, the kind of whole, you know, rough-tough hard-drinking....
> **ROSEANNE:** Oh yeah.
> **DANNY:** I mean it's kind of being set up I think quite mercilessly.
> **DEBBIE:** Yeah but if you try to imagine the same scene with Priscilla type of characters, very camp.[32]

In this exchange, the group highlights the way Captain Jack and John are "set up" to be heavily masculinized through "fighting" and "drinking." They discursively frame this by highlighting that the two fight and are rough, tough, and hard drinking. At the end, Debbie also highlights that to depict men in this context any other way would be problematic. In this way, she is perhaps referring to the pressures of genre: the strong male hero is part of what an audience expects to see as part of science fiction television. The depiction further highlights the distance that is placed both in representational and cultural terms, between the figure of the strong male hero and anything associated with femininity, including the notion of a male hero as camp (effeminate). Indeed, group talk from all the sessions suggested that my participants interpreted the masculinity of both characters as extreme.

HYPERMASCULINITY

The theme of hypermasculinity stands out in "Kiss, Kiss, Bang, Bang"; when Jack and John, the leading men and the focus of the episode's narrative, face each other in a bar fight scene, the visual centerpiece of the episode. This alpha male fight for dominance links men, traits of hypermasculinity, and the overall diegesis together. The title of the episode is also an innuendo: a kiss, followed by either a violent or sexual "bang" or a gun shot. Thus, the title and the narrative conflate masculinity with sex and violence. The phrase, "Kiss Kiss Bang Bang," also has its own cultural heritage. It became associated with James Bond in the 1960s and was the original title for the opening soundtrack to *Thunderball* before United Artists specified the song must have "thunderball" in the title, thus associating the phrase with the heterosexual, womanizing version of masculinity celebrated by the Bond movies of the time.[33] Moreover, the theme of hypermasculinity emerged unprompted from all my focus groups, suggesting that it is a meaning in the text that stood out for most participants:

> **SUE:** The non-aliens seem to be cast much more into that role (passive) versus the kind of hypermasculinity.
> **SHANE:** The two alien time drifters or whatever you call them who were bisexual or shagged anything that moved, were so very masculine guys you couldn't imagine anyone like that an alien or whatever actually wanting to have a relationship and there was the guy the ex-boyfriend and they started kissing and punching.[34]

Shane goes on to refer to Jack and John as "so macho."³⁵ In this exchange, the participants from Gr3 were in general agreement that Jack and John have "hypermasculine" traits, denoted by the use of terms such as "so macho" and "really masculine."

As some of the participants noted, on its own, hypermasculinity has been a mainstay of television and cinema superheroes. Therefore, its inclusion in a fantasy series is not that surprising. However, in the case of *Torchwood*, the two leading, hypermasculine supermen also happen to be queer. The foregrounding of a tough masculinity by the leading men of the episode reflects a shift in Western gay male culture from the 1970s that sought to distance itself from the camp and effeminacy that had acted as a cultural code among gay men before laws around gay sex were relaxed. As Levine notes of the gay clone cruising culture of the 1970s, sex was expected to be rough, heavy: "you gave it like a man and you took it like a man."³⁶ As Daniel Harris notes, the gay clone of the 1970s saw gay sex not only as different to straight sex but also as central to gay identity. Imagery of the 1970s clone, perhaps most famously embodied by Laaksonen's Tom of Finland erotic comic book character, overemphasized masculinity, drawing on military and biker gang culture iconography. Indeed, pornography of the time foregrounded the type of sex that gay clone culture reified. It was sex that emphasized "bestial couplings free of feminizing affection and tenderness."³⁷ While the appropriation of codes of heteromasculinity was in some way a liberation for gay men, a chance to challenge straight men at their own game, it also sent a message that straight men and their form of masculinity was aspirational and a natural version of masculinity that gay men could resume now that the dark years of camp subcultural codes were over. Harris summarizes the effect of this shift in gay male culture, embodied particularly through the pornography and fashion of the time:

> The dominant mythic figure of the post-Stonewall pornography is the non-gay homosexual . . . who, while engaging in gay sex, manages to retain the masculine identity of a straight man untouched by the look and sensibility of the subculture. The non-gay homosexual is gay only in the bedroom, while in public he easily passes as a dyed-in-the-wool heterosexual . . . Despite his formidable stamina and sex drive, he is a solitary sensualist who has no stake or interest in a collective homosexual identity but has eliminated all tell-tale signs of urban gay life from his behaviour.³⁸

This hypermasculinity which has dominated much of gay male culture for some time now could, as Tim Edwards has noted, also be read as camp in terms of its extreme parody of "straight" masculinity.[39] There are certainly elements of *Torchwood* that can be read as camp in terms of its style. Camp elements were identified by respondents through the sexual innuendos in the narrative; through Hart's outfit, reminiscent of the Napoleonic French military and emulating the style and camp of Adam Ant and the new romantic movement of the 1980s; and through the inclusion of John Barrowman and his extratextual cult camp associations to musicals.[40] But, camp is also evinced through the "playfulness" of the text in general, seen through, for example, throwaway comments in the script about fancying poodles or the inclusion of an alien character that looks like a blowfish driving a sports car at the opening of "Kiss Kiss, Bang Bang."[41] While aspects of the series can be read as camp, with its distancing from the camp effeminacy that once dominated underground gay culture, it is a camp that is less political in queer terms—what Moe Meyers has referred to as "pop camp."[42] Thus, we can say that in television terms, Jack and John represent what is a more acceptable form of queer masculinity to wider audiences—a hypermasculinity that both rejects some gay stereotypes (effeminate camp) while also confirming to, and even exceeding, ideas of traditional heteromasculinity.

HYPERMASCULINE BISEXUALITY

Some aspects of this hypermasculinity, outside of the context of this series as a queer text, would be unacceptable and fall into the category of what has recently been termed "toxic masculinity": "a (heterosexual) masculinity that is threatened by anything associated with femininity (whether that is pink yogurt or emotions)."[43] Jack and John often engage in humorous quips or "banter," linking them both back to a traditional heteronormative masculinity often associated with British "lad culture."[44] For example, in this exchange:

> **CAPTAIN JACK HARKNESS:** You were the wife.
> **CAPTAIN JOHN HART:** *You* were the wife.
> **CAPTAIN JACK HARKNESS:** No, you were the wife.
> **CAPTAIN JOHN HART:** Oh, but I was a *good* wife! (original emphasis).[45]

While Hart accepts in the end that he was the wife, the exchange connotes a wider cultural assumption that to be the wife (female) is something you should avoid as a man. If straight men were to suggest that being the "wife" is a secondary position in a relationship, this would be seen as misogynistic—a rejection of femininity that is characteristic of toxic masculinity.

When asked what the groups thought about the portrayal of sexuality when linked to the masculinity of the episode, aspects of Jack and John's characterizations as uber-masculine men carried different meanings in the context of their bisexuality:

> **HARRY:** Yeah but also it's a bit misplaced, he is an emotional being but then he is violent, I don't know as you said [*Shane*] if it was a representation of a heterosexual he would be horrible—I don't know whether it's preconceptions but it's like he is a little bit bi, so he'll be alright really. (my italics) [46]
>
> **SHANE:** Jack . . . he is a bisexual and can sleep with anyone, suggesting they are all crazy people and don't give a shit about feelings. They just want to fuck anything; but the ones who are definitely straight or gay, are the ones who are a bit boring and pedestrian.[47]

My participants make two points here worth analyzing further. First, the representation of hypermasculinity, such as misogynistic comments, are made acceptable through bisexuality—their sexual liberation acts as a smokescreen and somehow excuses them from reproducing oppressive heteromasculine discourses.[48] Second, the participants recognized the subtle suggestion that the leading men will sleep with anything; that to be bisexual is to be promiscuous, or at least performing a desire to sleep with everything. Not only is this problematic, reiterating the stereotype that bisexuality is often associated with being promiscuous, it is also a performance historically connected to the idea of men as "studs," where their sexual prowess is an achievement.[49] It connects a stereotypical version of bisexuality to Jack and John's characterizations as hypermasculine men. In doing so, it also becomes part of their hypermasculine superhero personas.

In his review of new queer comic book superheroes, Rod Lendrum welcomed the arrival of queer comic book superheroes including Midnighter, Apollo, Northstar, and the short-lived, queer Rawhide Kid.[50] However, he notes that both Rawhide Kid and Northstar, as effeminate superheroes, the queerest of the new superheroes, are both contained in their narratives, either through limited sex lives or through infrequent appearances. In other words, being camp or effeminate undermines your "abilities" as a long-running and successful comic queer male superhero.

In this short piece, I have been able to touch on only some of my respondents' comments about the masculinity of the two leading supermen in one episode of *Torchwood*. However, the responses suggest that other audience members also think *Torchwood* challenged the heteronormative idea of the male superhero as only interested in women. In doing so, however, the series simultaneously represents the new queer superhero as hypermasculine and reliant on performances of stereotypical masculinity and expressions of bisexuality as sexual power to carry queerness. It follows the trajectory of Western gay male culture, which through the clone culture of the 1970s and a process of foregrounding less emotional sex practices, created an initially subversive space within gay male culture to be less camp and to express a tough traditional masculinity. As Harris notes, this version of being a gay man was commercialized through pornography, replicating what was a subversive form of gay masculinity into a dominant mode of gay masculinity. Once separated from its social and political context, this dominant mode of gay masculinity became an acceptable and attractive (heteromasculine) version of being a gay man. In this way, the series reiterates traditional ideas of masculinity—a heteronormative version of gender that drives the heterosexual matrix and maintains its pervasive structures and influence. Indeed, it contributes to Lisa Duggan's notion of homonormativity, where LGBTQIA+ communities have replicated many practices of heterosexuality in order to fit in. *Torchwood* suggests that, in the same way as in the comic book sphere, queer television superheroes need to be hypermasculine to function uncontained in the text.

While these superheroes are bisexual with a fluidity to their sexual identities, any liberation offered here is offset by a reliance on associations to toxic forms of masculinity that require sexual dominance and a distaste for femininity, which are both aspects associated with hetero- and homonormative versions of masculinity. It reminds us, as Lynn Segal suggests that, "although the persecution of homosexuals is usually the act of men against a minority of other men, it is also the forced repression of the 'feminine' in all men."[51] With the creation of more and more new queer superheroes on our television screens, we should celebrate the opening out of superheroes' sexualities but ensure we are mindful of the potential hetero/homo normativity of their gendered sexual conditions.

NOTES

1. Catherine Johnson, "Doctor Who as a Programme Brand," in *New Dimensions of Doctor Who: Adventures in Space, Time and Television*, ed. Matt Hills (London, I. B. Tauris, 2013), 95.

2. Andy Medhurst, "Batman, Deviance and Camp," *The Superhero Reader*, ed. Charles Hatfield et al (University Press of Mississippi, 2013), 237–50. William Dozier, *Batman* (1966–1968; Los Angeles: 20th Century Fox Television). Harry M. Benshoff, *Monsters in the Closet: Homosexuality and the Horror Film*, Inside Popular Film (Manchester: Manchester University Press, 1997). Frederik Dhaenens, "The Fantastic Queer: Reading Gay Representations in *Torchwood* and *True Blood* as Articulations of Queer Resistance," *Critical Studies in Media Communication* 30, no. 2 (2013): 103. Stephen Greer, "Queer (Mis)recognition in the BBC's *Sherlock*," *Adaptation* 8, no. 1 (2015), 50–67. Steven Moffat, *Sherlock* (2010–present; Cardiff: BBC Television).

3. Nick Trujillo, "Hegemonic Masculinity on the Mound: Media Representations of Nolan Ryan and American Sports Culture," *Critical Studies in Mass Communication* 8, no. 3 (1991): 291.

4. Dhaenens, "The Fantastic Queer," 104. Rod Lendrum, "Queering Super-Manhood. Superhero Masculinity, Camp and Public Relations as a Textual Framework," *International Journal of Comic Art 7*, no. 1 (2005): 288. Gareth Schott, "From Fan Appropriation to Industry Reappropriation: The Sexual Identity of Comic Superheroes," *Journal of Graphic Novels and Comics* 1, no. 1 (2010): 17–29.

5. Scott Lobdel et al., *Alpha Flight#106*, (New York, Marvel Comics, 1992).

6. Schott, "The Sexual Identity of Superheroes," 18.

7. Russell T. Davies, *Torchwood* (2006–11: Cardiff: BBC Television). Dhaenens, "The Fantastic Queer," 104.

8. Although some of the characters only had same-sex relations with "human form" aliens.

9. Meg Barker et al., "British Bisexuality: A Snapshot of Bisexual Representations and Identities in the U. K.," *Journal of Bisexuality* 8, no. 1 (2008) 141–62.

10. Dee Amy-Chinn, "GLAAD to Be *Torchwood* ? Bisexuality and the BBC," *Journal of Bisexuality* 12, no. 1 (2012): 65. Andy Medhurst, "One Queen and His Screen," *Queer TV: Theories, Histories, Politics*, ed. Glyn Davis and Gary Needham, (United Kingdom: Taylor and Francis, 2008), 80, https://doi.org/10.4324/9780203884225. Dhaenens, "The Fantastic Queer," 114.

11. Judith Butler, *Gender Trouble: Feminism and the Subversion of Identity* (London and New York: Routledge, 1990).

12. Lisa Duggan, "The New Homonormativity: The Sexual Politics of Neoliberalism," *Materializing Democracy: Toward a Revitalized Cultural Politics*, ed. Russ Castronovo and Dana D. Nelson (Durham: Duke University Press, 2002).

13. For the anonymity of the participants, all names were changed as part of the study.

14. *Torchwood*, Episode 2.1, "Kiss Kiss, Bang Bang," directed by Ashley Way, aired January 16, 2008, on BBC Two.

15. Tamar Liebes and Elihu Katz, *The Export of Meaning: Cross-Cultural Readings of Dallas* (Cambridge: Polity, 1993).

16. Ian Parker, *Discourse Dynamics* (London and New York: Routledge, 1992).

17. *Doctor Who*, Episode 9, "The Empty Child," directed by James Hawes, aired May 21, 2005, on BBC One.

18. Lee Barron, "Out in Space," in *Illuminating Torchwood: Essays on Narrative, Character and Sexuality in the BBC Series* (Jefferson: McFarland and Company, 2010).

19. *Doctor Who,* Episode 13, "The Parting of the Ways," directed by Joe Ahearne, aired on June 18, 2005, on BBC One.

20. Peter Coogan, "The Hero Defines the Genre, the Genre Defines the Hero," in *Superhero: The Secret Origin of a Genre*, ed. Peter Coogan and Robin Rosenberg (Austin: Monkey Brain Books, 2006).

21. Tim Kring, *Heroes* (2006–10; New York City: NBC).

22. *Torchwood*, "Kiss Kiss Bang Bang."

23. Extract from Focus Group 1, July 30, 2012.

24. Extract from Focus Group 1, July 30, 2012.

25. Extract from Focus Group 4, August 4, 2012.

26. Extract from Pilot Focus Group, June 28, 2012.

27. Butler, *Gender Trouble*.

28. Myra J. Hird, "Gender's nature: Intersexuality, transsexualism and the 'sex'/'gender' binary," Feminist Theory 1, no. 3 (2000): 348.

29. Extract from Pilot Focus Group, July 30, 2012.

30. Extract from Focus Group 1, July 30, 2012.

31. Extract from Focus Group 2, August 2, 2012.

32. Extract from Focus Group 4, August 4, 2012.

33. *Thunderball*, directed by Terence Young (1965; Los Angeles: United Artists).

34. Extract from Focus Group 4, August 4, 2012.

35. Extract from Focus Group 3, August 3, 2012.

36. "Clones" refers to a dominant subcultural mode for gay men in the 1970s and 1980s that emerged in urban centers in the US and UK and was characterized by reproducing a hegemonic "macho" form of masculinity. Adam Isaiah Green, "Gay But not Queer: Toward a Post-Queer Study of Sexuality," *Theory and Society* 31, no. 4, (2002): 521–45. Martin P. Levine and Michael S. Kimmel, *Gay Macho: The Life and Death of the Homosexual Clone* (New York: New York University Press, 1998), 74.

37. Daniel Harris, *The Rise and Fall of Gay Culture* (New York: Ballantine Books, 1997), 148.

38. Harris, 151–52.

39. Tim Edwards, *Cultures of Masculinity* (London and New York: Routledge, 2006).

40. Before appearing in *Torchwood*, John Barrowman was known for his role in the camp musical film *The Producers* (2005).

41. *Torchwood*, "Kiss Kiss Bang Bang."

42. Moe Meyer, *Reclaiming the Discourse of Camp in the Politics and Poetics of Camp* (London and New York: Routledge, 1994).

43. Sarah Banet-Weiser and Kate M. Miltner, "#MasculinitySoFragile: Culture, Structure, and Networked Misogyny," *Feminist Media Studies* 16, no. 1 (2016): 171–74.

44. Alison Phipps and Isabel Young, "'Lad Culture' in Higher Education: Agency in the Sexualization Debates," *Sexualities* 18, no. 4 (2015): 459–79.

45. *Torchwood*, "Kiss Kiss Bang Bang."

46. *Torchwood*, "Kiss Kiss Bang Bang."

47. *Torchwood*, "Kiss Kiss Bang Bang."

48. Sadie E. Hale and T. Ojeda, "Acceptable Femininity? Gay Male Misogyny and the Policing of Queer Femininities," *European Journal Of Women's Studies* 25, no. 3 (2018).

49. Barker, "British Bisexuality." Jonathan Dollimore, "Bisexuality, Heterosexuality, and Wishful Theory," *Textual Practice* 10, no. 3 (1996): 523–39. Susan M. Jackson and Fiona Cram, "Disrupting the Sexual Double Standard: Young Women's Talk about Heterosexuality," *British Journal of Social Psychology* 42, no. 1 (2003): 113–27.

50. Lendrum, "Queering Super-Manhood," 302.

51. Lynn Segal, *Slow Motion: Changing Masculinities, Changing Men* (London, Virago, 1990), 16.

PART III

STRATEGIES OF RESISTANCE

EMMA FROST, THE WHITE QUEEN

Superpowers as the Performance of Gender

RICHARD REYNOLDS

> "After all, Ginger Rogers did everything that Fred Astaire did. She just did it backwards and in high heels."
> —[ATTRIBUTED TO ANN RICHARDS]

Emma Frost has been a key character and enigma within the Marvel Universe since her first appearance in 1979. Initially a ruthless and hypersexualized operative for the nefarious Hellfire Club, Frost transformed into a leading member of the X-Men. Her potent telepathic powers have been augmented by the ability to transform into invulnerable crystal. Frost has appeared in key X-Men stories of the twenty-first century, as well as television shows and movies. This chapter focuses chiefly on her original appearances as a villain (in the 1979–80 *Uncanny X-Men* story arc written by Chris Claremont and penciled by John Byrne), her youth and backstory (as told in Karl Bollers's 2003–4 miniseries, *Emma Frost*), her decision to join the X-Men, and the establishment of her relationship with Scott Summers/Cyclops (as detailed in Grant Morrison's 2001–5 stint as writer on *New X-Men*). It discusses her character arc as portrayed in Joss Whedon's *Astonishing X-Men* (2004–8) and her development during Matt Fraction's subsequent run on *Uncanny X-Men* (2009–11).

Frost has many facets: mutant, telepath, strategist, warrior, Machiavellian plotter, femme fatale, lover, and loyal friend. She engages with the world on her own terms, bypassing many of the stereotypes which have attached themselves to superheroines over the decades. She inverts many of the tropes of toxic sexuality, employing them for her own empowerment.[1] Her abrasive and manipulative personality functions as a dark mirror for other characters in the mutant saga, inscribing emotions and attitudes that implicitly question the values of the X-Men and the genre to which they belong. Frost personifies what Judith Butler has termed the "agreement to perform, produce, and sustain … genders as cultural fictions."[2] The nature and extent of Frost's powers facilitate a superpowered performance of both gender and sexuality. This performance undermines the normative codes of the female as an object of the male gaze, as well as the codes of patriarchy which these tropes support. Frost's self-empowering manipulation of the male gaze—and herself as the object of that gaze—not only subverts deeply inscribed conventions of the superhero genre, but also deregulates binary distinctions between object and subject.

FIRST APPEARANCE

The 1970s saw the emergence of several superheroines who were clearly created in response to the development of the feminist movement in the previous decade. Established superheroines were also fundamentally revamped. At DC, Wonder Woman, originally a heroine who fought in close combat, had been transformed in the 1960s into an Emma Peel–style secret agent without superpowers.[3] In 1972, Wonder Woman appeared on the cover of *Ms.* magazine's first issue with her full superpowers and original costume restored.[4] At Marvel, Chris Claremont developed Ms. Marvel and Storm, and reinvented Jean Grey (Marvel Girl) as the Phoenix.[5] But until Ms. Marvel's appearance in 1976, Marvel's superheroines were equipped with either what are sometimes called "stand and point" powers (such as The Scarlet Witch, or the original Marvel Girl) or with powers that required them to disappear from the action in order to be used, such as The Invisible Woman and The Wasp. Claremont's ambitions included changing the way that female supervillains were portrayed, and his introduction of Emma Frost (The White Queen) into the *X-Men* should be seen in this wider context.

Frost first appeared in *Uncanny X-Men #129* (1980), written by Chris Claremont and penciled by John Byrne.[6] Issue #129 marks the beginning of a six-part story arc which narrates the X-Men's first encounter with the Hellfire Club, a group of superpowered individuals in pursuit of global power from behind the cover of their eponymous and exclusive New York gentlemen's club.[7] The Hellfire Club narrative is itself part of a longer, nine-part story which culminates in the release of the Dark Phoenix from within the psyche

Our first sight of Emma Frost, as drawn by John Byrne
© 1980 Marvel Comics

of Jean Grey.[8] The overwhelming power of the Phoenix causes Jean to undergo extreme personality changes. Into this storyline, an example of the tendency to problematize the superheroine who possesses too much power, Frost is added, apparently already completely corrupted by the superpowers which she deploys.

Frost is introduced to us as the Hellfire Club's White Queen. Frost is also Chair of the Trustees of the Massachusetts Academy, an educational institution in competition with Professor Xavier's Westchester Academy for Gifted Youngsters. Both schools are in the business of recruiting and training young mutants. *Uncanny X-Men #129* sees the two academies competing head-to-head for another key character making her debut: thirteen-year-old Kitty Pryde.

The Hellfire Club storyline is deeply concerned with the sexuality of its characters. Wolverine comes close to murdering a drug store proprietor who asks him to pay for a copy of *Penthouse* he is exploring. Summers and Jean engage in passionate lovemaking in issue 132.[9] In the same issue, former X-Man Warren Worthington (Angel) provokes jealousy from his partner, Candy Southern, by kissing Jean a little too passionately at their reunion. Even the teenage Kitty Pryde is checking out Colossus's impressive physique: "that guy pushing the wheelchair is so huge ... kinda neat-looking too."[10]

Into this environment, the hypersexualized White Queen is inserted. We first glimpse her at a board meeting of the Hellfire Club, at which Jason Wyngarde (Mastermind) and Sebastian Shaw are plotting the capture of emerging mutants and the simultaneous elimination or capture of the X-Men.[11] The board meeting is conducted in a dark, mysterious space, with Wyngarde and Shaw depicted in profile, in shadow, or at long range, every panel emphasizing the threat which they represent. In the final panel of one page, the White Queen is clearly depicted for the first time, in a frontal, three-quarter-length pose.[12] Frost stands out from her surroundings as if spotlit from above, her body sculpted by Byrne's use of chiaroscuro. Her white cloak, basque, thigh boots and sharply bobbed blonde hair combine the superheroine's skin-tight fighting costume with well-established fetish signifiers. Frost's slender waist and powerful, muscled thighs also present an idealized dominatrix physique. The reader does not yet know anything about this new character's superpowers, but those with eyes to see can tell that the White Queen's power resides, at least partly, in the "hyper-sexualization ... of obvious sexual signifiers"—to use Jeffrey Brown's pertinent phrase.[13]

Pryde, however, is immune to Frost's seduction when Frost (now clad in a slit-skirted business suit) visits the Pryde's family home in Chicago, to recruit Kitty for the Massachusetts Academy. Kitty reflects, "Where'd they dredge up that 'Ms. Frost' anyway? She looked at me like I was something good to eat. >Ick< She gives me the creeps."[14] As the plot develops, Colossus, Storm, and Wolverine are captured by Frost. Storm is shackled to a high-tech St. Andrews cross (another staple of the BDSM world), while Colossus and Wolverine are suspended in cages.[15] Frost clearly relishes her power over the captured X-Men, taking particular delight in torturing (or "psychically probing") the helpless Storm with bolts of energy:

> **FROST:** I don't want to hurt you, my dear. I want us to be ... friends
> **STORM:** Haiearrrgh!![16]

The prisoners are liberated by Pryde's intervention. In a rematch with the X-Men, Frost and her henchmen are thoroughly defeated. Frost engages in a psychic duel with Jean, which provokes the only moment of heroism Frost displays during this story arc. Almost at the point of destruction from the fiery onslaught of the Phoenix, she thinks, "Only one chance ... must channel ... all remaining power ... into a telepathic psi-bolt ..."[17] This display, in extremis, of the "extra effort" or "all or nothing" strategy, is characteristic of superheroes at the crucial moment in any battle. But Frost's heroic, extra effort is insufficient, and she appears to have been killed.

FROM VILLAIN TO HEROINE

Reader responses in the letter column were positive and insightful about the achievements of Claremont and Byrne. The treatment of gender was much praised, and the X-Men emerged as a superhero comic of choice among the LGBT community and more widely, among those with almost any kind of nonmainstream identity.[18] Elizabeth Holden, writing from Ottawa in Canada, praises the Hellfire Club storyline in the following terms: "the sense of dangerous sexuality, Phoenix's inability to understand what is happening to her ... makes this plot very interesting indeed. ... this seems to be the only Marvel comic that is free of sexual stereotypes or bias. ... [The women] are not sex objects, or cowards, or perpetual hostages. Instead, you have made them individuals, and I heartily approve."[19] Under the influence of Wyngarde, who is able to project his optical illusions directly into Jean Grey's mind, this formerly conventional young woman begins to explore her darker sexual fantasies. At the same time, she gains almost limitless psychic superpowers.[20] Part of Frost's function in this story arc is to introduce the notion of what Angela Carter termed the "Sadean Woman" in 1979 book of the same name.[21] The literary model for Carter's sexual aggressors is the protagonist of De Sade's novel *Juliette*, who employs sex "as an instrument of terror ... [and] lobs her sex at men and women as if it were a hand grenade."[22] Frost's fully developed Sadean instincts demarcate the emotional and sexual territory which Jean may be destined to explore. Frost is the finished article, the sexual terrorist that Jean may become. By overtly surfacing the fetish subtext long encoded in superheroine (and villainess) costumes, Claremont and Byrne also devised a postmodernist puzzle (or trap) for all those who were to depict Frost in the future. Can such a hypersexualized superwoman subvert the established power structures of the genre while simultaneously being the object of the male gaze?

Despite having been created (and destroyed) in the service of a limited narrative function, Frost took on a life of her own. Having somehow survived her encounter with Phoenix, she returns in *Uncanny X-Men #151* and remains intent on enrolling Pryde in her Massachusetts Academy.[23] But without Byrne's artwork, Frost's return lacks the resonance of her first appearance and the character continued as an occasional guest villain, also appearing in the miniseries *Firestar*, with her Hellions—the team made up of students from Frost's Massachusetts Academy.[24]

Frost's role as a teacher and mentor of younger mutants has facilitated her gradual evolution from villain to heroine in *Generation X* (1994).[25] Now fighting on the side of the angels, Frost was dressed in form-fitting green instead of frosty white. But, she remained a sexual terrorist, as this exchange with the less-than-trusting Sean Cassidy (Banshee) exemplifies. Frost has brought Cassidy (a fellow reformed criminal) and other members of Generation X to her luxurious apartment:

> **CASSIDY:** Now tell us what ye hoped to accomplish by bringing us here. That is, if'n ye are through with trying to impress us?
> **FROST:** I have a whole list of things I can do to impress you, Mr Cassidy ... but there are children present.[26]

Frost may have undertaken her journey from the dark side, but she never completely lost her "bad girl" personality. Her dominant attitude provides a powerful counterpoint to the accumulated emotional baggage of "good girl" superheroines, who so often appear to be saddled with what Judith Butler describes as gender melancholia, manifested through ambivalent feelings towards their own superpowers.[27] Significantly, Frost soon returned to her signature white costumes.[28] After Generation X disbanded, Frost taught young mutants in the sanctuary of Genosha.[29] When the island was attacked by Sentinels, as depicted in Grant Morrison's *New X-Men #114* (2001), Frost survived the ensuing destruction of sixteen million mutants through the intervention of a secondary mutation: she acquires a coating of organic diamond.[30] This mutation visually expresses both Frost's vanity and acquisitiveness ("I do look rather spectacular in the light, don't I?"), and the hard, impermeable boundaries that she places between her emotions and the outside world.[31] It is her arch rival and antagonist, Jean Grey, who asks the killer question of this new, jewel-encrusted Frost:

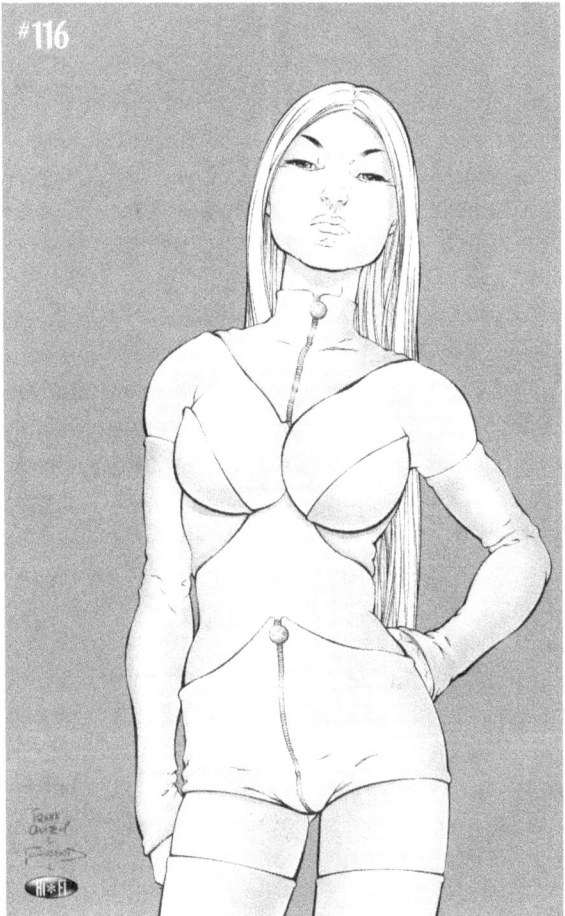

Emma Frost as re-imagined by Frank Quitely © 2001 Marvel Comics

JEAN: What makes you such a bitch, Emma?
FROST: Breeding, darling. Top class breeding. [32]

Frost's response is both provocative and to the point. Millions of mutants have been wiped out in the Sentinels' attack on Genosha, yet Frost holds herself aloof from the other X-Men, questioning Charles Xavier's policies of peaceful coexistence with *homo sapiens*. Frost's sexualized yet withdrawn presence is fittingly reinvented by artist Frank Quitely's meandering lines and "crinkly" detailing, which bring a deadpan flatness to Frost's otherwise blatantly erotic costume and physique. Quitely's cover for *New X-Men #116* (2001) is the definitive rendering of this polymorphous, pouting, and elusive Frost.

EMMA'S YOUTH

Frost's backstory had been sketched out before, but in 2003–4 her school and college years were explored in an eighteen-part miniseries, written by Karl Bollers and illustrated by Randy Green and Carlo Pagulayan.[33] As the offspring of a wealthy Massachusetts family, Frost's struggles to assert herself in the shark-tank environment of her WASP home: domineering father, oppressed mother, narcissistic (and also mutant) supermodel sister Adrienne, attention-seeking Emo sister Cordelia and closet-gay brother Christian. All the family compete in their different ways for paternal attention and approval. Frost's additional challenge is her emergent mutant mindreading power, which she initially has difficulty controlling. Not yet a blonde bombshell, Frost adopts and discards a series of different strategies in her relationships with authority figures: at home, in school, at university, at work, and in the criminal underworld. Bollers explores how an individual programmed by their environment to be a passive victim can escape their conditioning and acquire agency in their dealings with the outside world. The story's artwork capitalizes on the visual relationship between Frost's growing sense of her own personality and capabilities, and the evolving ways in which she learns to use her body as a beautiful weapon. Frost changes from a mousy-haired schoolgirl to a blonde temptress in a series of dramatic leaps. None is more dramatic than the first, when a spectacular white Gaultier ball gown launches a reinvented Frost at her school prom. As brother and confidante Christian observes: "white is definitely your color."[34]

Teenage Frost reinvents herself through her steadily more self-empowering performances of her gender and sex. As Judith Butler observes, "gender proves to be performative . . . gender is always doing, though not a doing by a subject who might be said to pre-exist the deed."[35] For Frost, occasions for such performance are offered at every turn: at the prom, family parties, a casino, and (most dramatically) when performing a staged bondage video for her kidnappers.[36] This crisis provokes Frost into using her telepathic abilities as a weapon for the first time, sowing distrust among the gang of amateur kidnappers, who consequently eliminate each other. Frost then collects the ransom money from the agreed drop point and uses it to fund her own college education. The kidnappers' payoff buys Frost's freedom from parental control. The next time we see Frost, she has transformed herself into a bleached blonde and is completing her education at New York's Empire State University.[37] At ESU, Frost is introduced to the complexities of both human-mutant and mutant-mutant relations. Frost's education, her emotions, and superpowers come together at this point to form the template of the future White Queen and beyond.

FROST AS A TEAM PLAYER

Grant Morrison, Joss Whedon, Matt Fraction, and Kieron Gillen have all used Frost as a key member of the X-Men and as the instigator of plotlines which expose the emotional vulnerabilities of other characters. But the development which embedded Frost at the emotional core of the X-Men was her relationship with Scott Summers, team leader and successor-elect to Professor Xavier.[38] Morrison shows Frost engaging Summers in sessions of telepathic therapy ("as the X-Men's only qualified sex therapist"), during which their relationship blossoms at the expense of Summers's deteriorating marriage to Jean Grey.[39] Morrison explicitly links Frost's telepathic powers with her performance of both gender and sex, drawing out a theme which had been implicit in Claremont's original villain. In *New X-Men #139* (2003), Jean enters Frost's mind and finds Summers already in residence, with Frost dressed up in Jean's Phoenix costume:

> **GREY:** I knew I'd find my husband here in your head, Emma.
> **SUMMERS:** It's not real … it's just thoughts …
> **FROST:** Well, you have to agree I look rather good in these old rags of yours, dear. But I can think myself into something a little more up-to-date if you like.

Psychically probed by Grey in the ensuing confrontation, Frost explains how she established herself as Shaw's right hand in their mutual takeover of the Hellfire Club:

> **FROST:** I became exactly what Sebastian wanted … the Ice Queen, the dominatrix from hell … and I watched how he did business. I learned how simple and predictable the desires of men can be. [40]

But Frost is moved to confess to Wolverine just a few pages later:

> **FROST:** Why did I allow myself to become so stupid and so vulnerable, Logan? Why did I have to fall in love with Scott bloody Summers? [41]

This dialogue captures Frost's doomed struggle, as a telepath, to experience authentic relationships. Immediately after Frost's confession of her love for Summers, she becomes the victim of a mysterious assassin and, for a time, appears to have been destroyed. Her diamond form is smashed into thousands of glittering fragments. In her writings on gender performativity, Butler asserts that it is meaningless to separate the performer from the performance. But the attack that shatters Frost's crystal form could be said to do precisely this. Frost's performances have transformed her body into a hypersexualized tool which she uses in her performances of power. The key is control. As Dawn Heinecken observes, women "seen as spectacle may be read as being in power as long as they place themselves as author, in control of their own image."[42] The emotional vulnerability afforded by love has the potential to shatter the integrity of such a performance, just as Frost's precious crystal form is shattered and thus rendered worthless by her attacker. Performance, objectification, and gender melancholia are thus elegantly linked together.

ASTONISH THEM!

In 2004, Joss Whedon and John Cassaday were announced as writer and artist for the new *Astonishing X-Men* series. Whedon had always acknowledged the influence of Chris Claremont's *Uncanny X-Men* on his own television creation, *Buffy the Vampire Slayer* (1997–2003), and Cassaday's work on Warren Ellis's *Planetary* (1998–2009) marked him as an artist adept at foregrounding the emotional subtext of his stories.

Cassaday renders Frost in a style that contrasts strongly with the work of Phil Jiminez, Frank Quitely, or Green and Pagulayan.[43] To appreciate the difference, it is helpful to move beyond the sexualized/non-sexualized binary distinction so often employed in critical writing on superheroine depictions. Cassaday's Frost is a highly sexualized creation, but in a radically different way to the work of the preceding artists. Earlier artists had placed Frost's body on display as an object for the reader's gaze. However, this gaze was regularly compromised or undercut by Frost's actions as the subject of her own narrative, inviting a reading of Frost as a powerful character who subverts the expectations aroused by her appearance. In contrast, Cassaday renders Frost as intensely introspective, the lines of her body consistently in debate with themselves as she articulates and reticulates poses, postures and facial expressions that blur distinctions between object and subject and thus constantly confound and contradict the expectations of our gaze.

Cassaday and Whedon's work explores how Frost's telepathic powers interact with her use of her body as a tool to draw the viewer's gaze and to exert her powers. Cassaday achieves this most explicitly through his depiction of Frost's eyes, both their appearance and the direction of their gaze. Wide set and enervated, the eyes are angled away from each other, surveying a wide field, never seeming to converge on a single vanishing point.[44] Frost's eyelids are frequently portrayed as partly closed, her gaze partially hooded and thus not inviting direct eye contact. Frost consistently stares straight out from the panel which contains her, her gaze fixed either on the reader or beyond, into the blank field implied by our presence in the extended narrative space of reader and text.[45] Sometimes, she glances sideways from the panel, into a space that does not formally exist within the narrative frame, occupied as it is by a previous or succeeding action.[46] Frost's eyes, as rendered by Cassaday, break the unwritten rules of sequential art. They explore the surface of the text as our own eyes do, as readers exploring the page and space that we are engaged with. And thus Frost's superpowers become subtly embedded within the texture of the medium itself.

Cassaday also accomplishes a radical transformation of Frost's face, hollowing it out and emphasizing her high forehead, overcoding the signs of sexuality imported via Frost's physique and costume with the signifiers of asceticism and piercing intellect. Her lipstick preference has also changed, from pink or red to a frosting in white, the same icy hue as her costume. The costume itself remains revealing and blatantly sexualized, although in a more crisply authoritarian way: tight pants and slit skirts are worn with high boots, replacing the front-laced basques and corsets that had previously been Frost's trademark fetish attire. This new-look Frost is an enigma.

The key to Frost's arc in the Whedon/Cassaday collaboration is the continuing development of her relationship with Summers. Frost's manipulation of Summers foregrounds the possibilities of the traditional, heterosexual male being controlled by the very signifiers of female sexuality to which he is inescapably lured. The male gaze is thus turned back upon itself. And yet Whedon allows doubt to be present at every turn: is Summers really in love with Frost or is the whole situation manipulated by her telepathic powers? Pryde, reintroduced into the team by Whedon, immediately references Frost's first appearance way back in *Uncanny X-Men #129*: "When I think about evil, yours is the face that I see."[47] Pryde acts as a proxy for the reader's lingering distrust of Frost and the motivation behind her relationship with Summers. Whedon and Cassaday bring these doubts explicitly to the surface in the dialogue between the characters in *Astonishing X-Men #3*:

The eyes of Emma Frost, as drawn by John Cassaday © 2004 Marvel Comics

FROST: Of course, Kitty thinks I'm mentally controlling everything you say . . .
[A theatrical beat, achieved by a dialogue-free panel, as Scott mulls over Emma's words]
SUMMERS: But you're *not*, right? (original emphasis)[48]

Cassaday splits this dialogue into three wide, shallow panels, progressively isolating Summers and Frost from their companions and their environment.

As the Whedon/Cassaday X-Men narrative develops, most of the key characters are given a defining moment of heroic self-sacrifice, which is not directly related to their specific superpowers. For Frost, this process is an extended one: as the X-Men's joint leader, she is required to win trust and cooperation without resorting to either her telepathic or sexual abilities. Such trust and leadership are definitively exhibited in the climactic action of the X-Men's battle with the Breakworld, spread over *Astonishing X-Men #19–24* (2007–8) and *Giant Size Astonishing X-Men* (2008). Frost becomes the force that knits the team together, the X-Men's real leader. The final demonstration of Frost's rehabilitation comes when it is she who comforts and strengthens Pryde through an act of self-sacrifice which nullifies the Breakworld's mortal threat to Planet Earth. Pryde's "face of evil" has become the face of consolation and empathy, although Frost in many ways remains as icy and abrasive as before.

"KNEELING BAGS MY NYLONS..."

Matt Fraction's 2008–11 run on *Uncanny X-Men* saw the mutant team relocate to San Francisco. This relocation is itself part of a wider rebuilding process, after the catastrophes which had overtaken the mutants in the Marvel Universe over the previous years. San Francisco becomes a sanctuary city for all mutants. Cyclops even uses the phrase "mutant sanctuary" in a Frost-powered telepathic address, inviting mutants everywhere to head west to the coast.[49]

Fraction's *Uncanny X-Men* became unpopular with certain sections of fandom, chiefly due to the hypersexualized bodies of most of the main protagonists. This hypersexualization is largely the product of Greg Land's artwork, with its glossy, airbrushed appearance. Land is known for his use of images taken directly from advertisements, fashion magazines, and other sources.[50] This copying or "swiping" process is especially apparent in Land's depiction of the glamorous women who populate these storylines: notable among these being Frost. Land has been especially criticized for swiping or tracing facial details from pornographic sources and reproducing these in depictions of violence against his female characters.[51] A well-documented example is the assault on the young mutant Pixie in *Uncanny X-Men #501*, where the expression on Pixie's face has been demonstrated to have been traced from a pornographic image of an orgasmic female face.[52] This apparent legitimizing of sexualized violence repelled many longtime fans and introduced an unprecedented toxicity into the series's portrayal of its female characters.

Land renders Emma Frost's face in an almost constant state of arousal. His treatment of her features and body language is in striking contrast to John Cassaday's equivalent work on *Astonishing X-Men*. A telling example is the sequence of panels which fill the first three pages of the "epilogue" to *Uncanny X-Men #500*.[53] In this sequence, Frost is engaged in "farcasting" Summers's thoughts: telepathically amplifying and broadcasting his words, so that mutants around the world can receive the invitation to seek sanctuary in San Francisco. The panels at the foot of pages 32 and 34 show Frost exhibiting an exaggerated, porno-starlet expression: long eyelashes swept upward at the tips, glossy lips catching the ambient light, mouth half open to display a semicircle of gleaming and predatory teeth. In both these panels, Frost touches the side of Summers head with her white-gloved hands. The resulting image is coyly, insistently sexual. It is all intended to be fun, of course, a new, postfeminist twist on the venerable traditions of "good girl" art. In Anna Peppard's view, such depictions are "quintessentially postfeminist, inasmuch as they're ostensibly tongue-in-cheek, but in a way that's ultimately at the expense of the women who—as fictional women written and drawn by men—can't consent to being 'in on the joke.'"[54] The Emma Frost as developed by Morrison, Bollers, and Whedon was sexualized to the tips of her white-gloved fingers, but this predatory sexuality was a *tool* used by Frost in the service of her own agenda. In Greg Land's work, Frost becomes a piece of eye candy.[55]

This farcasting scene in *Uncanny X-Men #500* is about summoning the mutants of the world to a sanctuary city. Its eroticization is gratuitous—and demeaning to the two central characters involved. But more demeaning to Emma than to Summers, as her sexuality is depicted here as a condition that is inseparable from her characterization, a force which she is incapable of controlling. We are not far away here from a very bleak and very traditional view of female sexuality. Such a view regards the sexually active woman as intrinsically dangerous, a source of social instability because she wields a power that she cannot fully control. Translated into superheroine terms,

The hypersexualized Emma Frost, as drawn by Greg Land © 2011 Marvel Comics

this theme has at various times informed the character arcs of Phoenix, the Scarlet Witch, and even Wonder Woman herself.[56] Implicitly, such a view opposes Butler's argument that both gender and sexuality are a performance. It is an essentialist view, running counter to many years of Frost's narrative as crafted by previous creative teams as well as established audience readings and responses to the character.

A telling moment occurs in *Uncanny X-Men #502* (2009), when Frost drops in on Kurt Wagner (Nightcrawler), keeping vigil in the unused chapel he has constructed in the X-Men's new Marin County headquarters.

WAGNER: Emma. Welcome to the chapel.
FROST: It's lovely, Kurt. I didn't know you were building it.
WAGNER: The way things are these days, I thought . . . maybe it could provide comfort. Faith isn't the kind of thing that can be inflicted, Ja? Better we have a holy place and not need it. . . . Do you pray, Emma?
FROST: These are two hundred dollar Italian cashmere Kiki De Montparnasse *stockings*, Kurt. I'll only kneel in them if *absolutely necessary* . . .[57]

Fraction is indulging his readers in a piece of movie-fan bricolage, his dialogue openly referencing a celebrated exchange between Kirk Douglas (Tatum) and Jean Peters (Lorraine) in Billy Wilder's 1951 film noir, *Ace in The Hole*.[58] Tatum, the hard-boiled journalist, encourages Lorraine, the hard-boiled blonde (whose husband is trapped in a life-threatening situation in a collapsed mine shaft) to seize a lucrative photo opportunity for the press by praying in church. She responds with, "I don't pray. Kneeling bags my nylons." This passage exemplifies the vexatious relationship of the Fraction/Land X-Men texts to postfeminism and the postmodernist irony which saturates their work. The dialogue and the bricolage that underpins it position Frost as a conventional femme fatale: a tease and a trophy. She is now merely the scheming woman whose empowered performance is for all men to witness, because there is no off switch to kill this compulsive acting out of one's gender. Kurt Wagner's next visitor to the chapel is the reborn Peter Rasputin (Colossus). Wagner is reading aloud from the Catholic Church's "Prayer for the Lost." Colossus enters, surveys the room, and asks Kurt if he is the first visitor to the chapel. To which Wagner replies, "Well, Emma Frost. But, you know. Filthy girl."[59] The phrase "Filthy girl" is a cleverly realized piece of dialogue, allowing as it does two quite opposed readings. We can side with Nightcrawler, in his bleak judgement of Frost's spiritual condition. Like Kurt, we can judge her as one of the "lost" who require to be led from the "domain of darkness." Or, reading the expression on Wagner's face as one of prurience rather than genuine concern or empathy, we could read the scene as an exposé of the hypocrisy of organized religion in the face of overt and unashamed female sexuality.

This tiny scene between Nightcrawler and Colossus is a setup for a plot development played out later, in *Uncanny X-Men Annual #2* (2009). A complicated storyline finds Frost in the middle of a struggle between Namor (the Sub-Mariner) and Shaw, her former business partner and chair of the Hellfire Club. Frost assists Namor, who has also become her lover, in his vendetta against Shaw.

FROST: Sebastian Shaw. I'll give you his *head* on a platter.
NAMOR: That's how you would earn my trust? Would you be my Salome? Is there an attendant Dance of the Seven Veils? (original emphasis)[60]

Frost is as good as her word—or so it seems. Dressed in her original Hellfire Club dominatrix attire, she distracts Shaw with some of his preferred "kinks and perversions," before appearing to sever his head with a ceremonial broadsword, which she gifts on a charger to the very impressed Prince Namor.[61] However, once Namor has departed, the reader learns that Frost has deceived both her current and former lovers. Shaw has not actually been decapitated: Frost has used her mental powers to hand Namor a pumpkin, which her powers tricked him into believing was his enemy's head. Frost then contacts Summers and informs him that she is bringing Shaw into custody "for his crimes against mutantkind."[62]

This is a radical rewriting of the Salome story, as it appears in both the Bible and in the work of Josephus. In the source material, Salome asks for the head of the imprisoned John the Baptist as a gift from her father, King Herod, who has promised her whatever she desires, as a reward for her exquisite dancing.[63] Aubrey Beardsley's famous print of Salome captures the narrative's essence of untethered female sexuality, the perceived motiveless and Sadean cruelty of the sexually empowered female.[64] But Fraction and his artist Mitch Breitweiser invert the Salome myth, by transforming the woman into the murderer and the King (Prince Namor) into the receiver of the gift. The myth is then further inverted through the revelation that Shaw's death has been a staged illusion.

The Salome myth, even when doubly inverted, still retains its power. Frost's double deception of both Prince Namor and Shaw is a categorical demonstration of the sexuality inseparable from her mental superpowers. She seduces both men, only to leave them deceived and impotent. Shaw is left trapped in his gimp-chair, immobilized by the power of Frost's mental gifts. He rages and threatens to kill her and then asks what authority or law gives Frost the right to restrain him. Frost's reply is as two-edged as the sword she still brandishes: "There is no law any more. Haven't you heard? Law is dead. The whole world is ending."[65] Whose world is ending? Could it be Shaw's patriarchal world of fetishized, commodified, and toxic sexuality, in which Frost herself has been a sometimes-willing participant and enabler? The key difference between Salome and Frost may be that Frost has agency to redefine her sexuality outside the family or the patriarchal system—to choose an audience for the performance of her sexualized superpowers. In the final panel, Breitweiser depicts Frost looking straight at the reader, her power once again conveyed through her gaze. Who is next?

WHAT DOES EMMA FROST REALLY WANT?

Since the departure of Matt Fraction, Frost's character arc has not developed significantly in the X-Men narratives. The *Avengers vs. X-Men* (2012) and *Inhumans vs. X-Men* (2016–17) crossover epics have added little subtlety to her characterization, although the latter saga required Frost to come to terms with the death of her lover, Summers. In a more recent story arc, *Secret Empire* (2017), Frost uses her mental gifts to attack Hydra from within. Trickery and manipulation are Frost's superpowers, an inescapable part of her being. But what is the intent behind all of this manipulation, this relentless and empowering performance of what others wish to see? What does Emma Frost want?

Frost is frequently trapped between the roles of object and subject, has surpassed all established norms, and has realized new superlatives in her performance of both her gender and sex. In a sense, her mental and sexual superpowers allow Frost to transcend the subject/object binary oppositions on which all codes of patriarchy and political power are supported.[66] Frost's entire existence is a performance of gender and sex, one which her superpowers make infinitely more effective. Frost traces a line that evades control. She is a jester, a trickster, a polished mirror for the male gaze. But the parameters of her performances are ultimately determined by established gender and sex roles. To paraphrase Michel Foucault, there is no performance which can take place outside of society. Or, as Susan Bordo puts it, "women may indeed contribute to the perpetuation of female subordination ... by embracing, taking pleasure in, and even feeling empowered by the cultural objectification and sexualization of the female body."[67]

Frost's freedom, Bordo might argue, depends on others' oppression, a lesson which Frost herself learns in Bollers's origin story. This may explain why the covers of each of the eighteen parts of *Emma Frost* show Frost, not as she appears at that stage of the story, but as the ultimate product of her evolving performance: the White Queen, the Dominatrix from Hell. Likewise, the diamond skin Frost gains in Morrison's text both protects her from physical harm, but nullifies her mental powers while simultaneously rendering her as a supremely valuable and desirable object. However, Morrison and all the other key chroniclers of Frost's development are male and are perhaps ready to see gender performance as something separable from personal identity. It would be both fascinating and enlightening to see what women writers and artists might accomplish with Emma Frost as their protagonist.

NOTES

1. As evidenced in the evolving iterations of Frost's characterization by Claremont, Morrison, Whedon, and others.

2. Judith Butler, *Gender Trouble: Feminism and the Subversion of Identity* (London and New York: Routledge, 1990), 25.

3. Carolyn Cocca, *Superwomen: Gender, Power and Representation* (New York: Bloomsbury, 2016), 31–34. Tim Hanley, *Wonder Woman Unbound: The Curious History of the World's Most Famous Heroine* (Chicago: Chicago Review Press, 2014), 168–73.

4. Cocca, *Superwomen*, 33. Hanley, *Wonder Woman*, 197–99.

5. Chris Claremont et al., *Uncanny X-Men #101* (New York, Marvel Comics, 1976).

6. Claremont and Byrne commenced their run as writer and artist on the *All-New All-Different X-Men* with issue 108. From issue 114 the title reverted to *Uncanny X-Men*.

7. As has been frequently pointed out, the storyline of *Uncanny X-Men #129–34* is deeply influenced by an episode of the British *Avengers* television series. Emma Peel (played by Diana Rigg) is transformed into the "Queen of Sin" by a modern-day Hellfire Club based in London, an organization which (like its namesake in the X-Men) is seeking political power through a combination of financial and political influence, and terrorism. See Clemens, Brian. "A Touch of Brimstone," *The Avengers*, season 4, Episode 21. Directed by James Hill. February 19, 1966. (London: ABC Canal +, 2000). DVD.

8. Chris Claremont et al., *Uncanny X-Men #129–137* (New York, Marvel Comics, 1980).

9. Chris Claremont et al., *Uncanny X-Men #132* (New York, Marvel Comics, 1980).

10. Chris Claremont et al., *Uncanny X-Men #129* (New York, Marvel Comics, 1980).

11. Claremont et al.

12. Frost is glimpsed in silhouette, two panels earlier.

13. Jeffrey A. Brown, *Dangerous Curves: Action Heroines, Gender, Fetishism and Popular Culture* (Jackson: Mississippi University Press, 2011), 67.

14. Chris Claremont et al., *Uncanny X-Men #129* (New York, Marvel Comics, 1980).

15. Chris Claremont et al., *Uncanny X-Men #131* (New York, Marvel Comics, 1980).

16. Claremont et al.

17. Claremont et al.

18. See, for example, Brown, *Dangerous Curves* and Cocca, *Superwomen*. Roz Kaveney, *Superheroes! Capes and Crusaders in Comics and Films* (London: I. B. Tauris, 2008). Jennifer Stuller, *Ink-Stained Amazons and Cinematic Warriors: Superwomen in Modern Mythology* (London: I. B. Tauris, 2010).

19. Chris Claremont et al., *Uncanny X-Men #136* (New York, Marvel Comics, 1980).

20. This process starts in *Uncanny X-Men #125* (1979), well before the main Hellfire Club story arc begins, in issue #129.

21. Angela Carter, *The Sadean Woman: An Exercise in Cultural History* (London: Virago Press, 1979).

22. Carter, 105.
23. Chris Claremont et al., *Uncanny X-Men #151* (New York: Marvel Comics, 1981).
24. Tom DeFalco et al., *Firestar #1–4* (New York: Marvel Comics, 1986).
25. Scott Lobdell et al., *Uncanny X-Men #316–318* (New York: Marvel Comics, 1994). Fabian Nicieza et al., *X-Men #36–37* (New York: Marvel Comics, 1994).
26. Claremont Chris et al., *Uncanny X-Men #317* (New York: Marvel Comics, 1980.
27. Judith Butler, *Gender Trouble*.
28. Scott Lobdell et al., *Generation X #6* (New York: Marvel Comics, 1994).
29. Brian Wood et al., *Generation X #75* (New York: Marvel Comics, 2001).
30. Grant Morrison et al., *New X-Men #114–154* (New York: Marvel Comics, 2001–5).
31. Morrison et al.
32. Morrison et al.
33. Karl Bollers et al., *Emma Frost #1–18* (New York: Marvel Comics, 2003–5).
34. Bollers, *Emma Frost*.
35. Butler, *Gender Trouble*, 25.
36. Bollers, *Emma Frost*.
37. Bollers.
38. Even the characters' names imply a preordained relationship: Frost = Ice and Summers = Heat.
39. Morrison, *New X-Men #131*.
40. Morrison.
41. Morrison.
42. Dawn Heinecken, *The Warrior Women of Television* (New York: Peter Lang, 2003), 27.
43. Joss Whedon et al., *Astonishing X-Men #1–24* (New York: Marvel Comics, 2004–8). Joss Whedon et al., *Giant Size Astonishing X-Men #1* (New York: Marvel Comics, 2008).
44. Whedon, *Astonishing X-Men #2*.
45. "There is always a certain excessiveness, a difficulty associated with women who appropriate the gaze, who insist upon looking." Mary Anne Doane, *Femmes Fatales: Feminism, Film Theory and Psychoanalysis* (New York: Routledge, 1991), 27.
46. Whedon, *Astonishing X-Men #2*.
47. Whedon.
48. Whedon.
49. Matt Fraction et al., *Uncanny X-Men #500–544* (New York: Marvel Comics, 2009–11).
50. I am indebted to Geoff Klock for pointing out to me the extent of Land's tracing from visual sources.
51. Derek J. Smith, "Porno, Crooks, and Comic Books," *UncannyDerek*, December 19, 2010, https://uncannyderek.com/2010/12/19/my-land-or-your-land/.
52. "Greg Land ripoff/tracing/recycling thread," *Comic Vine Forum*, May 20, 2018, https://comicvine.gamespot.com/forums/gen-discussion-1/greg-land-ripofftracingrecycling-thread-695764/.
53. Fraction, *Uncanny X-Men #500*.
54. Anna Peppard, quoted from an e-mail dated March 3, 2018.
55. Matt Fraction et al., *Uncanny X-Men #532* (New York: Marvel Comics, 2011).
56. Cocca, *Superwomen*, 31–34. Hanley, *Wonder Woman Unbound*, 168–73. Stuller, *Ink-Stained Amazons*, 37–39.
57. Matt Fraction et al., *Uncanny X-Men #502*, (New York: Marvel Comics, 2009).

58. *Ace in the Hole*, directed by Billy Wilder (1951; Los Angeles: Paramount Pictures).
59. Fraction, *Uncanny X-Men #504*.
60. Matt Fraction et al., *Uncanny X-Men Annual #2* (New York: Marvel Comics, 2009).
61. Fraction et al.
62. Fraction et al.
63. See Mark (6:17–29) and Matthew (14:3–11) for the Biblical Salome story.
64. Aubrey Beardsley, "Salome," *The Studio*, London, April 1893.
65. Fraction, *Uncanny X-Men Annual #2*.
66. Gilles Deleuze and Felix Guattari, *A Thousand Plateaus* (London, Athlone Press, 1988), 167–91.
67. Susan Bordo, *Unbearable Weight: Feminism, Western Culture and the Body* (Berkeley, University of California Press, 1993), 262.

ALBUS DUMBLEDORE AND THE CURSE OF TOXIC MASCULINITY

KAREN SUGRUE

> "Words are, in my not so humble opinion, our most inexhaustible source of magic. Capable of inflicting injury and remedying it."
> —J. K. ROWLING, *Harry Potter and the Deathly Hallows*

I grew up in Ireland in the 1980s. At that time, Ireland was homogeneous in all things—white, Catholic, heterosexual, and deeply misogynistic. There were very few women doing anything other than being wives and mothers, and masculine norms and expectations fell firmly into the category of traditional "hegemonic masculinity."[1] Difference of any sort was suppressed, violent homophobia was rife, and sexuality and gender performance were microcontrolled by the dual weapons of shame and fear. The Irish Catholic church controlled schools, hospitals, media, and government, and imposed their repressive dogma on all aspects of Irish life.[2] The Irish Censorship Board, once described as "the fiercest literary censorship this side of the Iron Curtain," was notorious.[3] The history of twentieth-century Ireland is the history of suppression of difference. In this bleak landscape, a few television programs that somehow escaped through the web of censorship talked about difference, love, equality, social justice, and inclusion. Almost invariably, these were science fiction and fantasy, embodying a seemingly impossible vision of utopian society and optimism about humanity, such as *The Incredible Hulk*, *Spiderman*, *Batman*, *Wonder Woman*, and of course, *Star Trek*. For better or for worse, my personal ideals, values, and social justice dreams were set by utopian science fiction and superhero genres, and I have never doubted the hugely important power of popular culture to validate, teach, model, and heal.

It has long been argued that popular culture, a key component of Louis Althusser's "Ideological State Apparatus," reveals "some of the most pressing problems confronting society."[4] Giroux contends that "the media in particular is a substantial, if not *the*, primary educational force in regulating meanings, values, and tastes that offer up and legitimate particular subject positions."[5] It is interesting therefore to look to popular cultural representations of what Judith Butler calls successful "gender performances" and the "signifying gestures through which gender is established" to get a sense of some of the "compulsory frames set by various forces that police the social appearance of gender."[6] In his discussion about his relationship with the band "Daniel Amos," Andrew Herrman argues that "pop culture impacts our identities indelibly and profoundly. Like people with synaesthesia who can see sound and taste color, we are embedded in popular culture. It impacts our emotional states and our differing tastes. Popular culture helps us to define who we are, what we believe and influences who we befriend."[7] If we are to look to popular cultural products to get a sense of "meanings, values and tastes," few have a wider spread than the enormously popular *Harry Potter* series. The seven books, released between 1997 and 2007, are the most successful book series of all time selling more than 500 million copies, translated into 78 languages, and made into eight multibillion dollar blockbuster movies and with dedicated fans of all ages.[8]

Harry Potter came into my life in my early twenties. I was a very grown up and serious adult by then and far too old, I felt, for stories about wizards. Forced on me by a much younger sibling, I started reading only out of love for her. Almost immediately, I found myself immersed in a world I recognized from youthful fangirling. People of good heart, fighting against overwhelming odds for what was right, with themes of love and friendship and community. The Dursleys' vicious suppression of and revulsion at Harry's differentness and their frantic efforts to hide and ignore that difference, had a particularly Irish Catholic feel to it. I felt like I had come home.

Working in education, I have been interested in the teaching strategies, and emotional labor and care work performed at Hogwarts by Dumbledore and all the staff, as well as the family form that they represent as a group. In more recent readings, I've been drawn to Rowling's use of blood politics throughout the texts. The phrases "Mudbloods," "filthy halfbloods," and "squibs" are used throughout the series as highly offensive, pejorative terms. Since my first reading, when such early twentieth-century notions of racial purity seemed impossibly historically distant, to the present day when we see marchers chanting "clean blood, clean minds" through the streets of Warsaw, we watch with horror as racial politics continue to be on the ascendency worldwide, and Rowling's tale takes on a new immediacy and relevancy.[9]

Well-known sociologist Michael Kimmel argues that the "aggrieved entitlement of white men" lies at the root of a great deal of contemporary, developed-world racial politics.[10] Voldemort, the great villain of the *Harry Potter* series, is the very embodiment of embittered white male entitlement. His fevered efforts to make himself immortal at the expense of his humanity, his aggressive belief in his own superiority, and his dismissal as unimportant those he views as "other," all have clear parallels in the contemporary white supremacist movement. With this lens in mind, it is on the representations of masculinity in the *Harry Potter* franchise that this chapter will focus.

Betty Friedan's eerily prescient work *The Second Stage* predicts that the gender revolution will stall unless we also fight to liberate men from gendered role expectations.[11] And so it has come to pass. In 2018, the gender pay gap, the second shift, the worry work, and the burden of care are all still firmly in place, and women are still dramatically underrepresented in positions of power, status, and influence.[12] It is very hard, as Friedan pointed out, to see how this can change until we change normative behavioral and lifestyle expectations for boys and men also. Anne-Marie Slaughter has argued that women were told we could do it all, if we did it all at the same time.[13] However, it is simply not possible to do everything, and while care work is still undervalued and carried out primarily by women, the revolution will remain stalled.[14] When reading the newest installment of the *Harry Potter* universe, *The Cursed Child* (2016), I was disappointed that although Hermione is the Minister for Magic, it was not explicitly stated that Ron had taken on the family care duties.[15] Traditional gendered notions abound, with Hermione commenting to Harry, "you know, Ron says he thinks I see more of my secretary Ethel than of him. Do you think there's a point where we made a choice—parent of the year or Ministry official of the year?"[16] Even when we have excellent role models of women in power, we have no popular cultural roadmaps for the logistics of how to achieve it and cannot seem to envisage any form of gender relations that do not involve traditional gendered behavior. Further adding to the disappointingly gendered performances being showcased is the scene where Hermione, the Minister for Magic, goes into Harry's (a subordinate) office:

> Hermione sits with piles of paper in front of her in Harry's messy office. She is slowly sorting through it all. Harry enters in a rush. He is bleeding.

> **HERMIONE:** Harry, I get it. Paperwork's boring.
> **HARRY:** Not for you.[17]

Paperwork, though vital, is clearly not heroic, and Harry must be a hero, needs to be a hero. The entire series is constructed around the idea that Harry must be heroic to save the world, or everyone he loves will die. Warren Farrell and Michael Kimmell have written extensively on what has been called "the boy crisis" in contemporary developed countries. This crisis is signposted by boys falling behind on indicators of health and education.[18] Farrell's analysis includes what he terms "heroic intelligence versus health intelligence" and he claims that boys, to their detriment, are taught one and not the other.[19] Through this lens, "heroic intelligence" is displayed when the day is saved, people are kept safe, and others provided for. "Health intelligence" then is displayed by behaviors that keep themselves alive, safe, and in happy, loving relationships. If we apply this lens to behaviors by key men and boys in the *Harry Potter* series, a clear pattern emerges.

> **HERMIONE:** You're bleeding.
> Harry checks his face in the mirror. He dabs at the wound with his robes.
> **HARRY:** Don't worry, it'll go with the scar.[20]

For so long women fought against the limited and demeaning representations of themselves in the media—which portrayed them only in the roles and gender performances that society deemed appropriate. When we look at the representations of boys and men in contemporary media, it is clear that similar work needs to be done to change how they are represented. In the *Harry Potter* universe, mirroring our own, we see very slow progress and only small changes in the expression of masculinity over the three generations of Dumbledore, Harry, and most recently, young Albus in the final installment, *The Cursed Child*. While all three display very clear heroic intelligence, Harry and Albus are saved by their friendships from the poison of undiluted toxic masculinity.

POLICING MASCULINITY

Michel Foucault discusses the power of discourse and its use by the powerful to regulate bodies through time and space.[21] Gender and sexuality are two key components of this system of regulation, as is the powerful discursive weapon of "normality" (read: acquiescence to socially accepted norms for behavior) that is used to beat people into compliance. Women have long campaigned and fought for recognition of the way in which society controls their behavior by enforcing rules of "normality." Since Raewyn Connell's discussion of hegemonic masculinity in her ground breaking *Masculinities*, it has increasingly been recognized that the same critical attention needs to be paid to the way this process operates for men.[22] One useful analytical tool that has been developed is the Policing of Masculinity which monitors the multiple ways in which hegemonic masculinity is established as the "ideal" or normative standard, for idealized male behavior.[23] According to Christopher Reigeluth and Michael Addis, "policing of masculinity (POM) operates as a primary gender socialization mechanism on young boys as they navigate adolescence. POM can be understood as any action that serves to prevent or punish behaviour perceived as insufficiently masculine based on contextually situated gender norms."[24] Hegemonic masculinity refers to the idea that men are not creatures of emotion. Instead, they are beings of logic and dispassion; calm, without needs of their own, desiring only to fulfill their manly obligations to home and country.[25] In this idealized light, men are brave and fearless, feeling neither pain nor cold. They understand the requirements of sacrifice; are physically fit and strong and enjoy sports. The role of these idealized masculine men in the family is to provide financial support and they do not want, nor are they able to perform, any "caring" (read: "women's") work. They are Kathleen Lynch's "Care Commanders" and their financial support gives them immunity from "care responsibilities," which are the duty of the "care foot soldiers" (women).[26] Likewise, hegemonic or idealized masculinity holds no space for what Arlie Hochschild calls "emotional work" (work done to manage one's own feelings or the feelings of another in an effort to benefit a relationship), that is also constructed as primarily a feminized domain.[27] Boys and men who have emotions and needs of their own and sometimes need to feel cared for are "policed" by peers and society in general, often being shamed, bullied, and abused.[28] Popular cultural representations of caregiving men who engage in emotional work are rare or discursively constructed negatively.[29]

When we look to representations of masculinity in the *Harry Potter* texts, what kind of gender role performances do we see being played out by key male characters? In one of the most emotionally resonant elements of the series, Dumbledore's gender performance of elements of hegemonic masculinity could be read almost as a cautionary tale. In *Harry Potter and the Philosopher's Stone* (1997), when Harry asks Dumbledore what he sees in the

Mirror of Erised (which shows your deepest desires), he replies, "I see myself holding a pair of thick, woollen socks. One can never have enough socks."[30] Although the reader suspects there is more to the story, Dumbledore holds Harry, and us, at a distance and continues to do so until after his death. Like Harry, we are forced to piece together the story from secondhand sources, frustrated and hurt that we were not told directly. As a psychotherapist, I have seen this story played out many times with clients endlessly grieving that they were held distant by a parent who was unwilling or unable to show vulnerability. Mindful of the damage it must do, it is difficult as a parent and a psychotherapist to read Harry's dreadful hurt in the fifth installment, *Harry Potter and The Order of the Phoenix* (2003), when Dumbledore will not talk to him or offer him support or reassurance when Harry is at his most vulnerable. The story ends in tragedy and regret. Dumbledore, verbalizing one of the most intergenerationally psychologically damaging elements of hegemonic, self-sacrificing masculinity, says, "So you see, I have been trying, in distancing myself from you, to protect you, Harry. An old man's mistake."[31]

What is vitally important about this construct of potentially harmful representations of hegemonic—or "toxic"—masculinity is the impact on the mental health of men being pressured to hold this space. Connell argues that men are educated to see dependence as weakness, and masculinity is defined in terms of dominance.[32] As Lynch articulates, "one of the results of the gendering of care is that men's emotional socialization undermines their ability to articulate the vulnerable emotional self."[33] We see this played out in *The Order of the Phoenix*: "Harry watched him, but this uncharacteristic sign of exhaustion, or sadness, or whatever it was from Dumbledore did not soften him. On the contrary, he felt even angrier that Dumbledore was showing signs of weakness. He had no business being weak when Harry wanted to rage and storm at him."[34] While there are many misconceptions about what constitutes these potentially harmful representations of hegemonic masculinity, Chimamanda Ngozi Adichie explains it succinctly when she says that, "masculinity is a hard, small cage, and we put boys inside this cage. We teach boys to be afraid of fear, of weakness, of vulnerability. We teach them to mask their true selves."[35] Toxic masculinity, or hegemonic masculine norms that have become poisonous to men, are the result of the repressive and contradictory expectations that our society puts on boys and men.

If we examine the statistics on men's health and well-being, they start to give us a sense of exactly what the impact of living in that small, hard cage might be, and what the so-called "boy crisis" looks like.[36] Across the developed world, alarming numbers of boys continue to be diagnosed with

ADHD and treated with psychostimulants from very young ages, despite significant evidence of overdiagnosis.[37] At the same time, 98 percent of mass shootings in the US are committed by men.[38] Globally, men die by suicide three to four times more often than women.[39] Men are more often the *victims* of accidents, crime and violence.[40] They get cancer more often than women and their survival rate is lower. They do worse in school, drop out more, get more dangerous jobs, and work longer hours, for more years. They die sooner than women. There is an expectation that they provide financial security for their families while family court systems around the world will overwhelmingly find in favor of women. In criminal justice settings, men are sentenced to jail more often and serve longer sentences than women.[41] Both Kimmel and Farrell note that men are reporting that they feel forgotten and undervalued by a world for whom their lives have been disposable.[42] Both these authors argue that the world has primed and used men as war and factory fodder for far too long and that there are very serious consequences to this. In country after country, many have been alarmed at the rise of racist and white supremacist movements populated by what Kimmel calls "the angry white men" of the alt-right.[43] Ngozi Adichie was understating when she said "we have a problem with gender."[44]

While there are a great many problems with the representation of gender in *Harry Potter*, the entire series makes a very strong statement about the fragmentation of community, the dangers of othering, and the lack of belonging and acceptance. Time and again, Dumbledore talks about the power of division and discord to help our enemies. In what could be read as a commentary on contemporary racial politics, in *Harry Potter and the Chamber of Secrets* (1998), he says that "it is our choices that show what we truly are, far more than our abilities."[45] In *Harry Potter and the Goblet of Fire* (2000), Dumbledore says that "differences of habit and language are nothing at all if our aims are identical and our hearts are open" and that "we are only as strong united, as we are weak, divided."[46] Respect, belonging, and community, rather than difference based on arbitrarily assigned identities—these are the recurring themes of *Harry Potter*. As a sociologist, I adore Dumbledore, whose life's work is a perpetual critique of neo-liberalism, advocating the social model of German philosopher Ferdinand Tonnies of developing a community based on friendship, trust, mutual respect, and inclusion.[47] Simultaneously, as a psychotherapist, I am horrified at the way in which Dumbledore models grief and the handling of difficult emotions—especially in his role as surrogate father figure for Harry. Despite his wisdom and kindness, Dumbledore is not a helpful role model for Harry or indeed any young reader. He is emotionally cut off and withdrawn, and in life cannot show his emotional vulnerability, ask for help, or allow himself to enjoy a loving, reciprocal relationship with Harry (or anyone). In the emotionally charged chapter entitled "King's Cross" at the end of *Harry Potter and the Deathly Hallows* (2007), we see that only in death does he allow himself to be vulnerable with Harry. How many adults read that chapter and imagine themselves and an unreachable father having that most nourishing of conversations? He leaves Harry with the advice not to "pity the dead, Harry. Pity the living, and, above all, those who live without love," which I read not only as a comment on his own life choices, as well as Voldemort's, but also as advice to Harry not to follow his example, not to cut himself off the way that Dumbledore did.[48]

Dumbledore personifies the idealized hegemonic notion of heroic masculinity—working to protect those he loves, never asking for help and having no emotional needs of his own. This lonely, "toxic" need to protect those he cares for eventually, literally, poisons him when, in book five, he touches a Horcrux he was searching for alone, and is mortally wounded, literally, poisoned. Displaying outwardly, none of the fear or grief he must have been feeling, Dumbledore passes off this life-limiting injury with stoic aplomb, "A withered hand does not seem an unreasonable exchange for a seventh of Voldemort's soul."[49] When Harry realizes that he too must die, he performs bravery in the face of death just as Dumbledore modelled for him: "'I thought he would come,' said Voldemort in his high, clear voice, his eyes on the leaping flame. 'I expected him to come. I was, it seems . . . mistaken.' 'You weren't.' Harry said it as loudly as he could, with all the force he could muster: he did not want to sound afraid."[50] Like his mentor, Harry knows that the only way to maintain his masculinity, his heroism, his identity and sense of worth, is by hiding his fear and facing death alone. It is only in the final book, and in death, that we finally get an insight into the inner world of Dumbledore.

> When I discovered it, after all those years, buried in the abandoned home of the Gaunts—the Hallow I had craved most of all—I lost my head Harry. I quite forgot that it was now a Horcrux, that the ring was sure to carry a curse. I picked it up and I put it on and for a second I imagined that I was about to see Ariana, and my mother and my father, and to tell them how very, very sorry I was.[51]

Literature on the "policing of masculinities" talks about the general use of punishing phrases such as "toughen up," "be a big man," and "boys don't cry."[52] But even aside from the explicit use of language like this, purposely designed to shame and vilify, there is a glaring absence of role models in popular culture whose gender performances include the implicit notion that the very normal emotions boys feel are acceptable. Very often, male roles in popular culture are celebrated when they do not display any emotions at all, especially in the face of overwhelming loss. In film, television, and advertising there are largely only poor, limited, and caricatured male roles. These roles rarely go beyond the limited scope of the "hero" who fixes everything, but has no personal or emotional needs of his own, and the "idiot dad" who is foolishly bumbling through domesticity and cannot be trusted to take care of the kids. These are the media representations of what is referred to as toxic masculinity, and they are as widespread and ubiquitous as the sexist and demeaning portrayals of women, objectified and valued only for their attractiveness and adherence to norms of beauty and body size. The Bechdel Test continues to be a useful (if limited) tool to critique and make visible the misogyny in television and movies.[53] We need a new test, the "Dumbledore Test" perhaps, that allows us to see just how widespread these toxic, limiting and emotion-shaming representations of boys and men are. The test would simply ask, "Does any key male character directly ask for support with an emotional issue without being ridiculed or shamed?"

When we examine contemporary popular cultural products through the lens of gender with a particular eye on how men are represented, we start to see quite a startling pattern of potentially harming representations of hegemonic masculinity. Six of the ten top-grossing movies last year were superhero movies.[54] Most of them fail even the very basic requirements of respectful female representation outlined in the Bechdel test and all of them feature the poisonously dangerous representations of hegemonic masculinity being discussed here. In this bleak terrain, almost entirely devoid of emotionally healthy role models for boys and men, where does the *Harry Potter* series sit? Returning to Farrell's notion of "heroic intelligence" versus "health intelligence" to examine the performance of masculinity of Dumbledore, Harry, and finally, young Albus, it is possible to read a progression, but a small one: "Harry thought fast. '*Secrets and lies, that's how we grew up, and Albus (Dumbledore). . . . He was a natural . . .* .' Was he turning into Dumbledore, keeping his secrets clutched to his chest, afraid to trust?"[55] The portrayal of Harry and young Albus and the way they survive their epic adventures, does deviate from Dumbledore's lonely story because they have friends with them.

In *Harry Potter and the Deathly Hallows*, Hermione, begging Harry to allow others to help, says with exasperation, "You don't have to do everything alone, Harry."[56] Completing the evolution of the characters, young Albus, in *Harry Potter and the Cursed Child*, actively asks for help, saying, "I'm going to do this Scorpius. I need to do this. And you know as well as I do, I'll entirely mess it up if you don't come with me."[57] The entire series could be read as a parable designed to illustrate the dangers of toxic representations of hegemonic masculinity and the health and happiness promoting properties of friendship, cooperation, reliance, and trust in others. In book one, Harry, Ron, and Hermione each solve enchantments that have been set to guard the Philosopher's Stone. In book five, Harry and Dumbledore are punished for their need to save the day, when Voldemort uses it against them, resulting in the death of Sirius. There is a strong message that trust and friendship are vital for health and survival. At the end of the series in the Great Battle of Hogwarts, where Harry asks Neville to "Kill the snake," and all the characters play vital roles in the final battle, it is possible to argue that community is the key value being promoted and presented, in stark opposition to Dumbledore's solitary crusades.

In a powerful scene at the end of *Harry Potter and the Deathly Hallows*, Harry finally realizes that Dumbledore has given him the Resurrection Stone and that by doing so, he has ensured that Harry will not have to face his death alone. At this most difficult time, he can be surrounded by loved ones with whom he can share his fears and take comfort. "'You've been so brave,' his mother Lilly tells him. 'We are. . . . so proud of you,' says his dad. 'Does it hurt?' The childish questions had fallen from Harrys lips before he could stop it. 'You'll stay with me?' he asks them. 'Until the very end,' they promise."[58] We are allowed to see Harry's fear and hurt and grief, that he is "all too human," and he is all the more heroic for it.

If we reject essentialist notions about women—which we do—then we must also reject essentialist notions about men.[59] As Shannon Wooden and Ken Gillam argue, "a monolithic construct of masculinity, left un-interrogated, is as false as one for femininity and must comprise as much of a trap for individuals as *femininity* has been."[60] While feminists have been working to change the script for girls, the cultural representations of boys have "remained relatively inelastic, while the world around them has changed fundamentally" and young boys are simply not prepared for the world they are about to enter or the burdens of contemporary adulthood.[61] Those burdens may not be an epic fight to the death at Hogwarts School for Witchcraft and Wizardry. They may be the far heavier burdens of everyday adult life: financial responsibility, grief, disappointment, and boredom, burdens that men often believe they must carry alone if they are to be "real" men. Like Harry, very often the message coming at boys is that their value lies in their role as protectors and problem solvers. This expectation does two very damaging things. It puts an unbearable weight on men's shoulders, devalues their other attributes, and it disrespects the strength and resilience of the women of the world. It is not a message of equality and it is poisoning gender relations. The message of *Harry Potter* is that no matter what the burden, it is lightened when we share it and realize that we do not have to save the world, Hogwarts—or our families—on our own.

The origin story of Dumbledore could be used to read the *Harry Potter* books as an examination of how generations of good men learned to hide and suppress their emotions, trying to carry the burdens of the world on their own. Dumbledore could be read as a personification of all the generations of twentieth-century men who survived war and trauma while internalizing the message that the job of "real men" was to fearlessly and tirelessly protect and provide. In his youth, Dumbledore made an error of judgement, which led to the death of his vulnerable sister. He never forgave himself and in life, did not speak of his remorse or share his guilt. He never allowed himself the joy of love and held his grief silently for a lifetime, until it poisoned him.[62] Throughout the series, I admired Dumbledore as much as Harry did. However, it is possible to argue that his life epitomizes the worst effects of harmful representations of masculinity and the personal loneliness and devastation it can bring: "'Can you forgive me?' he said. 'Can you forgive me for not trusting you? For not telling you? Harry, I only feared that you would fail as I had failed. I only dreaded that you would make my mistakes. I crave your pardon Harry. I have known, for some time now, that you are the better man.'"[63] He continues in a later scene, "'You cannot despise me more than I despise myself.'"[64] Finally, in direct opposition to the traditional, hegemonic masculine space held by him throughout the series while alive, "Dumbledore gave a little gasp and began to cry in earnest."[65] In a life dedicated to public service and good works at the expense of personal happiness, Dumbledore—like Superman and Batman—personifies the unattainable ideal of twentieth-century masculinity: powerful but moral, quietly protecting the weak and fighting the villains, never asking for anything in return and displaying no personal or emotional needs. Dumbledore represents many twentieth-century fathers who work themselves to illness and death to provide safety but are incapable of allowing themselves to be vulnerable. They live in perpetual fear of being hurt, keep themselves distant and emotionally removed, unable to accept care and ultimately, as Dumbledore did after Ariana died and Grindlewald fled, choose isolation and emotional safety, rather than open themselves to connection.[66]

The problems being caused by harmful representations of hegemonic masculinity are enormous and impact every one of us. We must begin to seriously and systematically look at the types of role models our children have in the media which will shape the kinds of gendered behavior they expect of themselves and of each other. We need to create new narratives for our children that do not define masculinity and femininity in opposition to one another and reimagine gender relations of mutual responsibility and care giving. If, as Lynch argues, "equality is a question of having equal access to love, care and solidarity and an equal sharing of the burdens and benefits of love and care work," we still have a long road ahead and the evolution of Dumbledore, Harry, and young Albus demonstrates how slow and painful these changes must be.[67]

NOTES

1. "Hegemonic masculinity ... embodied the current most honoured way of being a man, it required other men to position themselves in relation to it. Hegemony meant ascendancy achieved through culture, institutions and persuasion." Raewyn Connell and James W. Messerschmidt, "Hegemonic Masculinity: Rethinking the Concept," *Gender and Society* 19, no. 6 (2005): 832.

2. Tom Inglis, *Moral Monopoly: The Rise and Fall of the Catholic Church in Modern Ireland*, (Dublin: UCD Press, 1998).

3. Robert Graves, *Irish Times*, June 22, 1950, quoted in Brian Kennedy, *Dreams and Responsibilities: The State and the Arts in Independent Ireland* (London: The Arts Council, 1950).

4. Louis Althusser, *Lenin and Philosophy and Other Essays*, trans. Ben Brewster (New York: New York University Press, 2001). Henry A. Giroux and P. Freire, "Pedagogy, Popular Culture and Public Life: An Introduction," in *Popular Culture, Schooling and Everyday Life*, ed. Henry A. Giroux and Roger I. Simon (New York: Bergin and Carey, 1989), viii.

5. Henry A. Giroux, *The Mouse that Roared: Disney and the End of Innocence* (Lanham: Rowman and Littlefield, 1999), 2.

6. Judith Butler, *Gender Trouble: Feminism and the Subversion of Identity* (London and New York: Routledge, 2007), viii. Butler, *Gender Trouble*, 33.

7. Andrew Hermann, "Daniel Amos and Me: The Power of Pop Culture and Auto Ethnography," *The Popular Culture Studies Journal* 1, no. 1 (2013): 7.

8. Nicolas Rapp and Krishna Thakker, "Harry Potter at 20: Billions in Box Office Revenue, Millions of Books Sold," *Fortune*, June 26, 2017, http://fortune.com/2017/06/26/harry-potter-20th-anniversary/.

9. Paul Hockenos, "Poland and the Uncontrollable Fury of Europe's Far Right," *The Atlantic*, November 15, 2017, https://www.theatlantic.com/international/archive/2017/11/europe-far-right-populist-nazi-poland/524559/.

10. Michael Kimmel, *Angry White Men: American Masculinity at the End of an Era* (London: Hachette, 2017).

11. Betty Friedan, *The Second Stage* (Cambridge: Harvard University Press, 1998).

12. "Gender Equality," *United Nations*, August 12, 2018, https://www.un.org/sustainabledevelopment/gender-equality/.

13. Anne-Marie Slaughter, "Why Women Still Can't Have It All," *The Atlantic*, August 15, 2012, https://www.theatlantic.com/magazine/archive/2012/07/why-women-still-cant-have-it-all/309020/.

14. Anne-Marie Slaughter, *Unfinished Business: Women, Men, Work, Family* (New York: Random House, 2016).

15. J. K. Rowling, John Tiffany, and Jack Thorne, *Harry Potter and the Cursed Child* (London: Little Brown, 2016).

16. Rowling, Tiffany, and Thorne, 33.

17. Rowling, Tiffany, and Thorne.

18. "Boys are doing less, getting lower grades, they're two and a half times more likely to commit suicide, three and a half times more likely to be suspended and five times more likely to be expelled." Michael Kimmel, "Solving the 'Boy Crisis' in Schools," *Huffington Post*, April 30, 2013, https://www.huffingtonpost.com/michael-kimmel/solving-the-boy-crisis-in_b_3126379.html?guccounter=1. Warren Farrell and John Gray, *The Boy Crisis: Why Our Boys Are Struggling and What We Can Do About It* (Dallas: BenBella Books, 2018).

19. Kimmel.

20. Rowling et al., *Cursed Child*, 31.

21. Michel Foucault, *Discipline and Punish: The Birth of the Prison* (New York: Vintage Books, 1975).

22. Shannon Wooden and Ken Gillam, *Pixar's Boy Stories: Masculinity in a Post Modern Age* (New York: Rowman and Littlefield, 2014).

23. Christopher Reigeluth and Michael Addis, "'Adolescent Boys' Experiences with Policing of Masculinity: Forms, Functions, and Consequences," *Psychology of Men and Masculinity* 17, no. 1 (2015): 74–83.

24. Reigeluth and Addis.

25. Wooden and Gillam, *Pixar's Boy Stories*.

Jesper Anderson and Thomas Johansson, "Global Narratives of Fatherhood: Fathering and Masculinity on the Internet," *International Review of Sociology* 26, no. 3 (2016): 482–96.

26. Kathleen Lynch and Judy Walsh, "Love, Care and Solidarity: What Is and Is Not Commodifiable," in *Affective Equality: Love, Care and Injustice*, ed. Kathleen Lynch et al. (London: Palgrave Macmillan, 2009).

27. Arlie Russell Hochschild, *The Managed Heart: Commercialization of Human Feeling* (Berkeley: University of California Press, 1983). Amy S. Wharton, "The Sociology of Emotional Labour," *Annual Review of Sociology* 35, no. 1 (2009): 147–65.

28. Kimmel, "Solving the 'Boy Crisis' in Schools."

29. Wooden, *Pixar's Boy Stories*.

30. J. K. Rowling, *Harry Potter and the Philosopher's Stone* (London: Bloomsbury, 1997), 230.

31. J. K. Rowling, *Harry Potter and the Order of the Phoenix* (London: Bloomsbury, 2003), 726.

32. Connell and Messerschmidt, "Hegemonic Masculinity."

33. Kathleen Lynch et al., "Introduction," in *Affective Equality: Love, Care and Injustice*, ed. Kathleen Lynch et al (London: Palgrave Macmillan, 2009), 8.

34. Rowling, *Order of the Phoenix*, 735.

35. Chimamanda Ngozi Adichi, *We Should All Be Feminists* (London: Fourth Estate, 2014), 26.

36. Farrell, *The Boy Crisis*.

37. Megan Fresson et al., "Overdiagnosis of ADHD in Boys: Stereotype Impact on Neuropsychological Assessment," *Applied Neuropsychology: Child* (2018).

38. "Number of Mass Shootings in the United States between 1982 and June 2018, by Shooter's Gender," *The Statistics Portal*, June 2018, https://www.statista.com/statistics/476445/mass-shootings-in-the-us-by-shooter-s-gender/.

39. "Suicide Statistics Report 2017," *Samaritans*, August 12, 2018, https://www.samaritans.org/sites/default/files/kcfinder/files/Suicide_statistics_report_2017_Final.pdf.

40. Alexandra Laiou et al., "856 Comparative Analysis of Road Accidents by Gender in Europe," *Injury Prevention* 22, no. 2 (2016): A305.

41. "Mortality Statistics and Road Traffic Accidents in the UK," *RAC Foundation*, 2011, http://www.racfoundation.org/assets/rac_foundation/content/downloadables/road%20accident%20casualty%20comparisons%20-%20box%20-%2020110511.pdf. "Cancer Mortality for all Cancers Combined," *Cancer Research UK*, August 12, 2018, http://www.cancerresearchuk.org/health-professional/cancer-statistics/mortality/all-cancers-combined#heading-Zero =. "Cancer Mortality Statistics Ireland," *HSE*, 2016, http://www.hse.ie/eng/services/list/5/cancer/pubs/intelligence/registrydata.html. "Canadian Cancer Statistics," Canadian Cancer Research, 2015, http://www.hse.ie/eng/services/list/5/cancer/pubs/intelligence/registrydata.html. "Causes of Death. Catalogue NO. 3303.0,3 *Australian Bureau of Statistics*, 2016, http://www.mindframe-media.info/for-media/reporting-suicide/facts-and-stats. "Gender Indicators for Health," *Australian Bureau of Statistics*, 2015, http://www.abs.gov.au/ausstats/abs@.nsf/Lookup/4125.0main+features3210Jan%202013#Endnote.

42. Kimmel, *Angry White Men*. Farrell, *The Boy Crisis*.

43. Kimmel, *Angry White Men*.

44. Ngozi Adichi, *We Should All*.

45. J. K. Rowling, *Harry Potter and the Chamber of Secrets* (London: Bloomsbury, 1998).

46. J. K. Rowling, *Harry Potter and the Goblet of Fire* (London: Bloomsbury, 2000), 723.

47. Charles Loomis, *Fundamental Concepts of Sociology* (Oxford: American Books, 1940).

48. Rowling, *Deathly Hallows*, 578.

49. J. K. Rowling, *Harry Potter and the Half-Blood Prince* (London: Bloomsbury, 2005), 476.

50. Rowling, *Deathly Hallows*, 563.

51. Rowling, 576.

52. Reigeluth, "Policing of Masculinity."

53. Developed by Alison Bechdel in 1985, the Bechdel test is a method for evaluating the portrayal of women in fiction. It asks whether a work features at least two women who talk to each other about something other than a man.

54. Stephen Cho, "Here are the Top Ten Highest Grossing movies of 2018," *Paste Magazine*, December 31, 2018, https://www.pastemagazine.com/articles/2018/12/here-are-the-top-ten-highest-grossing-movies-of-20.html.

55. Rowling, *Deathly Hallows*, 469.

56. Rowling.

57. Rowling, *Cursed Child*, 57.

58. Rowling, *Deathly Hallows*, 561.

59. Butler, *Gender Trouble*.

60. Wooden, *Pixar's Boys Stories*, xv.
61. Wooden, xvii.
62. Rowling, *Deathly Hallows*.
63. Rowling, 571.
64. Rowling.
65. Rowling, 574.
64. Rowling.
67. Lynch, "Introduction," 2.

CONCLUSION

Reflecting on Toxic Masculinity

The phrase "toxic masculinity" is one loaded with many sociopolitical inferences. As such, it tends to polarize opinion. However, there is value in utilizing it to deconstruct instances where gender representations have the potential to do more harm than good. Hence, its place in our title, highlighting the potentially negative reflections of gender that can be found in various forms of popular culture—be they comic books, films, television shows, or plays. Our aim was not to merely present a narrow view of the impact negative representations have on masculinity, but also to examine the impact on femininity and subaltern masculinities to demonstrate how the Other must contort itself to conform in a patriarchal society, lest it be viewed as monstrous.

Asserting that the status quo is inherently damaging—for all concerned—is only part of the argument. What this collection has attempted to do is to impel a very simple idea: plurality. It considers the need for more than one type of gender. By removing the gender binary and, instead, considering a spectrum that includes all gender, monstrous Otherness can be eliminated. It is only through an ideology of the many—included, represented, brought center-stage—that the construct of hegemonic masculinity, so narrow in its discourse of what is and what should be, can be effectively dismantled. While this process has begun, there is much left do as we change, evolve, and deepen our understanding. Of course, considering hegemony's tendency to fold in those aspects of the Other that are palatable and marketable while maintaining conservative hegemonic hierarchies, it is likely that our work to excavate toxicity will never be done. For example, as Craig Haslop states, regarding his findings on Torchwood (2006–11), even though the sexual identities of these heroes are fluid, there remains a reliance on presentations of masculinity that highlight dominance and places femininity as comparatively unpalatable. Moving away from such stereotypical representations of gender is our first step, but there are many more to follow.

It is important to note that if the art of popular culture must maintain as large an audience as possible, gender conservatism will still be evident. As the economic and financial motivations behind storytelling remain in play, a large audience must be appealed to and appeased. Television shows aimed at what is perceived to be the political center are under less risk of sparking controversy and, therefore, potential financial ramifications, from either conservative or progressive forces. For example, compare *Torchwood* and *Sense8* (2015–18), the Wachowski-led series that follows eight psychically connected people. Whereas Torchwood was under constant pressure to perform due to being on public broadcasting and being connected to a BBC flagship show in *Doctor Who*, the Wachowskis had the major benefit of their name and the current climate of Netflix opening the floodgates both in terms of creativity and budget. One show needs to frame its heroes at least partially in terms of what went before, whereas the other can be more deliberately playful with the gender and sexuality of its characters. Of course, this freedom presents its own issues: *Sense8* was canceled in 2017 after two seasons—with a single feature-length episode commissioned about a month after cancellation—due to low audience numbers and high production costs. Furthermore, the show suffered from increased backlash from its fanbase due to its stereotypical portrayal of life in the Global South.

There is also the inevitable intersection between fiction and reality: the cult of machismo known as hypermasculinity, which drives actors like Stephen Amell to fully iterate Green Arrow, but also to document it via social media. It is fascinating to think that Amell is stuck in this hegemonic rut as much as Oliver when James C. Taylor suggests that, despite the increasing development of Oliver's extended world in terms of identities, it is that central, dominant masculinity that is reasserted and essentially protected. Arrow, as a serial format, is evidence of how hybrid masculinities can perform alternative masculinities individually by wielding progressiveness as a heroic trait (by fighting the rich elite) while reinforcing hegemonic values and masculinity on a structural level (the hero is still the white man imposing order onto a chaotic world). Although the filter in the fictional world is set by the writers, no such barrier exists on Twitter or Instagram. These men who are asked to become these characters, not only in spirit but in a physical sense, in turn become cyphers for the cause: empty vessels whose only narrative is to state, over and over again: "I am a man, and this is how men

Rob McElhenny Social Media © 2019 Instagram

should be." Such glorification and cultivation of online personas completely erases the real-life consequences of these bodies: actors who pass out from dehydration to increase muscularity, the widespread increase of steroid (ab)use among American men, and the longterm health effects of drastic and recurring weight fluctuation. However, the upside is that social media is also capable of highlighting this cost, such as the above Instagram post by Rob McElhenney (of *It's Always Sunny in Philadelphia* fame), where he highlights both the financial cost and time-consuming nature of becoming physically fit to the degree required by Hollywood.[1]

Of course, it is not just men who fall/are pushed into the trap. Through both Esther De Dauw and Richard Reynolds's chapters on Batwoman and the White Queen, respectively, we can see the inherent struggle to fulfill a preordained gender binary, whether the subject attempts to manipulate that gender performance or not. Where *Torchwood*'s bisexual heroes had to tether themselves to a veneer of macho masculinity, Kate Kane and Emma Frost are essentially persecuted for being both within and without the hegemonic space. As De Dauw illustrates, the one true path is conformity: Kate cannot flee, protest, or reject the military industrial complex. When she does try to reimagine the concept of the feminine soldier, her role becomes villainous and her femininity monstrous. Emma Frost, in comparison, offers a glimpse of freedom within the hierarchy of oppression, provided that the character's gender performance is perfectly heteronormative and can be turned against the hierarchies. But this strategy is not available to all, and even if it were, the question remains: is this real freedom? This is where something curious happens: gender performance on one level but on an underlying and all-consuming level, gender performativity. Reynolds suggests such when he writes that Frost is caught between being object and subject, her performance of gender and sex extending into a supranormal state as a consequence of this conflict. Such performance, as Judith Butler would argue, is misleading. Frost is, and never has been, in control of the performance; the performance has been in control of her. Where this disturbing idea takes an especially dark turn is, as Richards highlights, when male artists and writers construct the narrative of her performance, essentially guaranteeing the dominant societal norm is adhered to. This performativity is inherent in both Kane's and Frost's stories, the overarching narrative being one of male control over what is and isn't permissible.

Hard boundaries of gender conformity strangulate any notions of difference, stripping any variants of nuance down into a strict duality of Us and Other. As Janne Salminen notes, *Batman v Superman* serves as a calling card for this conservative gender binary. Its portrayal of male traits strictly adheres to a heteronormative, hypermasculine ideal, even in the faux conflict from which its title is gleaned. A simple hierarchy is presented as infallible and irrefutable. Even the presence of a potentially disruptive force in Wonder Woman is, as Salminen states, only accepted if it can adhere to the norm. Also, any changes represented by Wonder Woman are only acceptable if they do not upset the status quo. In the face of any truly disruptive force, the arbiters of this hypermasculine society would readily defend it from destabilization. We see this in the form of Lex Luthor, whom Salminen notes is a stand-in for the liberal tech industry, queerness, and subaltern masculinities in general. The gender threat Luthor poses negates our two hypermasculine heroes' fake battle for masculine dominance, as they mobilize to protect the society where they inhabit the highest realm.

This society, framed by hegemonic masculinity, is partly formed by a media that presents hypermasculinity as ubiquitous. As Daniel J. Connell outlines, these images not only present a damaging fantasy, they tear at the very fabric of reality in their depictions of hypermasculine ideals. This pressurizing pattern, pushing physical representation to the outer boundaries of possibility through actors such as Hugh Jackman, shows some signs of reducing as the final phase removes itself entirely from reality. In this state of unreality—through the fantastical Hulk, Thanos, and even Bautista's Drax—we are potentially clearing an era of unsettling hypermasculine normalization.

While these fantastical bodies are overtly hypermasculine with obscene levels of muscularity and hardness, they are also clearly marked as alien, impossible, and created by the green screen. Is that enough to invalidate the glorification of the hypermasculine?

The need to liberate men from toxic masculinity, from the pressures of prescribed gender conformity, is espoused very clearly in Karen Sugrue's analysis of the *Harry Potter* series. Chronicling the generational divides when it comes to the adoption of gender norms that both cripple the individual and perpetuate their own misery, Sugrue suggests that the inevitable conclusion the painful furrow of coded masculinity creates need not be handed down, leaving behind the pained and isolated masculinity of Dumbledore and accepting the example of Albus Potter in *Harry Potter and the Cursed Child*—open, willing to express himself, and unafraid to ask for help.

The dual notion of isolation and belonging is a key conceptual bridge in this discussion, for it allows acceptance of difference and a sharing of emotional crises. Toxic masculinity shuns such things at great cost. Drew Murphy examines this through the leadership of Cyclops. Using Raewyn Connell's framework of hegemonic masculinity as well as the work of Margaret Wetherell and Nigel Edley, Murphy's analysis demonstrates how Cyclops ultimately follows a narrative journey of attempting to overcome compulsory, hegemonic performance. The idealization of hypermasculinity and normative reality is a continuous theme in X-Men, and as Murphy says, resonates with those marginalized by the hegemony. This can be seen in the way many episodes in X-Men canon reflect the challenges, stigmas, and discrimination felt by the LGBTQIA+ community. The complex relationship between mutants, Inhumans, and humans, suggests the battle for acceptance can, paradoxically, prove divisive—especially when hegemony continually folds in specific elements as a way to include specific subaltern identities and prevent solidarity among oppressed groups, such as the pinkwashing of white nationalism. As Murphy mentions, some mutants pass as human as long as they suppress their own powers, and it is these mutants who tend to push for assimilation the most, inadvertently throwing their less human-passing peers under the bus.

Acceptance in a world where an unreal binary holds cultural dominance can be so very hard to achieve and maintain. With every progressive step lies the potential to perpetuate the status quo. As Craig Haslop says, we should celebrate the ever-increasing level of representation of gender identity in our popular culture, but we should also be mindful when they exhibit the model of the status quo.

This mindfulness is a crucial component of identifying and tackling the toxic element of masculinity as presented in popular culture and the media. Structuralists would argue that we are drawn to narratives whose form presents a comforting familiarity—but what happens when that familiarity places one type of person as a hero above all others? If we are to believe that hegemony is a hierarchical system that is propagated not just by those who profit most, but also by those who buy into its stratification, then we must consider what is true change and what is only surface-level, ephemeral shifts. James Taylor notes that, due to superhero conventions, as much as a story looks forward facing, if it is framed through conservative gender values no longer fit for the modern world, it maintains that toxicity.

In short, this collection proposes a current scenario that is far from evolved but also far from hopeless: an environment where a better future might germinate. It begins with better representation, more variety, less homogeneity. It ends with new possibilities, new stories that are fresh yet highly resonant, and new narratives that do not perpetuate a continued misery just to validate its cycle. When Reynolds said it would be a positive move to see in what direction women writers and artists might take Emma Frost, he was suggesting we revisit Baudrillard's first phase of the image—a reflection of a profound reality—and this time, make sure it is not the hardened, aggressive, taciturn face of a straight white man staring back at us over and over again. We are plural in our being, and representations of masculinity need to reflect that movement forward not just for men or for boys, but for all of us.

NOTE

1. Rob McElhenney, "Look, it's not that hard," *Instagram*, posted September 6, 2018. https://www.instagram.com/p/BnXtEz1BLFP/.

BIBLIOGRAPHY

Ahearne, Joe, dir. *Doctor Who.* Season 1, Episode 13, "Parting of the Ways." Aired June 18, 2005, on BBC One.

Alaniz, José. *Death, Disability, and the Superhero: The Silver Age and Beyond.* Jackson: University Press of Mississippi, 2014.

Allen, Judith A. "Men Interminably in Crisis? Historians on Masculinity, Sexual Boundaries, and Manhood." *Radical History Review* 82 (2002): 191–207.

Althusser, Louis. *Lenin and Philosophy and Other Essays.* Translated by Ben Brewster. New York: New York University Press, 2001.

Amell, Stephen. "Worth It." *Twitter.* August 23, 2015. https://twitter.com/StephenAmell/status/635620041317318656.

Amell, Stephen. "You Should See the Other Guy." *Facebook.* August 15, 2016. https://www.facebook.com/stephenamell/photos/a.976747499077184.1073741842.146921975393078/1118510381567561.

Amell, Stephen. "When You Go Through 3 Seasons of Hell." *Facebook.* August 15, 2016. https://www.facebook.com/stephenamell/photos/a.976747499077184.1073741842.146921975393078/1118510348234231.

Amell, Stephen. "He Should of Thought Twice." *Facebook.* February 15, 2016. https://www.facebook.com/stephenamell/photos/a.976747499077184.1073741842.146921975393078/999420560143211.

Amy-Chinn, Dee. "GLAAD to Be Torchwood ? Bisexuality and the BBC." *Journal of Bisexuality* 12, no. 1 (2012): 63–79.

Anderson, Jesper and Thomas Johansson. "Global Narratives of Fatherhood: Fathering and Masculinity on the Internet." *International Review of Sociology* 26, no. 3 (2016): 482–96.

Antjoule, Nick. *The Hate Crime Report 2016: Homophobia, Biphobia and Transphobia in the UK.* London: Galop, 2016.

Arxer, Steven L. "Hybrid Masculine Power: Reconceptualizing the Relationship between Homosociality and Hegemonic Masculinity." *Humanity and Society* 35, no. 4 (2011): 390–422.

Australian Bureau of Statistics. "Gender Indicators for Health." 2015. http://www.abs.gov.au/ausstats/abs@.nsf/Lookup/4125.0main+features3210Jan%202013#Endnote.

Australian Bureau of Statistics. "Causes of Death." Catalogue no. 3303.0. 2016. http://www.mindframe-media.info/for-media/reporting-suicide/facts-and-stats.

Bachmann, Chaka L. and Becca Gooch. *LGBT in Britain: Hate Crime and Discrimination.* London: Stonewall, 2017.

Banet-Weiser, Sarah and Kate M. Miltner. "#MasculinitySoFragile: Culture, Structure, and Networked Misogyny." *Feminist Media Studies* 16, no. 1, (2016): 171–74.

Barker, Meg, Helen Bowes-Catton, Alessandra Iantaffi, Angela Cassidy and Laurence Brewer. "British Bisexuality: A Snapshot of Bisexual Representations and Identities in the United Kingdom." *Journal of Bisexuality* 8, no. 1 (2008): 141–62.

Barron, Lee. "Out in Space." In *Illuminating Torchwood: Essays on Narrative, Character and Sexuality in the BBC Series*, edited by Andre Ireland, 178–92. Jefferson: McFarland and Company, 2010.

Baudrillard, Jean. *Simulacra and Simulation*. Translated by Sheila Faria Glaser. Michigan: The University of Michigan Press, 2000.

Beardsley, Aubrey. "Salome." *The Studio*. London, April, 1893.

Belkin, Aaron. *Bring Me Men: Military Masculinity and the Benign Façade of America Empire 1898–2001*. London: Hurst and Company, 2012.

Bendis, Brian Michael (writer), Jackson Guice (penciler and inker), Justin Ponsor (colorist), Chris Eliopoulos (letterer), Bill Rosemann (editor), Lauren Sankovitch (editor), and Ralph Macchio (editor). *Ultimate Origins #1*. New York: Marvel Comics, 2008.

Bendis, Brian Michael (writer), Jason Aaron (writer), Ed Brubaker (writer), Jonathan Hickman (writer), Matt Fraction (writer), John Romita Jr. (penciler), Olivier Coipel (penciler), Adam Kubert (penciler), Scott Hanna (inker), Mark Morales (inker), John Dell (inker), Laura Martin (colorist), Larry Molinar (colorist), Chris Eliopoulos (letterer), Tom Brevoort (editor), John Denning (editor), Lauren Sankovitch (editor), Nick Lowe (editor), and Jim Cheung (cover artist). *Avengers vs. X-Men #1–12*. New York: Marvel Comics, 2012.

Bendis, Brian Michael (writer), Stuart Immonen (penciler), Wade von Grawbadger (inker), Marte Gracia (colorist), Cory Petit (letterer), Nick Lowe (editor), and Jordan D. White (editor). *All New X-Men #1*. New York: Marvel Comics, 2013.

Bendis, Brian Michael (writer), Stuart Immonen (penciler), Wade von Grawbadger (inker), Marte Gracia (colorist), Cory Petit (letterer), and Nick Lowe (editor). *All New X-Men #3–4*. New York: Marvel Comics, 2013.

Benshoff, Harry M. *Monsters in the Closet: Homosexuality and the Horror Film*. Inside Popular Film. Manchester: Manchester University Press, 1997.

Blackman, W. Haden (writer), J. H. Williams III (writer, penciler and inker), Dave Stewart (colorist), Tod Klein (letterer), Mike Marts (editor), and Janelle Asselin (editor). *Batwoman #1*. Burbank: DC Comics, 2011.

Blackman, W. Haden (writer), J. H. Williams III (writer, penciler and inker), Dave Stewart (colorist), Tod Klein (letterer), Mike Marts (editor), Rickey Purdin (editor), and Harvey Richards (editor). *Batwoman #4*. Burbank: DC Comics, 2011.

Blackman, W. Haden (writer), J. H. Williams III (writer), Amy Reeder Hadley (penciler), Rob Hunter (inker), Guy Major (colorist), Todd Klein (letterer), Mike Marts (editor), Rickey Purdin (editor), and Harvey Richards (editor). *Batwoman #7*. Burbank: DC Comics, 2012.

Blackman, W. Haden (writer), J. H. Williams III (writer), Trevor McCarthy (penciler and inker), Guy Major (colorist), Tod Klein (letterer), Mike Marts (editor), Rickey Purdin (editor), and Harvey Richards (editor). *Batwoman #10*. Burbank: DC Comics, 2012.

Blackman, W. Haden (writer), J. H. Williams III (writer, penciler and inker), Dave Stewart (colorist), Tod Klein (letterer), Mike Marts (editor), Rickey Purdin (editor), and Harvey Richards (editor). *Batwoman #13*. Burbank: DC Comics, 2012.

Blackman, W. Haden (writer), J. H. Williams III (writer, penciler and inker), Dave Stewart (colorist), Tod Klein (letterer), Mike Marts (editor), Rickey Purdin (editor), and Harvey Richards (editor). *Batwoman #14*. Burbank: DC Comics, 2012.

Blackman, W. Haden (writer), J. H. Williams III (writer, penciler and inker), Dave Stewart (colorist), Tod Klein (letterer), Mike Marts (editor), Rickey Purdin (editor), and Harvey Richards (editor). *Batwoman #16*. Burbank: DC Comics, 2013.

Blackman, W. Haden (writer), J. H. Williams III (writer), Trevor McCarthy (penciler and inker), Walden Wong (inker), Guy Major (colorist), Tod Klein (letterer), Mike Marts (editor), and Darren Shan (editor). *Batwoman #19*. Burbank: DC Comics, 2013.

Bollers, Karl (writer), Randy Green (penciler), Carlo Pagulayan (penciler), Adriana Melo (penciler), Will Conrad (penciler and inker), Rick Ketcham (inker), Dennis Crisostomo (inker), Sean Parsons (inker), Andrew Pepoy (inker), Eric Cannon (inker), Pete Pantazis (colorist), Transparency Digital (colorist), Cory Petit (letterer), Rus Wooton (letterer), and Mike Marts (editor). *Emma Frost #1–18*. New York: Marvel Comics: 2003–5.

Bordo, Susan. *Unbearable Weight: Feminism, Western Culture and the Body*. Berkeley: University of California Press, 1993.

Box Office Mojo. "Batman v Superman: Dawn of Justice (2016)." Accessed March 14, 2018. http://www.boxofficemojo.com/movies/?id=superman2015.htm.

Braidotti, Rosi. *Metamorphosis: Towards a Materialist Theory of Becoming*. Cambridge: Polity, 2002.

Bridges, Tristan and C. J. Pascoe. "Hybrid Masculinities: New Direction in the Sociology of Men and Masculinities." *Sociology Compass* 8, no. 3 (2014): 246–58.

Bromesco, Charles. "Superman Only Has 43 Lines of Dialogue in *Batman vs. Superman*." *Screencrush*. April 18, 2016. http://screencrush.com/batman-vs-superman-dialogue/.

Brooker, Will. *Hunting the Dark Knight: Twenty-First Century Batman*. London: I. B. Tauris, 2012.

Brown, Jeffrey A. "Comic Book Masculinity and the New Black Superhero." *African American Review* 33, no. 1 (1999): 25–42.

Brown, Jeffrey A. *Dangerous Curves: Action Heroines, Gender, Fetishism and Popular Culture*. Jackson: Mississippi University Press, 2011.

Brown, Jeffrey A. *The Modern Superhero in Film and Television: Popular Genre and American Culture*. London and New York: Routledge, 2017.

Bukatman, Scott. *Matters of Gravity: Special Effects and Supermen in the 20th Century*. Durham: Duke University Press, 2003.

Burlingame, Russ. "What *Batman v Superman* Needs to Gross to Break Even." *Comicbook.com*. Accessed March 3, 2016. http://comicbook.com/2016/03/16/what-batman-v-superman-needs-to-gross-to-break-even/.

Burton, Tim, dir. *Batman*. 1989; Burbank: Warner Bros. Pictures.

Butler, Judith. "Gender is Burning." In *Feminist Film Theory: A Reader*, edited by Sue Thornham, 336–49. Edinburgh: Edinburgh University Press: 1999.

Butler, Judith. *Gender Trouble: Feminism and the Subversion of Identity*. London and New York: Routledge, 1990.

Butler, Judith. *Gender Trouble: Feminism and the Subversion of Identity*. London and New York: Routledge, 2007.

Canadian Cancer Research. "Canadian Cancer Statistics." 2015. http://www.hse.ie/eng/services/list/5/cancer/pubs/intelligence/registrydata.html.

Cancer Research UK. "Cancer Mortality for all Cancers Combined." August 12, 2018. http://www.cancerresearchuk.org/health-professional/cancer-statistics/mortality/all-cancers-combined#heading-Zero.

Carreiras, Helen and Gerhard Kümmel. "Off Limits: The Cults of the Body and Social Homogeneity as Discursive Weapons in Targeting Gender Integration in the Military." In *Women in the Military and in Armed Conflict*, edited by Helen Carreiras and Gerhard Kümmel, 29–48. Berlin: Springer, 2008.

Carter, Angela. *The Sadean Woman: An Exercise in Cultural History*. London: Virago, 1979.

Chambliss, Julian C. "Superhero Comics: Artifacts of the U.S. Experience." *Juniata Voices* 12, (2012): 145–51.

Chow, Broderick, Eero Laine, and Claire Warden. "Introduction: Hamlet Doesn't Blade: Professional Wrestling, Theatre, and Performance." In *Performance and Professional Wrestling*, edited by Broderick Chow, Eero Laine, and Claire Warden. London and New York Routledge, 2017, 1–6.

Craig, Steve. *Men, Masculinity, and the Media: Second Volume*. Austin: SAGE Publications, 1992.

Claremont, Chris (writer), Dave Cockrum (penciler), Frank Chiaramonte (inker), Bonnie Wilford (colorist), John Costanza (letterer) and Archie Goodwin (editor). *Uncanny X-Men #101*. New York: Marvel Comics, 1976.

Claremont, Chris (writer), John Byrne (writer and penciler), Terry Austin (inker), Bob Sharen (colorist), Glynis Wein (colorist), Tom Orzechowski (letterer), Roger Stern (editor) and Jim Salicrup (editor). *Uncanny X-Men #129–137*. New York: Marvel Comics, 1980.

Claremont, Chris (writer), John Byrne (writer and penciler), Terry Austin (inker), Glynis Wein (colorist), Tom Orzechowski (letterer) and Louise Jones (editor). *Uncanny X-Men #141*. New York: Marvel Comics, 1981.

Claremont, Chris (writer), Jim Sherman (penciler), Bob McLeod (penciler), Josef Rubinstein (inker), Bonnie Wilford (colorist), Tom Orzechowski (letterer) and Louise Jones (editor). *Uncanny X-Men #151*. New York: Marvel Comics, 1981.

Cocca, Carolyn. *Superwomen: Gender, Power and Representation*. London and New York: Bloomsbury, 2016.

"Comic Heroine Ms. Marvel Saves San Francisco from Anti-Islam Ads." Asian America, *NBC News*. January 27, 2015. https://www.nbcnews.com/news/asian-america/comic-heroine-ms-marvel-saves-san-francisco-anti-islam-ads-n294751.

Comic Vine Forum. "Greg Land ripoff/tracing/recycling thread." Accessed May 20, 2018. https://comicvine.gamespot.com/forums/gen-discussion-1/greg-land-ripofftracing recycling-thread-695764/.

Connell, Raewyn. *Masculinities*. Cambridge: Polity, 1995.

Connell, Raewyn. *Masculinities: Second Edition*. Cambridge: Polity, 2005.

Connell, Raewyn and James W. Messerschmidt. "Hegemonic Masculinity: Rethinking the Concept." *Gender and Society* 19, no. 6 (2005): 829–59.

Connell, Raewyn and Rebecca Pearse. *Gender: In World Perspective (Third Edition)*. Cambridge: Polity, 2015.

Coogan, Peter. "The Hero Defines the Genre, the Genre Defines the Hero." In *Superhero: The Secret Origin of a Genre*, edited by Peter Coogan and Robin Rosenberg, 3–10. Austin: Monkey Brain Books, 2006.

Copus, Nick, dir. *Arrow*, Season 1, Episode 18, "Salvation." Aired March 27, 2013, on The CW.

Cornell, Paul (writer), Miguel Sepulveda (penciler and inker), Alex Sinclair (colorist), Pete Pantazis (colorist), Rob Leigh (letterer) and Pat McCallum (editor). *Stormwatch #3*. Burbank: DC Comics, 2011.

Darowski, Joseph J. *X-Men and the Mutant Metaphor*. Lanham: Rowman and Littlefield, 2014.
Darowski, Joseph J. "When Business Improved Art: The 1975 Relaunch of Marvel's Mutant Heroes." In *The Ages of the X-Men: Essays on the Children of the Atom in Changing Times*, edited by Joseph Darowski, 37–45. Jefferson: McFarland and Company, 2014.
Davies, Russel T. *Torchwood*. Created by Russel T. Davies. 2006–11; Cardiff: BBC Television
DeFalco, Tom (writer), Mary Wilshire (penciler), Steve Leialoha (inker), Bob Wiacek (inker), Daina Graziunas (colorist), Tom Orzechowski (letterer), Lois Buhalis (letterer) and Ann Nocenti (editor). *Firestar #1–4*. New York: Marvel Comics, 1986.
Deleuze, Gilles and Felix Guattari. *A Thousand Plateaus*. London: Athlone Press, 1988.
Demetriou, Demetrakis Z. "Connell's Concept of Hegemonic Masculinity: A Critique." *Theory and Society* 30, no. 3 (2001): 337–61.
Dhaenens, Frederik. "The Fantastic Queer: Reading Gay Representations in *Torchwood* and *True Blood* as Articulations of Queer Resistance." *Critical Studies in Media Communication* 30, no .2 (2013): 102–16.
Dittmer, Jason. *Captain America and the Nationalist Superhero: Metaphor, Narrative, and Geopolitics*. Philadelphia: Temple University Press, 2013.
Doane, Mary Anne. *Femme Fatales: Feminism, Film Theory and Psychoanalysis*. London and New York: Routledge, 1991.
Dollimore, Jonathan. "Bisexuality, heterosexuality, and wishful theory." *Textual Practice* 10, no. 3 (1996): 523–39.
Dow, Bonnie. *Prime-Time Feminism: Television, Media Culture, and the Women's Movement since 1970*. Philadelphia: University of Pennsylvania Press, 1996.
Dozier, William. *Batman*. Created by William Dozier. 1966–1968; Los Angeles: 20th Century Fox Television.
Duggan, Lisa. "The New Homonormativity: The Sexual Politics of Neoliberalism." In *Materializing Democracy: Toward a Revitalized Cultural Politics*, edited by Russ Castronovo and Dana D. Nelson, 175–94. Durham: Duke University Press, 2002.
Duncanson, Claire. "Forces for Good? Narratives of Military Masculinity in Peacekeeping Operations." *International Feminist Journal of Politics* 11, no. 1 (2009): 63–80.
Dyer, Richard. "Don't Look Now." *Screen* 23, no. 3–4 (2014): 61–73.
Eck, Beth A. "Compromising Positions: Unmarried Men, Heterosexuality, and Two-phase Masculinity." *Men and Masculinities* 17, no. 2 (2014): 147–72.
Eco, Umberto. "The Myth of Superman." *Diacritics* 2, no. 1 (1972): 14–22.
Edwards, Tim. *Cultures of Masculinity*. London and New York, Routledge, 2006.
Faludi, Susan. "Reagan's America: The Backlash Against Women and Men." In *Movies and American Society*, edited by Steven J. Ross, 314–36. Oxford: Blackwell: 2002.
Faludi, Susan. *Stiffed: Betrayal of the American Man*. New York: William Morrow and Company, 1999.
Faludi, Susan. *The Terror Dream: Fear and Fantasy in Post-9/11 America*. New York: Metropolitan Books, 2007.
Fancher, Peggy, Kathryn K. Knudson and Leora N. Rosen. "Cohesion and the Culture of Hypermasculinity in U.S. Army Units." *Armed Forces and Society* 29, no. 3 (2003): 325–51.
Farrell, Warren and John Gray. *The Boy Crisis: Why Our Boys Are Struggling and What We Can Do About It*. Dallas: BenBella Books, 2018.
Favreau, John, dir. *Iron Man 2*. 2010; Burbank: Marvel Studios.

Feasey, Rebecca. *Masculinity and Popular Television*. Edinburgh: Edinburgh University Press, 2008.

Feige, Kevin, dir. *Ant-Man*. 2015; Burbank: Marvel Studios.

Fiske, John. *Television Culture*. London and New York: Routledge, 1987.

Foucault, Michel. *Discipline and Punish: The Birth of the Prison*. New York: Vintage Books, 1975.

Foucault, Michel. *The History of Sexuality: Volumes 1–3*. London: Penguin, 1990.

Fraction, Matt (writer), Mitch Breitweiser (penciler and inker), Daniel Acuna (penciler, inker and colorist), Elizabeth Breitweiser (colorist), Joe Caramagna (letterer) and Nick Lowe (editor). *Uncanny X-Men Annual #2*. New York: Marvel Comics, 2009.

Fraction, Matt (writer), Ed Brubaker (writer), Kieron Gillen (writer), Greg Land (penciler), Terry Dodson (penciler), Yanick Paquette (penciler), Whilce Portacio (penciler), Harvey Tolibao (penciler), Paul Renaud (penciler and inker), Leonard Kirk (penciler and inker), Ibrain Roberson (penciler and inker), Jay Leisten (inker), Rachel Dodson (inker), Karl Story (inker), Edgar Tadeo (inker), Sandu Florea (inker), Cam Smith (inker), Dan Green (inker), Nathan Lee (inker), Frank D'Armata (colorist), Justin Ponsor (colorist), Jim Charalampidis (colorist), Joe Caramagna (letterer), Cory Petit (letterer), Nick Lowe (editor), Axel Alonso (editor), Jake Thomas (editor), Alan Fine (editor), Jordan D. White (editor) and Daniel Ketchum (editor). *Uncanny X-Men #500–544*. New York: Marvel Comics, 2009–11.

Fradley, Martin. "What Do You Believe In? Film Scholarship and the Cultural Politics of the Dark Knight Franchise." *Film Quarterly* 66, no. 3 (2013): 15–27.

Fresson, Meggan, Thierry Meulemans, Benoit Dardenne and Marie Geurten. "Overdiagnosis of ADHD in Boys: Stereotype Impact on Neuropsychological Assessment." *Applied Neuropsychology: Child* (2018). Online. DOI 10.1080/21622965.2018.1430576.

Friedan, Betty. *The Second Stage*. Cambridge: Harvard University Press, 1998.

Gattis, Mark and Steven Moffat. *Sherlock*. Created by Mark Gattis and Steven Moffat. 2010–present; Cardiff: BBC Television.

Genette, Gérard. *Palimpsests: Literature in the Second Degree*. Translated by Channa Newman and Claude Doubinsky. Lincoln: University of Nebraska Press, 1997.

Gillen, Kieron (writer), Carlos Pacheco (penciler), Rodney Buchemi (penciler), Greg Land (penciler), Billy Tan (penciler), Michael Del Mundo (penciler), Brandon Peterson (penciler and inker), Paco Diaz (penciler and inker), Dustin Weaver (penciler and inker), Ron Garney (penciler and inker), Luke Ross (penciler and inker), Daniel Acuña (penciler, inker and colorist) Jorge Molina (penciler, inker and colorist), Roger Bonet (inker), Walden Wong (inker), Cam Smith (inker), Jay Leisten (inker), Craig Yeung (inker), Frank D'armata (colorist), Rachelle Rosenberg (colorist), Jim Charalampidis (colorist), Dommo Sanchez Amara (colorist), Rex Lokus (colorist), Justin Ponsor (colorist), Larua Martin (colorist), Guru-eFX (colorist), Morry Hollowell (colorist), Matt Milla (colorist), Joe Caramagna (letterer), Nick Lowe (editor), Jordan D. White (editor), Daniel Ketchum (editor) and Sebastian Girner (editor). *Uncanny X-Men #1–20*. New York, Marvel Comics, 2011–12.

Giroux, Henry A. and P. Freire. "Pedagogy, Popular Culture and Public Life: An Introduction." In *Popular Culture, Schooling and Everyday Life*, edited by Henry A. Giroux and Roger I. Simon, 1–30. New York: Bergin and Carey, 1989.

Giroux, Henry A. *The Mouse that Roared: Disney and the End of Innocence*. Lanham: Rowman and Littlefield, 1999.

Gledhill, Evan Hayles. "Twenty Percent of His Body: Scar Tissue, Masculinity and Identity in *Arrow*." In *Arrow and Superhero Television*, edited by James F. Iaccino, Corey Barker and Myc Wiatrowski, 78–94. Jefferson: McFarland and Company, 2017.
Graves, Robert. *Irish Times*. June 22, 1950. Quoted in Brian Kennedy, *Dreams and Responsibilities: The State and the Arts in Independent Ireland*. London: The Arts Council, 1950.
Gray, Jonathan. *Show Sold Separately: Promos, Spoilers, and Other Media Paratexts*. New York: New York University Press, 2010.
Graydon, Danny. Conversation at 2nd The Superhero Project Global Meeting. September 9, 2016.
Green, Adam Isaiah, "Gay but Not Queer: Toward a Post-Queer Study of Sexuality." *Theory and Society* 31, no. 4 (2002): 521–45.
Greer, Stephen. "Queer (Mis)recognition in the BBC's *Sherlock*." *Adaptation* 8, no. 1 (2015): 50–67.
Guerrasio, Jason. "The 10 Highest-Grossing Movies of 2017 that Ruled the Box Office." *Business Insider UK*. December 19, 2017. http://uk.businessinsider.com/highest-grossing-movies-of-2017-list-2017-12?r=USandIR=T/#5-guardians-of-the-galaxy-vol-2-8635-million-6.
Gunn, James, dir. *Guardians of the Galaxy*. 2014; Burbank: Marvel Studios.
Hale, Sadie E. and T. Ojeda. "Acceptable Femininity? Gay Male Misogyny and the Policing of Queer Femininities." *European Journal of Women's Studies* 25, no. 3 (2018): 310–24.
Hall, Kelley, J. and Betsy Lucal. "Tapping into Parallel Universes: Using Superhero Comic Books in Sociology Courses." *Teaching Sociology* 27, no. 1 (1999): 60–66.
Hampf, Michaela M. *Release a Man for Combat: The Women's Army Corps during World War II*. Köln: Böhlau Verlag, 2010.
Hanley, Tim. *Wonder Woman Unbound: The Curious History of the World's Most Famous Heroine*. Chicago: Chicago Review Press, 2014.
Hans, Ann P. and Andrew Lane. "Collecting Sexual Orientation and Gender Identity Data in Suicide and Other Violent Deaths: A Step toward Identifying and Addressing LGBT Morality Disparities." *LGBT Health* 2, no. 1, (2015): 84–87.
Harding, Maebh. "Marriage Equality: A Seismic Shift for Family Law in Ireland." In *International Survey of Family Law: 2016 Edition*, edited by Bill Atkin, 255–76. London: Family Law, 2016.
Harris, Daniel. *The Rise and Fall of Gay Culture*. New York: Ballantine Books, 1997.
Harrison, Kelby. *Deceit: The Ethics of Passing*. Plymouth: Lexington Books, 2013.
"Harry Rulon-Miller '51 Invitational." *Princeton Day School*. December 8, 2017. https://issuu.com/princetondayschool/docs/hrm_program_17_for_issuu.
Hawes, James, dir. *Doctor Who*, Season 1, Episode 9, "The Empty Child." Aired May 21, 2005, on BBC One.
Heinecken, Dawn. *The Warrior Women of Television: A Feminist Cultural Analysis of the New Female Body in Popular Media*. New York: Peter Lang Publishing, 2003.
Hermann, Andrew. "Daniel Amos and Me: The Power of Pop Culture and Autoethnography." *The Popular Culture Studies Journal* 1, no. 1 (2013): 6–17.
Hermes, Joke. "Father Knows Best? The Post-Feminist Male and Parenting in *24*." In *Reading 24: TV against the Clock*, edited by Steven Peacock. London: I. B. Tauris, 2007.
Hill, James, dir. *The Avengers*. Season 4, Episode 21, "A Touch of Brimstone." Aired February 19, 1966, on ABC.
Hird, Myra J. "Gender's Nature: Intersexuality, Transsexualism and the 'Sex'/'Gender' Binary." *Feminist Theory* 1, no. 3 (2000): 347–64.

Hochschild, Arlie Russell. *The Managed Heart: Commercialization of Human Feeling*. Berkeley: University of California Press, 1983.

Hockenos, Paul. "Poland and the Uncontrollable Fury of Europe's Far Right." *The Atlantic*. November 15, 2017. https://www.theatlantic.com/international/archive/2017/11/europe-far-right-populist-nazi-poland/524559/.

Holland, Janet, Caroline Ramazanoglu, Sue Sharpe, and Rachel Thomson. *The Male in the Head: Young People, Heterosexuality and Power*. London: The Tufnell Press, 1998.

HSE. "Cancer Mortality Statistics Ireland." HSE. 2016. http://www.hse.ie/eng/services/list/5/cancer/pubs/intelligence/registrydata.html.

hUltacháin, Ciarán Ó, Rachel Mathews-McKay and Bego Urain. *Burning Issues 2, Responses*. Dublin: National LGBT Federation, 2016.

IMDb. "Christopher Reeve." August 12, 2018. https://www.imdb.com/name/nm0001659/bio?ref_=nm_ov_bio_sm.

Inglis, Tom. *Moral Monopoly: The Rise and Fall of the Catholic Church in Modern Ireland*. Dublin: UCD Press, 1998.

Jackson, Susan M., and Fiona Cram. "Disrupting the Sexual Double Standard: Young Women's Talk about Heterosexuality." *British Journal of Social Psychology* 42, no. 1 (2003): 113–27.

Jarvis, Nigel. "The Inclusive Masculinities of Heterosexual Men within UK Gay Sports Club." *International Review for the Sociology of Sport* 50, no. 3 (2015): 238–300.

Jeffords, Susan. *Hard Bodies: Hollywood Masculinity in the Reagan Era*. New Brunswick: Rutgers University Press, 1994.

Jenkins, Henry. *The Wow Climax: Tracing the Emotional Impact of Popular Culture*. New York: New York University Press, 2006.

Johnson, Catherine. "*Doctor Who* as a Programme Brand." *New Dimensions of Doctor Who: Adventures in Space, Time and Television*, edited by Matt Hills. London: I. B. Tauris, 2013.

Johnson, Paul Elliott. "The Art of Masculine Victimhood: Donald Trump's Demagoguery." *Women's Studies in Communication* 40, no 3 (2017): 230–34.

Learned Hand, Billings. Quoted in Peter Coogan. "The Definition of the Superhero." In *A Comic Studies Reader*, edited by Jeet Heer and Kent Worcester. 77–93. Jackson: University Press of Mississippi, 2009.

Kaveney, Roz. *Superheroes! Capes and Crusaders in Comics and Films*. London: I. B. Tauris, 2008.

Kimmel, Michael. *Angry White Men. American Masculinity at the End of an Era*. London: Hachette, 2017.

Kimmel, Michael. "Solving the 'Boy Crisis' in Schools." *Huffington Post*. April 30, 2013. https://www.huffingtonpost.com/michael-kimmel/solving-the-boy-crisis-in_b_3126379.html?guccounter=1.

Klapp, Orrin E. "Heroes, Villains and Fools, as Agents of Social Control." *American Sociological Review* 19, no. 1 (1954): 56–62.

Klein, Alan. "Comic Book Masculinity." *Sport in Society* 10, no. 6 (2007): 1073–119.

Korte, Gregory. "Military Draft: Judge Rules Male-Only Draft is Unconstitutional." *USA Today*, February 24, 2019. https://eu.usatoday.com/story/news/nation/2019/02/24/military-draft-judge-rules-male-only-registration-unconstitutional/2968872002/.

Kring, Tim. *Heroes*. 2006–10; New York. NBC Studios.

Krueger, Jim (writer), Alex Ross (writer), John Paul Lennon (penciler), Bill Reinhold (inker), Matt Hollingsworth (colorist), Marie Javins (editor), and Polly Watson (editor). *Earth X #0*. New York: Marvel Comics, 1999.

Lacey, Brian. *Terrible Queer Creatures: Homosexuality in Irish History*. Dublin: Wordwell, 2015.

Laiou, Alexandra, Katerina Folla, George Yannis, Robert Bauer, Klaus Machata, Christian Brandstaetter, Pete Thomas, and Alan Kirk. "Comparative Analysis of Road Accidents by Gender in Europe." *Injury Prevention* 22, no. 2 (2016): A305.

Lane, Anthony. "Duels and Rules." *The New Yorker*. April 4, 2016. http://www.newyorker.com/magazine/2016/04/04/batman-v-superman-and-francofonia.

Lanier, Trevor Matthew. "The Supermen of the Justice League and X-Men: Comic Book Representations of Masculinity for Today's Audience." Cambridge: Emmanuel College, 2010. Thesis.

Lemire, Jeff (writer), Humberto Ramos (penciler), Victor Olazaba (inker), Edgar Delgado (colorist), Joe Caramagna (colorist), Daniel Ketchum (editor), Christina Harrington (editor), and Mark Paniccia (editor). *Extraordinary X-Men #1*. New York: Marvel Comics, 2016.

Lemire, Jeff (writer), Charles Soule (writer), Leinil Francis Yu (penciler and inker), Gerry Alanguilan (inker), David Curiel (colorist), Clayton Cowles (letterer), Wil Moss (editor), Daniel Ketchum (editor), Charles Beacham (editor), Chris Robinson (editor), Nick Lowe (editor), and Mark Paniccia (editor). *Inhumans vs. X-Men #6*. New York: Marvel Comics, 2017.

Lendrum, Rod. "Queering Super-Manhood. Superhero Masculinity, Camp and Public Relations as a Textual Framework." *International Journal of Comic Art* 7, no. 1 (2005): 287–303.

Levine, Martin P. and Michael S. Kimmel. *Gay Macho: The Life and Death of the Homosexual Clone*. New York: New York University Press, 1998.

Lewis, David A. "Save the Day." In *What Is A Superhero?* edited by Robin S. Rosenberg, 31–42. New York: Oxford University Press, 2013.

Light, Claire. "Sense8 and the Failure of Global Imagination." *Nerds of Colour*. June 10, 2015. https://thenerdsofcolor.org/2015/06/10/sense8-and-the-failure-of-global-imagination/.

Liebes, Tamar, and Elihu Katz. *The Export of Meaning: Cross-Cultural Readings of "Dallas."* Cambridge: Polity, 1993.

Llamas-Rodriguez, Juan. "Working Out as Creative Labor, or the Building of the Male Superhero's Body." In *Arrow and Superhero Television*, edited by James F. Iaccino, Corey Barker, and Myc Wiatrowski, 61–77. Jefferson: McFarland and Company, 2017.

Lobdell, Scott (writer), Tom Morgan (penciler), Chris Ivy (inker), Bob Sharen (colorist), Janic Chiang (letterer), and Bobbie Chase (editor). *Alpha Flight #102*. New York: Marvel Comics, 1992.

Lobdell, Scott (writer), Mark Pacella (penciler), Dan Panosian (inker), Bob Sharen (colorist), Janic Chiang (letterer), Bobbie Chase (editor), and Chris Cooper (editor). *Alpha Flight #106*. New York: Marvel Comics, 1992.

Lobdell, Scott (writer), Joe Madureira (penciler), Terry Austin (inker), Dan Green (inker), Steve Buccellato (colorist), Chris Eliopoulos (letterer), and Bob Harras (editor). *Uncanny X-Men #316*. New York: Marvel Comics, 1994.

Lobdell, Scott (writer), Joe Madureira (penciler), Dan Green (inker), Steve Buccellato (colorist), Chris Eliopoulos (letterer), and Bob Harras (editor). *Uncanny X-Men #317*. New York: Marvel Comics, 1994.

Lobdell, Scott (writer), Roger Cruz (penciler), Tim Townsend (inker), Steve Buccellato (colorist), Chris Eliopoulos (letterer), and Bob Harras (editor). *Uncanny X-Men #318*. New York: Marvel Comics, 1994.

Lobdell, Scott (writer), Chris Bachalo (penciler), Mark Buckingham (inker), Richard Starkings (letterer), Comicraft (letterer), and Bob Harras (editor). *Generation X #6*. New York: Marvel Comics, 1995.

Loomis, Charles. *Fundamental Concepts of Sociology*. Oxford: American Books, 1940.

Lynch, Kathleen, John Baker, and Maureen Lyons. "Introduction." In *Affective Equality: Love, Care and Injustice*, edited by Kathleen Lynch, John Baker, and Maureen Lyons, 1–11. London: Palgrave Macmillan, 2009.

Lynch, Kathleen and Judy Walsh. "Love, Care and Solidarity: What Is and Is Not Commodifiable." In *Affective Equality: Love, Care and Injustice*, edited by Kathleen Lynch, John Baker and Maureen Lyons, 35–53. London: Palgrave Macmillan, 2009.

Mahdawi, Arwa. "The Trouble of the LGBT Right Wing." *The Guardian*. October 26, 2017. https://www.theguardian.com/commentisfree/2017/oct/26/ascent-lgbt-right-wing-afd

Mahn, Gerri. "Fatal Attractions: Wolverine, the Hegemonic Male and the Crisis of Masculinity in the 1990s." In *The Ages of the X-Men: Essays on the Children of the Atom in Changing Times*, edited by Joseph J. Darowski, 335–56. Jefferson: McFarland and Company, 2014.

Malkin, Marc. "Spider-Man's Shirtless Audition." *E!News*. May 7, 2007. https://www.eonline.com/news/59203/spider-man-s-shirtless-audition.

Mangold, James, dir. *The Wolverine*. 2013; Los Angeles: 20th Century Fox.

Mangold, James, dir. *Logan*. 2017; Los Angeles: 20th Century Fox.

Massumi, Brian. *A User's Guide to Capitalism and Schizophrenia: Deviations from Deleuze and Guattari*. Cambridge: MIT Press, 1992.

McElhenny, Rob. "Look, it's not that hard." *Instagram*. September 6, 2018. https://www.instagram.com/p/BnXtEz1BLFP/.

McNally, Victoria. "Why 2016 is the Year We Need to Stop Pretending Women Aren't Geeks." *MTV*. December 22, 2015. http://www.mtv.com/news/2683640/geek-media-numbers-breakdown/.

Medhurst, Andy. "One Queen and His Screen." In *Queer TV: Theories, Histories, Politics*, edited by Glynn Davis and Gary Needham, 79–88. Abingdon: Taylor and Francis, 2008.

Medhurst, Andy. "Batman, Deviance and Camp." In *The Superhero Reader*, edited by Charles Hatfield, Jeet Heer, and Kent Worcester, 237–50. Jackson: University Press of Mississippi, 2013.

Metacritic. "Batman V Superman: Dawn of Justice." Accessed July 4, 2018. http://www.metacritic.com/movie/batman-v-superman-dawn-of-justice.

Meyer, Moe. *Reclaiming the Discourse of Camp in the Politics and Poetics of Camp*. London and New York: Routledge, 1994.

Miklaszewski, Jim and Halimah Abdullah. "All Combat Roles Now Open to Women, Pentagon Says." *NBC News*. December 3, 2015. https://www.nbcnews.com/news/us-news/pentagon-nbc-news-all-combat-roles-now-open-women-n473581.

Miller, Mark (writer), Steve McNiven (penciler), Dexter Vines (inker), Mark Morales (inker), Jay Liesten (inker), Morry Hollowell (colorist), Christina Strain (colorist), Justin Ponsor (colorist), Jason Kieth (colorist), Paul Mounts (colorist), Nathan Fairbairn (colorist), Cory Petit (letterer), John Barber (editor), Michael Horwitz (editor), Aubrey Sitterson (editor), Axel Alonso (editor), and Jody Lehoup (editor). *Wolverine #66–72*. New York: Marvel Comics, 2008–9.

Miller, Mark (writer), Steve McNiven (penciler), Dexter Vines (inker), Mark Morales (inker), Molly Hollowell (colorist), Cory Petit (letterer), Jeanine Schaefer (editor), John Barber (editor), Jody Leheup (editor), and Axel Alonso (editor). *Wolverine: Old Man Logan Giant Size #1*. New York: Marvel Comics, 2009.

Mittell, Jason. *Complex TV: The Poetics of Contemporary Television Storytelling*. New York: New York University Press, 2015.

Morris, Max, and Eric Anderson. "Charlie is So Cool Like: Authenticity, Popularity and Inclusive Masculinity on Youtube." *Sociology* 49, no. 6 (2015): 1200–1217.

Morrison, Grant (writer), Frank Quitely (penciler), Ethan Van Sciver (penciler), Tom Derenick (penciler), John Paul Leon (penciler), Phil Jiminez (penciler), Keron Grant (penciler), Chris Bachalo (penciler), Marc Silvestri (penciler), Igor Kordey (penciler and inker), Frank Quitely (penciler and inker), Tim Townsend (inker), Mark Morales (inker), Dan Green (inker), Prentiss Rollins (inker), Scott Hanna (inker), Sandu Florea (inker), Richard Perrotta (inker), Danny Miki (inker), Bill Sienkiewicz (inker), Andy Lanning (inker), Norm Rapmund (inker), Avalon Studios (inker), Al Vey (inker), Aaron Sowd (inker), Simon Coleby (inker), Matt Banning (inker), Joe Weems (inker), Billy Tan (inker), Eric Basaloua (inker), Brian Haberlin (colorist), Hi-Fi Design (colorist), Dave McCraig (colorist), Chris Chuckry (colorist), Steve Firchow (colorist), Matt Milla (colorist), John Starr (colorist), Comicraft (letterer), Richard Starkings (letterer), Saida Temofonte (letterer), Albert Deschesne (letterer), Chris Eliopoulos (letterer), Rus Wooton (letterer), Pete Franco (editor), Mark Powers (editor), Mike Raicht (editor), Nova Ren Suma (editor), Warren Simons (editor), Anne Thornton (editor), Stephanie Moore (editor), Cory Sedlmeier (editor), and Mike Marts (editor). *New X-Men #114–154*. New York: Marvel Comics, 2001–5.

Morrison, Grant. *Supergods: Our World in the Age of the Superhero*. London: Jonathan Cape, 2011.

Mosher, Donald L., and Silvan S. Tomkins. "Scripting the Macho Man: Hypermasculine Socialization and Encultration." *The Journal of Sex Research* 25, no. 1 (1988): 60–84.

Mulder, James. "'Believe It or Not, This is Power': Embodied Crisis and the Superhero Film." *Journal of Popular Culture* 50, no. 5 (2017): 1047–64.

Mulvey, Laura. "Visual Pleasure and Narrative Cinema." *Screen* 16, no. 3 (1975): 6–18.

Neale, Steve. "Masculinity as Spectacle: Reflections on Men and Mainstream Cinema." *Screen* 24, no. 6 (1983): 2–16.

Ngozi Adichi, Chimamanda. *We Should All Be Feminists*. London: Fourth Estate, 2014.

Nicieza, Fabian (writer), Andy Kubert (penciler), Matt Ryan (inker), Kevin Somers (colorist), Bill Oakley (letterer), and Bob Harras (editor). *X-Men #36*. New York: Marvel Comics, 1994.

Nicieza, Fabian (writer), Andy Kubert (penciler), Matt Ryan (inker), Mike Sellers (inker), Kevin Somers (colorist), Bill Oakley (letterer), and Bob Harras (editor). *X-Men #37*. New York: Marvel Comics, 1994.

Nicieza, Fabian (writer), Andy Kubert (penciler), Matt Ryan (inker), Mike Sellers (inker), Kevin Somers (colorist), Bill Oakley (letterer), and Bob Harras (editor). *X-Men #37*. New York: Marvel Comics, 1994.

Nolan, Christopher, dir. *The Dark Knight Rises*. 2012; Burbank: Warner Bros. Pictures.

Obedin-Maliver, Juno. "Time for OBGYNs to Care for People of All Genders." *Journal of Women's Health* 24, no. 2 (2015): 109–11.

Pachankis, John. "Socially Anxiety in Young Gay Men." *Journal of Anxiety Disorders* 20, no. 8 (2006): 996–1015.

Pak, Greg (writer), Greg Land (penciler), Matt Ryan (inker), Justin Ponsor (colorist), Clem Robins (letterer), Sean Ryan (editor), Mike Marts, Nick Lowe (editor), and Stephanie Moore. *X-Men Phoenix Endsong #1–5*. New York: Marvel Comics, 2005.

Pagello, Federico. "The 'Origin Story' is the Only Story: Seriality and Temporality in Superhero Fiction from Comics to Post-Television." *Quarterly Review of Film and Video* 34, no. 8 (2017): 725–45.

Parke, Cole. "The Christian Right's Love Affair with Anti-Trans Feminists." *Political Research Associates*. August 11, 2016. https://www.politicalresearch.org/2016/08/11/the-christian-rights-love-affair-with-anti-trans-feminists/.

Parker, Ian. *Discourse Dynamics*. London and New York: Routledge, 1992.

Pascoe, C. J. *Dude, You're A Fag: Masculinity and Sexuality in High School*. Berkeley: University of California Press, 2007.

Peppard, Anna. Qtd. from a personal email exchange. March 3, 2018.

Philips, Rosemary R. "The Battle over Bathrooms: Schools, Courts, and Transgender Rights." *Theory in Action* 10, no 4 (2017): 100–104.

Phipps, Alison and Isabel Young. "'Lad Culture' in Higher Education: Agency in the Sexualization Debates." *Sexualities* 18, no. 4 (2015): 459–79.

Piacenza, Joanna. "Superhero Movies Possess Staying Power with Viewers, but Moviegoers Say They Want to Wee More Diverse Characters." *Morning Consult*. April 26, 2018. https://morningconsult.com/2018/04/26/superhero-movies-possess-staying-power-with-viewers/.

RAC Foundation. "Mortality Statistics and Road Traffic Accidents in the UK." 2011. http://www.racfoundation.org/assets/rac_foundation/content/downloadables/road%20accident%20casualty%20comparisons%20-%20box%20-%20110511.pdf.

Raimi, Sam, dir. *Spider-Man*. 2002; Los Angeles: Sony Pictures.

Rapp, Nicolas, and Krishna Thakker. "Harry Potter at 20: Billions in Box Office Revenue, Millions of Books Sold." *Fortune*. June 26, 2017. http://fortune.com/2017/06/26/harry-potter-20th-anniversary/.

Reeser, Todd W. *Masculinities in Theory: An Introduction*. Sussex: Wiley-Blackwell, 2010.

Rehling, Nicola. *Extra-Ordinary Men: White Heterosexual Masculinity in Contemporary Popular Cinema*. Plymouth: Lexington Books, 2009.

Reigeluth, Christopher and Michael Addis. "'Adolescent Boys' Experiences with Policing of Masculinity: Forms, Functions, and Consequences." *Psychology of Men and Masculinity* 17, no. 1 (2015): 74–83.

Renfrow, Daniel. "A Cartography of Passing in Everyday Life." *Symbolic Interaction* 27, no. 4 (2011): 485–506.

Riedel, Sam. "Batman v Superman v Misogyny: The Antifeminism of Dawn of Justice." *Bitch Media*. March 13, 2016. https://www.bitchmedia.org/article/batman-v-superman-v-misogyny-antifeminism-dawn-justice.

Rosenberg, Matthew (writer), Leinil Francis Yu (penciler), Gerry Alanguilan (inker), Rachelle Rosenberg (colorist), Travis Lanham (letterer), Mark Paniccia (editor), Christina Harrington (editor), Chris Robinson (editor), and Darren Shan (editor). *Phoenix: Resurrection #1*. New York: Marvel Comics, 2018.

Rotten Tomatoes. "Batman v Superman: Dawn of Justice." Accessed 28 April 2018. https://www.rottentomatoes.com/m/batman_v_superman_dawn_of_justice/?search=Batman V Superman.

Rottenberg, Catherine. "Neoliberal Feminism and the Future of Human Capital." *Signs: Journal of Women in Culture and Society* 42, no. 2 (2017): 329–48.
Rowling, J. K. *Harry Potter and the Philosopher's Stone*. London: Bloomsbury, 1997.
Rowling, J. K. *Harry Potter and the Chamber of Secrets*. London: Bloomsbury, 1998.
Rowling, J. K. *Harry Potter and the Goblet of Fire*. London: Bloomsbury, 2000.
Rowling, J. K. *Harry Potter and the Order of the Phoenix*. London: Bloomsbury, 2003.
Rowling, J. K. *Harry Potter and the Half Blood Prince*. London: Bloomsbury, 2005.
Rowling, J. K. *Harry Potter and the Deathly Hallows*. London: Bloomsbury, 2007.
Rucka, Greg (writer), J. H. Williams III (penciler), Tod Klein (letterer), Dave Stewart (colorist), and Michael Siglain (editor). *Batwoman: Elegy*. Burbank: DC Comics, 2010.
Ryan, Michael, and Douglass Kellner. *Camera Politica: The Politics and Ideology of Contemporary Hollywood Film*. Bloomington: Indiana University Press, 1988.
Samaritans. "Suicide Statistics Report 2017." August 12, 2018. https://www.samaritans.org/sites/default/files/kcfinder/files/Suicide_statistics_report_2017_Final.pdf.
Scharrer, Erica. "Men, Muscles, and Machismo: The Relationship between Television Violence Exposure and Aggression and Hostility in the Presence of Hypermasculinity." *Media Psychology* 3, no. 2 (2001): 159–88.
Scharrer, Erica. "Hypermasculinity, Aggression, and Television Violence: An Experiment." *Media Psychology* 7, no. 4 (2005): 353–76.
Schott, Gareth. "From Fan Appropriation to Industry Re-Appropriation: The Sexual Identity of Comic Superheroes." *Journal of Graphic Novels and Comics* 1, no. 1 (2010): 17–29.
Schreckinger, Ben. "Trump on Protester: 'I'd like to punch him in the face.'" Politico. February 23, 2016. https://www.politico.com/story/2016/02/donald-trump-punch-protester-219655.
Schumacher, Joel, dir. *Batman Forever*. 1995; Burbank: Warner Bros. Pictures.
Schumacher, Joel, dir. *Batman and Robin*. 1997; Burbank: Warner Bros. Pictures.
Schur, Michael, and Greg Daniels. Parks and Recreation. Created by Michael Schur and Greg Daniels. 2009–15; New York: NBC Studios.
Scott, Anthony Oliver. "Review: Batman v Superman . . . V Fun?" *The New York Times*. March 23, 2016. http://www.nytimes.com/2016/03/25/movies/review-batman-v-superman-dawn-of-justice-when-super-friends-fight.html?_r=0.
Segal, Lynne. *Slow Motion: Changing Masculinities, Changing Men*. London: Virago, 1990.
Serpe, Nick. "Trump Disrupts the Valley." *Dissent* 64, no. 4 (2017): 75–81.
Singer, Bryan, dir. *X-Men*. 2000; Los Angeles: 20th Century Fox.
Singer, Bryan, dir. *X2*. 2003; Los Angeles: 20th Century Fox.
Singer, Marc. "The Myth of Eco: Cultural Populism and Comics Studies." *Studies in Comics* 4, no. 2 (2013): 355–66.
Slaughter, Anne-Marie. "Why Women Still Can't Have It All." *The Atlantic*, August 15, 2012. https://www.theatlantic.com/magazine/archive/2012/07/why-women-still-cant-have-it-all/309020/.
Slaughter, Anne-Marie. *Unfinished Business: Women, Men, Work, Family*. New York: Random House, 2016.
Smith, Clancy. "Days of Future Past: Segregation, Oppression and Technology in X-Men and America." In *The Agency of the X-Men: Essays on the Children of the Atom in Changing Times*, edited by Joseph J. Darowski, 63–76. Jefferson: McFarland and Company, 2014.
Smith, Derek J. "Porno, Crooks, and Comic Books." *UncannyDerek*. December 19, 2010. https://uncannyderek.com/2010/12/19/my-land-or-your-land/.

Snape, Joel. "Hugh Jackman Workout: How He Got Ripped for Wolverine." *Coach Mag.* March 31, 2016. http://www.coachmag.co.uk/exercises/celebrity-workouts/146/exclusive-hugh-jackman-wolverine-workout.

Snyder, Zack, dir. *Batman v Superman: Dawn of Justice*. 2016; Burbank: Warner Bros. Pictures.

Stuller, Jennifer. *Ink-stained Amazons and Cinematic Warriors: Superwomen in Modern Mythology*. London: I. B. Tauris, 2010.

Strass, Bob. "Interview: Stan Lee." *The Guardian*. August 11, 2000. https://www.theguardian.com/film/2000/aug/12/features.

Stray Melanie. *Online Hate Crime Report 2017: Challenging Online Homophobia, Biphobia and Transphobia*. London: Galop, 2017.

Stroman, Susan, dir. *The Producers*. 2005; Los Angeles: Brooksfilms.

Sherman, Yael D. "Miss Congeniality." In *Feminism at the Movies: Understanding Gender in Contemporary Popular Cinema*, edited by Hilary Radner and Rebecca Stringer, 80–92. London and New York: Routledge: 2011.

Taneja, Amit. "From Oppressor to Activist: Reflections of a Feminist Journey." In *Men Speak Out: Views on Gender, Sex and Power*, edited by Shira Tarrant, 243–51. London and New York: Routledge, 2013.

Taylor, Aaron. "'He's Gotta Be Strong, and He's Gotta Be Fast, and He's Gotta Be Larger Than Life': Investigating the Engendered Superhero Body." *Journal of Popular Culture* 40, no. 2 (2007): 344–76.

The Statistics Portal. "Number of Mass Shootings in the United States between 1982 and June 2018, by Shooter's Gender." June 2018. https://www.statista.com/statistics/476445/mass-shootings-in-the-us-by-shooter-s-gender/.

Trujillo, Nick. "Hegemonic Masculinity on the Mound: Media Representations of Nolan Ryan and American Sports Culture." *Critical Studies in Mass Communication* 8, no. 3 (1991): 290–308.

United Nations. "Gender Equality." August 12, 2018. https://www.un.org/sustainabledevelopment/gender-equality/.

Vokey, Megan, Bruce Tefft, and Chris Tysiaczny. "An Analysis of Hyper-Masculinity in Magazine Advertisements." *Sex Roles* 68, no. 9 (2013): 562–76.

Ward, Jane. *Not Gay: Sex Between Straight White Men*. New York: New York University Press, 2015.

Warner Bros. Pictures. "Batman v Superman: Dawn of Justice—Official Trailer 2." *Youtube*. December 2, 2015. http://www.youtube.com/watch?v=fis-9Zqu2Ro.

Warren, Ellis (writer), John Cassaday (artist), and Laura Martin (colorist). *Planetary*. Burbank: Wildstorm [DC Comics], 1998–2009.

Waters, Emily, Larissa Pham, and Chelsea Convery. *A Report on Lesbian, Gay, Bisexual and Queer Hate Violence Homicides in 2017*. New York: National Coalition of Anti-Violence Programs, 2017.

Way, Ashley, dir. *Torchwood*. Season 2, Episode 1, "Kiss Kiss, Bang Bang." Aired January 16, 2008, on BBC Two.

Weis, Don, dir. *Batman*. Season 1, Episode 5, "The Joker is Wild." Aired January 26, 1966, on ABC.

Weldon, Glen. *The Caped Crusade: Batman and the Rise of Nerd Culture*. New York: Simon and Schuster, 2016.

Wetherell, Margaret, and Nigel Edley. "A Discursive Framework for Analyzing Men and Masculinities." *Psychology of Men and Masculinity* 15, no. 4 (2014): 355–64.

Wetherell, Margaret, and Nigel Edley. "Negotiating Hegemonic Masculinity: Imaginary Positions and Psycho-Discursive Practices." *Feminism and Psychology* 9, no. 2 (1999): 335–56.

Wharton, Amy S. "The Sociology of Emotional Labour." *Annual Review of Sociology* 35, no. 1 (2009): 147–65.

Wheatley, Helen. *Spectacular Television: Exploring Televisual Pleasure*. London: I. B. Tauris, 2016.

Wheeler, Andrew. "House of Xavier: How the X-Men Represent Queer Togetherness [Mutant and Proud]." *Comics Alliance*. June 16, 2014. http://comicsalliance.com/mutant-proud-xmen-lgbt-rights-family-community-identity/.

Whedon, Joss. *Buffy the Vampire Slayer*. Created by Joss Whedon. 1997–2003; Los Angeles: Twentieth Century Fox Television.

Whedon, Joss (writer), John Cassaday (penciler and inker), Laura Martin (colorist), Chris Eliopoulos (letterer), Joe Caramagna (letterer), Mike Marts (editor), Nick Lowe (editor), Andy Schmidt (editor), and Axel Alonso (editor). *Astonishing X-Men #1–24*. New York: Marvel Comics, 2004–8.

Whedon, Joss (writer), John Cassaday (penciler and inker), Laura Martin (colorist), Chris Eliopoulos (letterer), Axel Alonso (editor), Nick Lowe (editor) and Will Panzo (editor). *Giant Size Astonishing X-Men #1*. New York: Marvel Comics, 2008.

Whedon, Joss, dir. *Avengers Assemble*. 2012; Burbank: Marvel Studios.

Wilder, Billy, dir. *Ace in the Hole*. 1951; Los Angeles: Paramount Pictures.

Williams, Raymond. *Problems in Materialism and Culture*. London: Verso, 1980.

Wood, Brian (writer), Ron Lim (penciler), Sandu Florea (inker), Randy Elliott (inker), VLM (colorist), Richard Starkings (letterer), Comicraft (letterer), and Matt Hicks (editor). *Generation X #75*. New York: Marvel Comics, 2001.

Wooden, Shannon, and Ken Gillam. *Pixar's Boys Stories: Masculinity in a Post Modern Age*. New York: Cowman and Littlefield, 2014.

WWE Raw. Event RAW #1159. USA Network, August 10, 2015.

Young, Terence, dir. *Thunderball*. 1965; Los Angeles: United Artists.

CONTRIBUTORS

ESTHER DE DAUW is a Comic Studies scholar who focuses on the intersection of gender and race. Awarded her PhD by the University of Leicester in 2018, she teaches and provides student support at the University of Leicester.

DANIEL J. CONNELL is an independent researcher whose work focuses on deconstructing hypermasculinity in various mediums. His PhD, awarded by Brunel University in 2011, focuses on the hypermasculine phenomenon in the fledgling comic book literary fiction genre.

CRAIG HASLOP is a Lecturer in Media Studies at the University of Liverpool. Craig currently researches digital toxic masculinities and queerness in cult television.

DREW MURPHY is a postgraduate researcher with the Genders and Sexualities research group in the Limerick Institute of Technology. His current focus is on the ways in which gay and bisexual men in Ireland negotiate masculine identities and how these men use language to perform and modify their identities in various settings. His research interests are focused on the areas of identities, the LGBTQ experience, and gendered performances.

RICHARD REYNOLDS teaches at Central Saint Martins in London. He is a writer, lecturer, occasional broadcaster, and ex-publisher. His best-known work on comics is *Superheroes: A Modern Mythology*.

JANNE SALMINEN is a doctoral student at the University of Helsinki. He is currently writing his dissertation on the gender narratives of serialized blockbuster films. While most of his research revolves around gender, his other interests include diversity, popular culture, queer narratives, US politics, technology, and fandom.

KAREN SUGRUE is sociology lecturer with the Limerick Institute of Technology since 2002 and a practicing psychotherapist since 2013. She has a research interest in the areas of equality and social justice, digital media, and popular culture and is an advocate and activist in the area of mental health and wellness. She is currently researching wellness and political activism.

JAMES C. TAYLOR is a Teaching Fellow at the University of Warwick's Department of Film and Television Studies. He is currently working on his forthcoming book, *The Superhero Blockbuster: Adaptation, Style, and Meaning* (University Press of Mississippi).

INDEX

Page numbers in **bold** indicate an illustration.

AIDS crisis, 94
Albus Dumbledore. *See* Dumbledore
Albus Potter, 150–51, 153, 161
All New X-Men, 95, 98
Amell, Stephen, 12, 34, 35, 39–49, **43**, **47**, 158; as Arrow/Oliver, 34, 35, 41–42, **42**, 45–49; "Meme Monday," 46–48; physicality, 41, **43**, 45, 46, 47, **47**; social media, 12, 35, 45–48; wrestling persona, 45–48. *See also* Arrow/Oliver
Andy Dwyer, 26, **26**
Ant-Man (2015), 32
antifeminism, 52
Arrow (2012–2020), 12, 34, 35, 39–49, **42**, 49n2
Arrow/Oliver, 12, 39–49, **42**, **43**, 49n13, 158; hegemonic masculinity, 34–35, 38–40, 41, 46, 48, 49; heteronomy, 43; male bodies, 41–43; male emotion, 38–39; origin story, 38–39; seriality, 36–37; Team Arrow, 39, 40, 43–44, 49; television masculinity, 37
Astonishing X-Men series, 130–31, **132**, 133
Avengers, The (2012), 29
Avengers vs. X-Men (2012), 94, 96, 97, 100n9, 138

Bale, Christian, 44–45
bat chevron, 83–84
Batman, 12, 44–45, 52–65, **59**, 80–81, 88n30; Adam West, 52; bat chevron, 83–84; Batman Incorporated, 83, 84; Bat-Signal, 83, 88n30; Ben Affleck, 53; Bruce Wayne, 53, 54–55, 56–57, 58, 62; Christian Bale, 44–45, **56**; crisis of masculinity, 54, 60–61, 62, 64–65; fragile masculinity, 54, 55–56; George Clooney, **56**; heteronormativity, 57, 58; hybrid masculinity, 55; hypermasculinity, 53, 55, 64, 160; Michael Keaton, **56**; origin story, 53; physicality, 55, 58; Superman dynamic, 53–54, 60, 61–62, 64–65; Val Kilmer, **56**
Batman (1966–1968), 52, 60, 67n33
Batman Begins (2005), 44–45
Batman Incorporated, 83, 84
Batman v Superman: Dawn of Justice (2016), 12, 52–65, **59**, 160
Bat-Signal, 83, 88n30
Batwoman, 13, 71–87, **85**; alignment with Batman, 80, 81, 83–84; family, 71–72, 74–76, 77, 81; Flamebird, 83–84; homosexuality, 78–79; masculine portrayal, 75–76, 77, 85, 86–87; military service, 77–79; monstrous femininity, 85–87, 159; origin story, 71–72, 77; paternal relationship, 71, 75–76, 77, 79–81; rejection of femininity, 75–76, 78–79, 80, 81; soldier identity, 77–79, 80, 84–87, 159; vigilantism, 79–80, 83, 84
Batwoman (2010–2015 comics), 71–87
Batwoman: Elegy (Rucka), 71–87
Baudrillard, Jean, 11–12, 19–21, 23, 31, 162
Bechdel Test, 150, 155n53
Beth Kane, 75–76, 77, 81
bisexuality, 13, 104, 113, 114
blood politics, 143–44
boy crisis, 144, 147–48, 154n18
Breitweiser, Mitch, 137–38

180

Bruce Wayne, 53, 54–55, 56–57, 58, 62. *See also* Batman
Butler, Judith, 3, 14, 62, 122, 126, 128, 130, 143, 160
Byrne, John, 122, **123**, 125, 126

camp, 4, 56, 103, 108, 109–10, 111–12, 114
Cassaday, John, 130, 131, **132**, 133
CGI, 19, 29, 32n3
Claremont, Chris, 89, 121, 122, 125
Colossus, 124, 136
Connell, Raewyn, 4, 35, 55, 59, 63, 146, 147, 161
Coogan, Peter, 106
crisis of masculinity, 14–15, 54, 60–61, 62, 64–65
cult of the body, 72
CW, 41–42, 43
Cyclops, 90, 96, 97–99, 100, 133, 161

Dark Phoenix Saga (1980), 95
Days of Future Past (2014 film), 93, 96, 99
Days of Future Past (comic), 91–93, 94, 95
DC, 6, 20, 81, 83, 122
Decimations (2005), 94
domestic spaces, 13, 79, 81–83, 84
Doomsday, 62–63
Dumbledore, 14–15, 143–53, 161; and Harry Potter, 146–47, 148–49, 150, 151; gender performance, 146–47; hegemonic masculinity, 147, 149; male emotion, 147, 148–49; origin story, 152; as role model, 148–49

Eco, Umberto, 12, 38
Emma Frost, 14, 121–39, **123**, 127, **132**, 159–60, 162; depictions, **123**, 124, 125–26, 127, **127**, 130–31, **132**, 133–34, **135**, 137–38, 160; Frank Quitely, 127, **127**; gender performance, 128, 129–30, 135, 138–39, 159–60; Greg Land, 133–34, **135**; Hellfire Club, 14, 121, 122–23, 129, 137; hypersexualization, 124, 125–26, 130–31, 133–34, **135**, 160; John Byrne, 122, **123**, 125, 126; John Cassaday, 130, 131, **132**, 133; Joss Whedon, 130, 131, 133; Kitty Pryde, 123–25, 126, 131, 133; Massachusetts Academy, 123–24, 126; Mitch Breitweiser, 137–38; origin stories, 128; Sadean Woman, 125; Scott Summers, 129–30, 131, 133, 134, 137, 138; secondary mutation, 126, 130, 138; sexual terrorist, 126; telepathic powers, 124, 128–29, 130, 131, 133, 134, 137, 138; villian to heroine, 126
Everyman, 21–22, 23, 24, 25, 26–28, 33n7
Extraordinary X-Men, 93, 95

Felicity (Team Arrow), 41, 43, **43**
female gaze, 11, 42, 43–44
female soldier/warrior, 72–73, 74–75, 77–79, 83, 84, 85–86, 87n5, 159
feminine identity, 71
femininity, 37, 39, 55, 58–59, 62, 65, 76, 77, 85, 110, 158
Flamebird, 83–84
Flash, The (2014–), 47, 49

Gabi Kane, 71–72, 74–75, 77
gay clone culture, 111, 114, 116n36
Gay Liberation Movement, 89–90
gender binary, 84, 108, 157, 159, 160
gender equality, 58–59
gender melancholia, 126, 130
gender performance, 14, 128, 129–30, 135, 138–39, 143, 146, 150, 159–60
gender roles, 3, 4, 36, 62, 63, 64, 65, 72–73, 75, 77, 86–87, 108–9, 142, 144, 146, 151–52, 157, 160
Generation X (1994), 126
Genosha, 126–27
Gotham, 81–83, 84, 85, 86
Guardians of the Galaxy (2014), 25–28, **27**, 30

Hank McCoy, 92, 93
hard masculinity, 82–83
Harry Potter, 15, 144–53
Harry Potter and the Chamber of Secrets (Rowling), 148
Harry Potter and the Cursed Child (2016), 144–45, 151, 161
Harry Potter and the Deathly Hallows (Rowling), 149, 150–51

Harry Potter and the Goblet of Fire (Rowling), 148
Harry Potter and the Order of the Phoenix (Rowling), 147, 151
Harry Potter and the Philosopher's Stone (Rowling), 146–47, 150
Harry Potter series, 143–53, 160
health intelligence, 145, 150
hegemonic masculinity, 4, 5–6, 10, 12–13, 34–35, 38–40, 41, 46, 48, 49, 52, 58, 59–61, 63, 65, 71, 87, 97, 98, 142, 146, 147, 149, 150, 151, 152, 153, 153n1, 157, 160, 161
Hellfire Club, 14, 121, 122–23, 129, 137
Hermione Granger, 144–45, 150
Heroes (2006–2010), 106
heroic intelligence, 145, 150
heteronormativity, 14, 40, 43, 57, 58, 62, 104, 114, 160
heterosexual masculinity, 57, 58, 61, 92, 98–100, 103, 109, 111, 112
hierarchical systems, 39, 84–85, 93, 162
homonormativity, 14
homosexuality, 57, 78, 92
House of M (2005), 94
Hulk, 29
hybrid masculinities, 5, 55, 158
hypermasculinity, 4–5, 11, 12, 14, 20–21, 22, 23, 25, 28, 29, 30–32, 53, 55, 64, 99, 109–14, 158, 160, 161
hyperreality, 19, 20–21, 32

Inhumans, 93–94, 95, 96–97, 101n18, 161
Inhumans vs. X-Men, 94, 95, 96, 138
intertext, 35, 48
Iron Man, 9, 23, 32, 33n7

Jack Harkness, 9, 13, 104–14
Jackman, Hugh, 21–25, **22**, **25**, 29–32, 41, 160
Jacob Kane, 71–72, 74–76, **75**, 77, 79–81, **80**, 83
Jason Wyngarde (Mastermind), 124, 125
Jean Grey, 95, 101n26, 122, 123, 124, 125, 126–27, 129
Jessica Jones (2015–2019), 9
John Hart, 13, 105–14
Joker, 61, 67n33

Kate Kane, 71–72, 74–87, **80**, 159. *See also* Batwoman
Kitty Pryde, 123–25, 126, 131, 133
Kurt Wagner (Nightcrawler), 135–36

Land, Greg, 133–34, **135**
Lee, Stan, 89
Legacy Virus, 94
Legends of Tomorrow (2016–), 49
Lex Luthor, 60–63, 65, 160
LGBTQIA+, 13, 63, 90, 92, 93, 95–97, 99–100, 104, 114, 161
Logan. *See* Wolverine
Logan (2017), 21, 29–31
Lois and Clark: The New Adventures of Superman (1993–1997), 34, 36
Lois Lane, 36, 59, 61, 63
Loki, 29
lone wolf narrative, 6
Lynch, Jessica, 72

Magneto, 97
Maguire, Tobey, 22, 23
male bodies, 6–7, 11–12, 21–24, 28, 30, 40–42, 43–44, 55, 58, 159, 160–61
male emotion, 38–39, 145, 146, 147–49, 150, 152
male gaze, 42, 122, 126, 131, 138
male savior/protector, 6, 12, 53, 58, 59–60, 62, 63, 73, 81–82, 83, 86, 88n28, 149, 151, 152, 160
male soldier/warrior, 72, 74–75, 77–78, 80, 84, 85, 86
Man of Steel (2013), 53, 60
Martha Kent, 59, 61
Marvel, 6, 14, 20, 89, 90, 91, 93, 97, 103, 121, 122, 125, 133
masculine authority, 45–46, 48
masculine ideals, 4, 6–7, 152
masculine/feminine dichotomy, 36, 37, 45, 53, 58, 59, 63, 65, 76, 77, 78, 86–87
Massachusetts Academy, 123–24, 126
McElhenney, Rob, 159, **159**
militaristic masculinity, 13, 39, 55, 57, 62, 66n18, 71, 73, 74, 76–78, 79, 80, 81, 84, 86–87, 159

monstrous femininity, 11, 13, 62, 85–87, 159
Ms. Marvel, 7, 7, 122
mutants, 89–100, 161

Natalia Mitternacht, 85
New X-Men #139 (2003), 129
Nolan, Christopher, 56
Northstar, 103–4

origin stories, 38, 39, 53, 71–72, 93–94, 101n19, 105–6, 128, 152
Other/Otherness/Othering, 13, 54, 58, 62, 76, 89, 90, 92, 94, 157

Pagello, Federico, 12, 38
paratext, 35, 45, 48
Parks and Recreation (2009–2015), 26, **26**
passing, 13, 90, 92–93, 94, 99–100, 114, 161
patriarchy, 4, 14, 32, 39, 58, 59, 65, 66n7, 82, 122, 137, 157
Peter Quill/Starlord, 25–28, **27**, **30**
Pixie, 134
plural masculinities, 107–8
plurality, 157
Policing of Masculinity, 146, 149–50
popular culture, 3–4, 5, 7, 10, 15, 52, 65, 73, 95, 142–43, 146, 150, 157–58, 161–62
post-feminism, 58–59, 65, 134, 136
Pratt, Chris, 25–28, **26**, **27**, **30**
Prince Namor, 136–37
Professor Xavier, 92
propoganda, 72

queer masculinity, 13, 106, 107–14
queerness, 14, 60–61, 62, 66n25, 90, 92, 94, 95, 96, 97, 98–99, 100, 103–4, 105, 106, 107–14
Quitely, Frank, 127, **127**

"real man," 57–58, 66n25, 151, 152
Reeve, Christopher, 19, 32n3
rejection of femininity, 75–76, 78–79, 80, 81
representation, 15
Rowland vs Tarr (1971), 72
Rudd, Paul, 32

Sadean Woman, 125
Salome myth, 137–38
Scott Summers, 129–30, 131, 133, 134, 137, 138
Sean Cassidy, 126
Sebastian Shaw, 124, 129, 136–37
Sentinels, 95, 126–27
Silver Age, 89
simulacrum, 11, 19, 21, 29, 31
Smallville (2001–2011), 34, 37
social media, 12, 35, 45–48, 158, 159, **159**
Spiderman (2002), 22
Star Trek franchise, 8
Stardust, 45, 47–48
status quo, of society, 38, 65, 66n25, 157, 160, 161
steroids, 29, 33n10
Storm, 8, 93, 122, 124
Stormwatch comics (2011–14), 81
subaltern masculinities, 4, 10, 55, 61, 65, 157–58, 160
superheroes: hypermasculinity, 11, 12, 21, 22–23, 30–31, 53, 55, 64, 110–12; market saturation, 7–8; mortality, 31, 55, 63, 94–95, 99, 101n26, 133, 147, 149, 151; origin stories, 38–39, 53, 71–72, 77, 93–94, 101n19, 105–6, 128, 152; physical transformation, 22, 23, 24–25, 26–27, 29, 32, 41; physicality, 7, 11–12, 21–24, 28, 30, 40–42, 43–44, 55, 58 (*see also* physical transformation); queer, 103, 104, 106–14; seriality, 36, 38, 41, 44–49; team, 39, 40, 83, 84; television, 7, 12, 19–34, 52
Superman, 12, 19, 36, 54, 55, 57–65, **59**, 106; Batman dynamic, 53–54, 60, 61–62, 64–65; Christopher Reeve, 19, 32n3; Dean Cain, 36; death, 55, 63; immigrant narrative, 54, 57–58; Lex Luthor, 60–63, 65; physicality, 58, 63
Superman/Batman dynamic, 53–54, 60, 61–62, 64–65

Team Arrow, 39, 40, 43–44, 49
television masculinity, 37
Tony Stark, 9, 23, 32, 33n7

Torchwood (2006–2011), 13, 103–14, 157, 159; bisexuality, 104, 113, 114; hypermasculinity, 109–14; Jack Harkness, 9, 13, 104–14; John Hart, 13, 105–14; "Kiss Kiss, Bang Bang," 105–14; origin story, 105–6; queer supermen/superheroes, 103, 104, 106–14
toxic femininity, 83, 84–85
toxic masculinity, 4–5, 10–11, 12, 15, 30, 112–14, 147, 149, 150, 157–62
transgender people, 63
Triple H, 45–46
Trump, Donald, 54–55, 96

Uncanny X-Men #129 (1980), 122, 123, 139n7
Uncanny X-Men #151, 126
Uncanny X-Men series (2008–2011), 133–38
United States Military Academy, 77–78

vigilantism, 12, 39, 58, 79–80, 83, 84
Voldemort, 144, 149, 151

Whedon, Joss, 130, 131, 133
white male ideal, 40, 54, 58, 60, 82, 88n28, 144
White Queen. *See* Emma Frost
Wolverine, 21–25, **22**, **25**, 29–32, 42, 124, 129; decline/death, 30–31; hypermasculinity, 22, 23, 30–31; physique, 22, 24–25, 30; simulacrum, 30–31

Wolverine, The (2013), 24–25, **25**
Women's Armed Services Integration Act (1948), 72
Women's Army Corps (WAC), 72
Wonder Woman, 12, 58–60, **59**, 62, 63, 64, 65, 122, 160
workout scenes, 24, 41, **43**, 44, 58
WWE wrestling, 12, 45–46

X-24, 30–31
X-Men, 13, 14, 20, 21–25, 29–32, 41, 89–100, 121–39; belonging, 96–97, 161; Inhumans, 93–94, 95, 96–97, 101n18, 161; Legacy Virus, 94; LGBTQIA+, 13, 92–93, 161; mortality, 94–95, 99; mutants, 89–100, 161; origin stories, 93–94, 101n19; passing, 90, 92–93, 94, 99–100, 161; prejudice, 91–93, 94, 96, 161; societal metaphor, 89–90, 91–93, 94, 95–97, 99–100, 161
X-Men (2000), 21, **22**
X-Men Origins: Wolverine (2009), 25
xenophobia, 54

www.ingramcontent.com/pod-product-compliance
Lightning Source LLC
Chambersburg PA
CBHW070402240426

43661CB00056B/2502